Intermediate Examination Paper 6

ELEMENTS OF INFORMATION SYSTEMS

Published May 1992 by Financial Training, 136-142 Bramley Road, London W10 6SR

Copyright © 1992 The Financial Training Company Limited

ISBN 1 85179 435 2

Printed in England.

0107z

Contents

657ELE
L
WYC

0107z

0107z

0107z

0107z

Introduction

General

This Study Pack has been written specifically for students preparing for Paper 6 *Elements of Information Systems* at the intermediate examination of the Association of Accounting Technicians.

In writing this Study Pack our aim has been threefold:

(a)   to provide the student with an up-to-date and comprehensive guide to present day data processing methods as required by the syllabus of this paper;

(b)   to provide copious examples of the practical aspects of information processing systems;

(c)   to provide a grounding for answering Paper 11 *Analysis and Design of Information Systems*.

The text is totally comprehensive and contains numerous examination style questions. It is important that you attempt these under examination conditions or much of their value will be lost.

Syllabus and examination

This subject relates to the normal, 'real-world' office. It will help your study if you look at the office in which you work (or recall offices you have seen in the past) and see how the topics discussed relate to it.

Is the office 'automated' electronically? Are the PCs linked to a distant minicomputer or mainframe? What are they actually used for? Is there a central database?

You do not have to study the electronic complexity of the computer and its devices but you do have to know the broad operational principles, including how and when information technology is used, and for what.

You will encounter numerous technical terms: you must understand them and be able to refer to their meaning and application in the exam. Make a special note of any new term you meet, and its definition; if you read your list regularly you will be able to remember these points.

The examiners have repeatedly said that candidates must have a thorough comprehension of the topics and their real-life relevance; it is not enough merely to repeat the facts memorised. You should read widely round the subject, including the computer news items and notes in the newspapers and journals.

Candidates will have to answer *five* questions out of *seven*, and should be prepared to produce simple diagrams to supplement their narrative as necessary.

Approach to your studies

Constant revision is essential to link the various topics together.

Try to relate the study area to illustrations and examples: for example, what would the practical use of database be to the accountant? When would batch processing be useful?

Syllabus

Aims

To develop an understanding of:

(a)   the role of information technology in business, with special reference to the accounting function;

(b)   the methods used to capture, store, process and transmit that information.

Syllabus

20%   **Information:**   the nature of data and information; the role of information in business; general characteristics of information; methods of information processing from manual to batch, on-line and interactive methods; general concepts of files, structure, content and organisation.

30%   **Hardware:**   input equipment for batch, on-line and other data capture methods;   the central processor unit, structure and function; file hardware and implications for processing methods; output equipment in both hard and soft form; data transmission, modems, multiplexors and local area networks.

30%   **Software:**   using and acquiring packages; computer language and utilities; problem definition and flowcharting; programming, principles and good practice.

20%   **Organisation and control:**   procedures for data vet and validations; staff tasks in a DP department; security and controls; standards and documentation.

Questions will not be set on the analysis and design of information systems, which will be examined in Paper 11 *Analysis and Design of Information Systems*.

Exam format

Students will be required to answer *five* questions out of *seven*.

Publisher's note

This Study Pack is closely tailored to the needs of students studying for the exam for Paper 6 at the intermediate stage. Studied properly, it will help you cover all parts of the syllabus in detail. However, the AAT examiners have repeatedly stressed the need for candidates to have a real understanding of the topics being examined, and of their relevance in real-life situations, rather than merely reproduce information from memory.

You should try to read round the subject as widely as you can; and, ideally, work through the Study Pack in the structured context provided by a distance learning programme or (even better) classroom tuition.

Financial Training offers a range of distance learning, revision and link courses tailored to the individual student's needs. For full details, write or phone us at 136-142 Bramley Road, London W10 6SR. Telephone: 081 960 4421. Fax: 081 960 8355.

0107z

Introduction to management information systems

In this first session we shall consider the role of information technology in business, particularly in providing information to management.

1.1 Aim and scope of syllabus

The accounting technician is faced with a bewildering variety of computerised systems in business today. In addition to computerised systems there are also a variety of developments in the office which are themselves computer-based. Information processing can enhance not only the computational tasks associated with accounting systems, but also the processing of the printed word in such applications as word processing and the communication of information through systems such as Electronic Mailbox and Videotex. The term *information technology* (IT) has been coined to encompass all these various developments. The proficient technician therefore should be able to demonstrate the ability to make use of up-to-date systems without necessarily possessing a deep and detailed knowledge of the technology. The purpose of this syllabus therefore is to equip the student with a good grounding in the systems and methods of information processing.

1.1.1 The structure of this Study Pack

The assumption made by the writers of this Study Pack is that the student is totally innocent of any data processing knowledge. This is, of course, doing the student an injustice as there is considerable awareness of computers and their applications in the world today. However the technician must know something about the detail of computer operations as well as being aware of the 'state of the art' with regard to computer equipment (hardware) as well as computer programming and applications (software). The technician needs to be able to think and write like a critic. It is not enough to demonstrate a knowledge, however superficial, of the hardware. The application of the hardware to various business situations is what is likely to interest the examiner. The Study Pack is therefore structured as follows:

(a) the nature of information;
(b) computer hardware;
(c) the 'electronic office';
(d) logical analysis and problem-solving;
(e) software;
(f) organisation and control.

1.1.2 The accounting technician and management

The nature of the technician's task is to organise the collection and processing of the various facts about the business organisation so that they can be given to the management. It is useful here, to consider what the management actually do.

The tasks associated with 'management' are generally these:

(a) forecasting;
(b) planning;
(c) organising;
(d) co-ordinating;
(e) decision-taking;
(f) controlling.

Management do not do these things intuitively! They need information about the business, their suppliers, their customers, their competitors and the world at large. The accounting technician is often the person who has the immediate responsibility of gathering the raw facts (the data) and ensuring that they are processed in order to provide management with the information that they need to discharge their duties. The accounting technician therefore will, typically, be in charge of a group of clerks, clerical assistants or machine operators who are front-line staff concerned with capturing the source data and maintaining the mechanics of information processing.

The technician must also be aware of the *raison d'être* of information processing. The following questions have to be considered:

(a) What information is required?
(b) How should it be collected and by whom?
(c) When and where should it be collected?
(d) How should it be processed, manually or by using computers?
(e) How should it be presented and when?
(f) How much will it cost and is it worth it?

Having set out how to satisfy management's requirements for information you will inevitably proceed to consider the use of computers and the techniques of systems analysis and design.

1.1.3 Definitions

A glossary of computer terms appears at the end of this Study Pack. Before starting on the detailed study of the material it will be helpful to define some of the principal terms relating to management and these are defined below in the sense in which they are used in this Study Pack.

(a) *Data* - facts, based on measurement, and recorded.

(b) *Information* - data communicated before or after processing.

(c) *Management* - the planning and control of the use of a set of resources to achieve one or more objectives.

(d) *Policy* - a course of management action agreed as a guide to decisions to be taken in achieving one or more objectives.

(e) *Objective* - a desired result defined for managers as a group or individually.

(f) *Manager* - a person responsible for management.

(g) *System* - a set of things connected, associated or interdependent so as to form a complex unity.

(h) *Structure* - a formal system of relationships.

(i) *Management information system* - a system in which defined data are collected, processed and communicated to assist those responsible for the use of resources.

(j) *Information structure* - a system defining the relationships between the information provided to managers which corresponds with their responsibilities.

(k) *Management process* - a sequence of activities by which a manager attempts to achieve one or more objectives.

(l) *Security* - preservation of information for further use, or to enable subsequent records to be re-constructed; control of access to confidential information.

(m) *Installation* - a collection of computer elements (input, calculation, storage, output and associated equipment) brought together to carry out data processing functions.

1.2   The management of an organisation

1.2.1   People and organisations

(a) An organisation consists of at least two people working together in some way to satisfy a need - the need might be their own or someone else's. All people have certain needs and the closer people work together the more likely it is that the organisation will be effective in meeting those needs.

(b) To be effective it is necessary to do certain things in any organisation. Such things might include:

   (i)   defining and agreeing upon the need which is to be satisfied;

   (ii) deciding what each person in the organisation is to do, when and where he is to do it and what resources he requires;

   (iii) communicating the decisions to all concerned;

   (iv) recording what subsequently happens and checking it against what was intended.

(c) The process of deciding such things, communicating the decisions and controlling the organisation's progress in order to achieve its purpose is commonly referred to as the *process of management*. We can see this process at work in both large and small organisations. Firstly, there are certain people called managers and secondly such people will be discussing problems with each other perhaps by letter or telephone, giving instructions and producing information at various intervals on all sorts of activities. In carrying out this process the people will be using a great variety of equipment such as telephones, copying machines and computers. The people, the equipment and the supplies form part of differing systems and sub-systems which may be either simple or very complex.

1.2.2   The process of management

(a)   *Definition* - The process of management is perhaps familiar to everyone and numerous definitions exist. We have chosen a short one. Management is 'the planning and control of the use of a set of resources to achieve one or more objectives'.

(b)   *Four essential steps* - It is useful to consider the basic process of management and this can be reduced to four essential steps where a manager will:

(i)	Agree to carry out the instruction of his superior.	*Accept task.*
(ii)	Decide upon the best way to carry out the task.	*Decide how.*
(iii)	Give instructions to his staff.	*Give instructions.*
(iv)	Set up a reporting mechanism to judge progress towards completion.	*Check results.*

(c)   If when the manager checks the results he finds that the task has not been completed satisfactorily (perhaps because of changed circumstances), he will probably go back to Step (ii) and decide again how to carry out the task. Finally, if the task cannot be completed, or when it is completed satisfactorily, the manager will report back to his superior.

(d)   *Motivating and controlling*

You will often find that the terms *motivating* and *controlling* are used when describing the process of management. While these activities are carried on, motivating really describes how managers might take certain steps, and controlling is no more than carrying out two of the steps (for example, deciding and checking results). Another term *co-ordination* is really the handling of the various steps in more complex situations. It will be seen that the control process described above is cyclical in nature and could be repeated several times until the task is satisfactorily completed. The cycle is fundamental to the concept of control, and we will be considering this aspect in more detail in future sessions.

At each stage, managers will require information and this is where management information systems can provide the necessary facts and figures to assist managers in carrying out their work.

(e)   *Summary* - To summarise, while the process of management may be infinitely complex (and the tasks different), the underlying principles remain and each manager from the chief executive down to the foreman on the shopfloor will go through the same basic four stages, ie:

(i)   accept task;
(ii)   decide how;
(iii) give instructions;
(iv) check results.

1.3   The decision-making process

1.3.1   Planning

Before deciding the best way to carry out a task and prior to giving instructions, a manager needs to think about the task facing him. If it is a simple task, such as a works manager querying with the accountant a point on a petty cash payment, this could be done very quickly by making a short telephone call. But if the task were more complex (say, 'introduce a costing system into this manufacturing business as soon as possible') then the works manager would need to do a number of things. For example:

(a)   ascertain why the system is required;
(b)   ask his accountant to consider the alternative systems of costing, for example, batch or processing;
(c)   select the most appropriate system;
(d)   draw up a plan indicating the likely resources, the timing for the introduction of the new system, the costs and the benefits.

In practice there would be a considerable number of questions to be answered and the plans for the costing system could, for example, involve a phased approach, whereby the system is introduced on a department by department basis over many months. The example merely indicates that a considerable amount of work needs to be undertaken before the introduction of the costing system.

Planning has often been defined as taking decisions before one takes action - our definition is: 'The identification of objectives and the selection of policies and methods necessary to achieve the objectives'. Planning implies a process of taking deliberate care when making a decision - for instance, we often talk of 'laying a plan' when we spend time carefully thinking out each aspect before coming to a decision. Again we can recognise that information is required in order to assist managers in the planning process, the end result of which is a set of instructions or a plan.

1.3.2   Decision-making

(a)   The operation of any organisation or the running of a business involves making many decisions. These can be made instantly or carefully as a result of systematic planning. Despite all the advances in information systems and the use of computers the ultimate decisions are still made by managers. The information can only assist the manager - it might even improve the quality of the decision - but it will still not remove the necessity of making the decision. Furthermore, you must never forget that in making a decision the manager is exercising his judgment. This may be based on his instinct. For example, we are all familiar with those managers who 'play it by ear' and in certain circumstances this approach may be acceptable. Very often a manager may have to take a decision when he has no information or when it is not quantifiable.

(b) After careful consideration of the type, level and frequency of decisions and the time available for collecting information, we might decide to use a computer to assist us in the decision-making process. As an illustration, many firms now operate a computerised stock control system whereby an order for fresh supplies is automatically issued whenever the stock falls below a stated reorder level.

(c) When considering the decision-making process you should remember that there are a number of different features, including the following:

   (i) decisions are made at various levels within an organisation;

   (ii) a time scale exists between the making of a decision and the resultant action which in turn leads to the completion of the task - ie, there are long-term, medium-term and short-term aspects;

   (iii) a decision situation is made up of two aspects:

   a decision where a choice is made between alternatives;

   an event which occurs and over which we have little or no control, for example the effect of adverse weather conditions on the output of the farming industry;

   (iv) a number of unquantifiable factors and influences are involved, for example 'stock market rumours' may be very important to the finance director of a large public company, but these are hardly quantifiable;

   (v) the choice between different alternatives involves risk because we are considering things in the future. Someone once said that the only certain thing we can say about the future is that it is unknown!

(d) Where information can be collected and organised in numerical and logical terms then you can calculate the value and consequences of the various alternatives before making the decisions. You are thus concerned with developing information systems to aid the decision maker.

1.3.3 Control

(a) Under **the process of management** it was suggested that control might involve us in two of the basic stages in our four-step process - for example, deciding and checking results. In addition, it was implied that the control process is cyclical in nature so that we might repeat the same process on several occasions before completing the necessary task.

(b) You should recognise that control in the more common usage of the word has certain connotations which imply a sense of coercion, for example a policeman on traffic-control would be making decisions probably on too little information but we are all aware that to ignore his signals could involve us more directly with the law.

(c) It is normal to think of control as including all the steps carried out in order to ensure that the actual results or the processes conform with what was planned. The control process is an important area in your studies and many information systems are in existence to help management, for example:

(i)   production control;
(ii)   stock control;
(iii) quality control;
(iv)   budgetary control.

(d)   The basic principles of any control process and the reporting of control information represents a major aspect of the course and will therefore be dealt with in more detail in the following sessions.

1.3.4   The levels of management

When designing an information system it is preferable that each report issued should be suitable to the needs of the recipient. Furthermore, you should be aware that there are different levels of management in any organisation. The principal levels of management in most companies are broadly as follows.

(a)   *The main board* of directors is responsible for developing company policy, having been appointed by the shareholders for ensuring, amongst other things, that an adequate rate of return is achieved on the ordinary share capital employed.

(b)   *Functional directors and senior managers* are responsible for the defining and controlling of functional plans. They are primarily concerned with implementing company policies as laid down by the board of directors. For example, a production director would be responsible for the manufacturing operations.

(c)   *Line managers* are responsible for controlling detailed performance and general day-to-day operations. This level often includes those staff who are not necessarily called managers (eg, supervisors or chargehands). However, their work still involves management.

The task of communicating between the various levels of management and providing the necessary information for planning and control purposes is where accountants have a vital role to play.

1.4   The organisation

1.4.1   Size of the organisation

Organisations come in many shapes and sizes. They range from the one-man business where all functions of management reside in one person, to a large public company or a nationalised industry employing many thousands of employees. Size alone demands a greater co-ordinating effort in respect of administrative systems and procedures. In smaller firms the management information service is often combined with the finance and accounting function. As the business grows, there is a need for improved communication to provide accurate and timely information for planning and control.

It will be appreciated that not all relationships between managers are formal and this can hinder systematic information flows. These informal relationships are often just as important but in view of the trend towards larger and larger groups of companies it has been found that more formal organisation structures require the necessary co-ordinated management information systems.

7

1.4.2   Organisation structure

In all but the smallest businesses or entities, it is an established principle that responsibilities for various functions are delegated within the business hierarchy. You would not expect the Managing Director of a substantial company to be concerned with the preparation of accounting information. Nor would you expect a busy chief accountant to be concerned with the detail of day-to-day recording. The various functional areas of management are allocated between key members of staff who, in turn, may delegate some of these functions to their sub-ordinates. This process of delegation may be depicted diagrammatically as shown in Figure 1.1

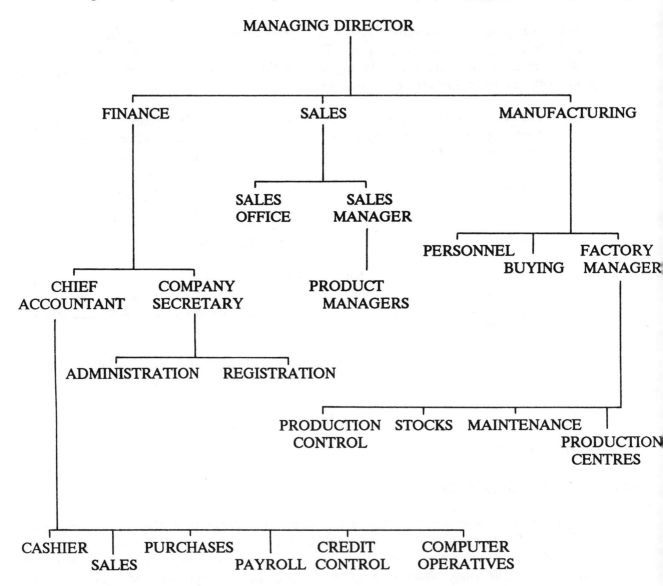

Figure 1.1: An organisation chart for a medium-sized manufacturing company

1.4.3   Communication

(a)   *Definition* - Communication in an organisation provides a means of planning the objectives of the firm, deciding upon courses of action and measuring performance of the actions taken. For our purposes communication is defined as the capacity of an individual or group to convey ideas and feelings to another individual or group and where appropriate to obtain a response. It is a subject that should be close to you. In the context of an organisation, communication may be considered as:

0108z

> (i)   an individual's ability to express himself;
> (ii)   the method of circulating information within the organisation.

(b)   The information may be circulated in a number of ways, for example:

> (i)   verbally, as feedback of information such as lunchtime conversations;
> (ii)   as written reports and schedules, for example, monthly accounts;
> (iii) as forms for processing such as goods inwards notes;
> (iv) as graphs, charts and diagrams;
> (v)   as visual presentations, for example, closed-circuit TV.

(c)   While it is customary to indicate the hierarchy of relationships through the medium of an organisation chart, your studies in communication should have taught you that the exchanges of data and information are considerably more flexible and complicated. The managing director may well be in contact with every manager in the business in order to be able to carry out his tasks. A communication network is shown in Figure 1.2.

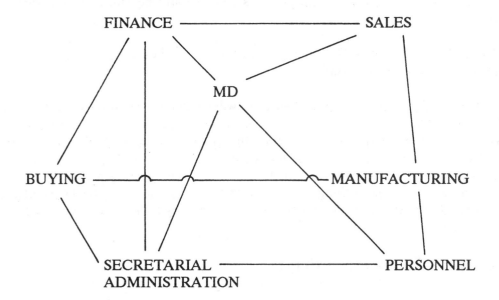

Figure 1.2: Communication network

Any study of information systems must include the differing information needs of the 'key staff' in the organisation and consider how these needs can be satisfied.

1.4.4   Accounting controls

One important reason for delegating responsibility between various staff members is that such a subdivision ensures that no one person has too much responsibility. It can also ensure that one person's work is reviewed by another. Regrettably errors and fraud do occur in businesses and even more regrettably accountants are often the people with immediate concern to prevent or detect fraud, as they are concerned with that most portable asset - cash. Errors, of course, arise whenever there is any employment of human effort. The errors attributed to computers can usually be traced to human errors either in designing the processing system or in handling the raw data. It is important to note that no function concerned with information processing can be carried out without regard for controls and security. When you approach the study of auditing, the study of control systems will be covered in more detail. However it will be sufficient for our purposes if you consider the following points:

(a) *Division of duties* - Most tasks are arranged so that the responsibility for authorisation, custody, recording and execution functions are segregated.

(b) *Reliable records* - The records of the entity must be preserved. A public limited company is required to keep its records for six years. The statute of limitations would require records to be kept for this length of time.

(c) *Custodial controls* - Suitable controls should exist for the custody of assets and records. You can imagine the chaos that could result if your computer files were destroyed or corrupted by a saboteur.

(d) *Supervisory systems* - These are set up to prevent errors and fraud or to facilitate their detection. Essentially one person's work should be checked or reviewed by another.

(e) *Managerial supervision* - The managers of the entity should review and control the activities of subordinate staff.

While the subject of controls and security will be dealt with in detail in Session 14, it is important for you to realise that no data processing task should take place without some concern to ensure that the process is controlled and reasonably secure from the risks of fraud and error. The old hackneyed slogan GIGO (garbage in, garbage out) often holds true, with distressing results for all concerned. There is nothing more damaging to morale than the knowledge that you cannot depend upon the information produced by a data processing system.

1.5   Management information systems

1.5.1   Definition

A management information system (MIS) has been defined as 'a system in which defined data are collected, processed and communicated to assist those responsible for the use of resources'.

We shall consider MIS in four principal sections:

(a)   management information requirements;
(b)   design of MIS;
(c)   development and installation of MIS;
(d)   organisational aspects.

It is essential to adopt a systematic approach, and, to assist you, each section describes in considerable detail all you need to know. The approach adopted is to consider what might be described as the more conceptual aspects in the first two sections such as why information is needed, its value and use and then gradually to move on to more practical topics, for example, the setting up of MIS project teams and the training of staff.

1.5.2   Definition

A management information system (MIS) has been defined as 'a system in which defined data are collected, processed and communicated to assist those responsible for the use of resources'.

The study of MIS cannot be undertaken in a vacuum and it is therefore essential to be aware of certain basic facts such as:

(i)   the type of organisation or business, the products or services offered and the principal markets;
(ii)   the principal objectives;
(iii)   the organisation structure and reporting relationships;
(iv)   the principal users of information and the use to which the information is put.

These basic facts operate within the organisation whose information is collected, processed and communicated. Such systems will therefore operate within:

(i)   different levels from the board of directors down to shop floor supervisors;
(ii)   different functions for example production, marketing and finance.

Although we are concerned with MIS and the integral part played by the computer it is not essential to use a computer as part of information systems and many parts of a system can be manual. Indeed, in a small organisation there may well be little or no automation at all.

1.5.3   Scope

To give you an idea of the scope of MIS some typical reports produced in a medium-sized manufacturing company might include the following.

(a)   *Production and material control*

    (i)   forward loading plans for production cycles;
    (ii)   machine capacity forecast;
    (iii)   departmental operating statements;
    (iv)   stock and work-in-progress reports;
    (v)   wastage report;
    (vi)   labour utilisation report.

(b)   *Marketing including distribution*

    (i)   market surveys;
    (ii)   order reports by product and geographical area;
    (iii)   discount trends;
    (iv)   transport and warehouse cost statements;
    (v)   salesman performance;
    (vi)   product service and support costs.

(c)   *Personnel*

    (i)   numbers employed by category;
    (ii)   overtime hours;
    (iii)   sickness, absence, lateness;

(iv) training requirements;
(v)   career development plans;
(vi) recruitment policy;
(vii) job descriptions.

(d) *Financial and management accounting*

(i)   annual statutory accounts;
(ii)   budgets and forecasts;
(iii) sales and contribution analyses;
(iv)   cash, management and working capital evaluation;
(v)   capital project appraisal;
(vi)   standard cost and variance analysis reports;
(vii) returns to government departments eg, VAT.

The above list of reports provides us, at a glance, with an overall view of what MIS is all about. What initial conclusions might be drawn from the above list? Write down your own thoughts and then check them against the following list:

(i)   information is needed for many different purposes;
(ii)   the information produced is a mixture of financial and statistical data;
(iii) there are different groups of users who work at different levels within the firm;
(iv)   the information is produced at different times and frequencies in the form of both *ad hoc* and regular reports;
(v)   information is required on internal and external factors;
(vi)   there are likely to be common pieces of information that are required in different functions;
(vii) information is required for decision making, planning and control.

1.6   Management information requirements and use

1.6.1   Why information is needed

It is always useful to start any consideration of a subject or a problem by asking the question 'Why?' Why is information needed? A moment's thought might produce this initial attempt at an answer:

(a) to assist management to plan the most effective use of resources such as labour and materials;

(b) to assist management to choose between alternative courses of action, for example whether to make a product or purchase it from an outside supplier;

(c) to aid management in controlling day-to-day operations, for example a comparison statement between actual results achieved and those planned.

The functions - such as planning and controlling - involved in managing an organisation therefore require knowledge that is relevant to the particular situation. How many of us have heard the cry, 'If only I had known that at the time'? Managers' judgments will be greatly enhanced by receiving the appropriate information on which to base their decisions.

Another way to look at why information is needed is to consider the definition of the management process. We have previously defined the management process as: 'A sequence of activities by which a manager attempts to achieve one or more objectives'. It can therefore be argued that managers first need information about objectives before they can do anything at all. However, there are many instances where a manager is not given any objectives or they are not clear and as such most managers would use their experience in effect to choose their own objectives. Despite the lack of clear objectives all situations would in practice involve the use of resources such as a certain number of staff or a factory of a particular size. When a manager accepts a task, by implication, he either has, or has not the opportunity to obtain the necessary resources to carry out the task. The type of information needed is therefore very much linked up with the manner in which resources are used, the results achieved and the progress being made towards the objectives. It could, for example, be important to know the profitability of the resources currently employed, whether such profitability could be improved, and if so, by how much. An improvement could be achieved by a major change in the relative inputs between, for example, labour and machines.

You should now be clear that a manager is a user of resources **in the light of information**. Futhermore, the whole complex process of management can be broken down into manageable sections or problems. The problem facing the chairman of a large group might be to decide how much of group funds to allocate to a particular activity whereas a foreman in the machine shop might be deciding which machine to use and which operators should be asked to operate it to turn out a particular job. Information is necessary at each level to help decide what to do and in due course to measure the skill and effectiveness of what is eventually done.

In the above discussion we have not considered the users of information in the wider sense, such as the general public or government departments, as our primary interest is in management information. Additional notes on the different information groups are set out in the next section.

1.6.2   The form of information

As an accountant, you may be forgiven for thinking that all information consists of figures and reports which are written on paper and appear on someone's desk, perhaps once a month, setting out last month's performance. Accountants obviously produce a lot of information which is evaluated in financial terms because money is the universally accepted measure and provides a common standard. But you should realise that any information system must include non-accounting information; for example, quantities alone might serve a useful purpose in many instances, particularly where managers are used to thinking in these units.

Most managers who walk round a factory can easily see whether there are piles of unfinished work accumulating even if the work-in-progress reports show otherwise. In some industries you can certainly smell and/or hear what is being produced. The point being made is that a manager can use all his senses to obtain information provided he knows what he is trying to do and is able to absorb it. For most of us the amount of information which can be absorbed visually is much greater than by any of the other senses and therefore communication is normally carried out in this manner. Within the visual framework we can, of course, use accounting and statistical reports, graphs, diagrams, closed circuit TV and many other forms of presentation. One of the main reasons for managers receiving written reports is that it is impossible in a large organisation for them actually to observe what is going on all the time in every department and therefore some form of reporting is necessary. Our monthly accounting reports might well be the most appropriate form for certain types of information after all.

1.6.3 Information flows

Normally, most organisations develop around major functional areas, for example, the functions of production, finance, distribution etc, and within each area there are additional sub-divisions. In the past managers were usually held responsible for obtaining the information they needed and such information was prescribed by the manager at the top and his decisions influenced reports at all levels. In addition, statutory requirements such as annual accounts provided the other main source of information. As organisations grew, more data was required than individual managers could handle and systems and data processing departments began to develop in order to collect, route and manipulate data. The information flowed up the channels of management largely by summarisations from varying levels of detail.

With the gradual introduction of company-wide systems, many organisations began to recognise the information systems' function as separate from the normal lines of responsibility/authority. We can often see this where basic data gathered, for example, by the sales representatives could well be of value to the manufacturing staff when they consider the volume of production. Futhermore, improved efficiency often requires departmental coordination within functions, geographical areas and divisions and the cost of collecting data could also force us into consideration of improved methods and flows. The information flows, if traced from one responsibility unit to another, present an information network which reflects horizontal and vertical flows of data.

1.6.4 Using the information

It perhaps seems too obvious to say that management information should be used. But this is not always the case. We often hear managers complain that they cannot understand the figures and so the interpretation and use of information is just as important as the methods chosen to provide it. When considering management information it is useful to determine whether managers are given any guidance, (eg, by written instructions or training courses) on how to use the information provided. In particular, managers must know:

(a)   which items of information should be monitored;
(b)   the principal reasons for differences between planned and actual results;
(c)   the possible action that could be taken on the information provided;
(d)   which person is responsible for taking the action described at (c) above.

If asked what happens when a piece of information is received, most of us would immediately think of comparing it with some other knowledge we already have. It might for example be a plan or budget or last month's results. The ability to check information by reference to experience and knowledge is said to be one of the qualities of a good manager. You should never ignore the possibility that information may be wrong so it is often an important task to check data although this is usually considered to be the responsibility of the person providing the data rather than the recipient.

1.6.5   Value of information

In general it is more than likely that all information has a cost and hopefully some benefit, although it is not always possible to quantify these. While a major effort to improve information is attractive, money is a scarce resource and investment in systems must be justified to ensure that progress is obtained and that the returns are worth the cost of development work. In the previous section we outlined the use of information and it could be argued that unless the information is used it can have no value at all. Positive action could result in the following:

(i)   minimising and/or elimination of losses;
(ii)   savings in cost;
(iii)   improved use of resources;
(iv)   increase in sales and/or profit;
(v)   prevention of fraud by improving audit controls.

Several companies have developed formal procedures for requesting moneys for information systems, improvements and changes and such a request might usefully include:

(i)   department and date of request;
(ii)   proposed change or addition;
(iii)   project number;
(iv)   application (discussion of problem and proposed solution);
(v)   equipment requirements:
        - additional;
        - to be replaced;
(vi)   comparison of present and proposed annual operating costs;
(vii)   quantifiable benefits;
(viii) non-quantifiable benefits;
(ix)   development costs;
(x)   time required to develop system;
(xi)   approved by (signature of authorised officers).

Non-quantifiable benefits might include such matters as improvements in response time and improved quality of service. It should be appreciated that in general it will be difficult, if not impossible, to claim direct cost savings as a result of the introduction of management information systems. Benefits are more likely to be achieved as a result of a more comprehensive approach to MIS thereby minimising overall cost while preventing excessive cost due to a fragmented approach. You will be considering the evaluation of costs and benefits in more depth in subsequent sessions.

1.6.6   Acid test for management information

The following simple check can often be applied to any information.

Key questions

(a)   The positive approach.

        Does the information:

        (i)   serve a useful purpose?
        (ii)   increase management effectiveness?

    (b)   The negative approach.

        If the information is not available:

        (i)   does anything suffer?
        (ii)   is it available in another form?

1.7 Design of MIS

1.7.1 Introduction

There are three basic questions to be answered when considering design, namely:

(a)   who will need the information and what groups can they be divided into?
(b)   what functional patterns can they be divided into and how can their needs be met within the overall objectives of the organisation?
(c)   what should be the frequency and content of the information provided?

Having answered the above three questions you will then proceed to see how MIS requirements might be met using either conventional methods or some form of data processing.

Finally it will be necessary briefly to consider the cost factors involved.

While it is possible to set out the general principles of MIS design you should never forget that businesses are as different as individuals and each case should be carefully considered before recommending a particular system.

1.7.2 Information groups

The different groups requiring information from and within, say, a limited company can be classified as follows:

(i)   level 1 -   the general public, national and international;
(ii)   level 2 -   national and local governmental agencies and other statutory bodies, national and international;
(iii)   level 3 -   the shareholders and their advisers;
(iv)   level 4 -   the board of directors;
(v)   level 5 -   functional directors and senior managers;
(vi)   level 6 -   line managers;
(vii) level 7 -   employees and their representatives.

In addition, while perhaps not levels in the MIS sense, a company will also be providing information to its suppliers and its customers.

It is worth noting a few points on some of the above levels which *for our purposes here* may be conveniently divided into three main groups:

(i)   *Group A*   Levels 1, 2 and 3 are in effect external to the business and would not be concerned with planning, control and the decision-making process. However from time to time such levels could have a major influence on the business, for example, government policy changes. The work of a public relations department would be primarily directed towards the general public. Shareholders' advisers include stockbrokers and financial analysts and their principal means of communication would be the annual published report and accounts. Those in Group A are more and more concerned with the information provided and their requirements must be considered in the MIS study. For example, the content of the annual report is currently under consideration by the government.

(ii) *Group B*   Levels 4, 5 and 6 are part of the management structure and information is vital to them for planning and control. The lack of information would effectively prevent them from carrying out their tasks and this is therefore the primary area for which MIS must provide. For example, the outputs from a management accounting system would be directed at this group.

(iii) *Group C*   Level 7 while having no management responsibility must nevertheless be considered in terms of information requirements. Indeed recent UK legislation such as the Employment Protection Act requires information to be given to Trade Unions without which they would be seriously impeded in carrying on collective bargaining. Furthermore, worker participation is likely to increase in the future which will present new and different demands for information.

Within Group B it is normal to sub-divide persons requiring information into the principal functional areas such as:

(i)   marketing including distribution and advertising promotion;
(ii)   production and material control;
(iii)   finance and company secretarial duties;
(iv)   personnel;
(v)   research and development.

However, some care should be exercised when considering the functional approach as it is likely that greater coordination of functions and increasing use of common basic data will blur the more traditional functional lines within most organisations. Additionally you must never forget that while we can often generalise about management functions each business is likely to be organised in a particular way, for example, the style of management could range from a dictatorship to a completely participative style and it is likely that such different firms would have different requirements.

The past decade has seen a rising volume of pressure for the business community to take a more active and responsible role in society's social and economic problems. No longer can a business claim that its only interest is the shareholders and the designer of an information system must now take full account of the requirements of these new groups of information users. As a student and future practitioner, you should therefore be aware of these new demands. To keep yourself up-to-date you should read the various professional journals and magazines which contain informative articles on recent trends and new legislation.

The principal risks in relation to information groups when designing new information systems are:

(i)   to forget groups A and C;
(ii)   to allow group B to become snowed under in a wealth of details;
(iii) to ignore some of the information currently received by recipients;
(iv)   to incur excessive cost by adopting a fragmented approach concentrating solely on one level or functional group;
(v)   to generalise too much and pay insufficient attention to different requirements.

1.7.3   Frequency and content

It should be recognised that many management information systems have not been carefully designed but have evolved over a period of many years. The frequency and content of existing information could be purely a result of personal preference of the managing director based on his problems and decisions perhaps 10 years before. In most organisations the main reason for the content and frequency of information returns is therefore likely to be the effective bargaining power and pressure exerted by the recipients.

Again different firms behave in different ways: some organisations have not changed the management reports for years while others seem to change them every month. A reasonable solution should be your objective.

It is important to ascertain when information will be required from the MIS and again this requires an investigation into the types of decisions that managers have to make. For example, if a distribution manager is responsible for sending goods on a routine basis once a month to different branches in a national organisation, he would only need notifications of changes of address as and when these occur. There is no requirement to receive a complete new listing, say, every month.

For the purposes of control, it is important to ascertain the time scale within which control can be effected; for example, material wastage information on a 'shift basis' could be significant if the shift leader can actually adjust the volume of material in order to reduce wastage.

You should never forget the cost and effort that goes into the preparation of information. The only reason why some firms can claim to have the 'figures' on the desks of their managers by 9.00 am each morning is because of the night shift in the computer operations department. It is usually difficult to recruit staff who are willing to work at night, so never overlook the effort required, particularly where a high level is required.

Most companies nowadays tend to produce monthly management accounts within, say two weeks of the month-end. The urgency of information needs may vary considerably from business to business.

1.7.4   Flexibility and adaptability

This is perhaps one of the most difficult areas of design. Flexibility might be defined as 'the ability to call on data from within the organisation in whatever form stored and wherever held and to obtain it in the form required by the decision maker'. This implies that provided we have collected the data in sufficient detail at the lowest level of management we could perhaps merely summarise it accordingly. However, there is perhaps more to it than that. In the past many systems were inflexible because:

(a)   continual summarisation of information moved upwards from one level to another without accompanying detail;

(b)   there was lack of communication and coordination between different functional groups so that access to other departments' data was non-existent;

(c)   there was lack of techniques and equipment to;

      (i)   select specific pieces of information from masses of data;
      (ii)   rearrange available data into a form suitable for a specific situation;
      (iii)   recall selected information in a short period of time - a day or less.

The development of computers in terms of storage capacity and speed of processing has presented the opportunity for greater flexibility. However, the strict discipline imposed by computer science means that considerable skill and extensive systems work is required in specifying requirements and in designing more flexible systems - but it can be done. We have already discussed information flows and information levels and also indicated that the provision of information is likely to require a more formalised approach in the future.

1.7.5   Conventional methods

This term is used solely to describe what might be termed various 'non large computer' systems that exist. In this context conventional methods include:

(a)   manual and manually aided systems;

(b)   mechanised systems (automatic data processing):

      (i)   adding and calculating machines;
      (ii)   accounting machines including visible record computers;
      (iii)   punched card equipment (now obsolete).

1.7.6   Electronic data processing

This term is used in the widest sense to include the processing data using electronic equipment such as a computer. At this stage we are only concerned with the use of computers and electronic data processing (EDP) in outline from an MIS design viewpoint. Historically there can be said to be four different approaches to the use of computers:

(a)   the experimental approach (let's buy a computer and see what we can do with it);

(b)   the office machinery approach (let's speed up our present clerical procedures, reduce the drudgery and cut staff numbers);

(c)   the functional approach (can we use the computer to solve a major problem such as maintaining adequate finished goods stocks in each of our warehouses?);

(d)   the integrated systems approach (after careful examination of all our information needs we have decided that using a computer is the most appropriate and we are therefore designing and developing suitable systems).

The first two approaches have tended to become obsolete and the third and fourth approaches are in common use. In general, it can be said that computers should be used either for processing large volumes of data of relatively few different types or for carrying out complex calculations. We are concerned with commercial as opposed to scientific applications and commercial applications may be classified as:

(a)   *Traditional systems* - as previously stated many of the first applications transferred to computers were of an accounting nature. The computer was used to carry out routine repetitive work, the primary benefit being faster and more accurate throughput. Typical applications included:

     (i)   payroll;
     (ii)   invoicing;
     (iii) sales and purchase ledger;
     (iv)   stock control records.

    There was no real coordination or integration of the different applications and output in terms of management information was often poorly conceived and organised.

(b)   *Integrated systems* - theoretically, the greatest benefits from using a computer arise from the introduction of large integrated systems in which the procedures for several separate applications, which are in some way related, are planned as a whole and developed as a closely knit group. Needless to say, a high degree of skill is required to develop a fully integrated system and the systems planning and designing together with the programming of the computer takes a lot of time and effort. Nevertheless many organisations now develop each application in such a way that these can be integrated, for example, a common format is adopted for the various files of data held within the system.

(c)   *Database systems* - this approach emphasises that if all the information generated by an individual transaction can be recorded and filed away, it can then subsequently be accessed to answer any question that a manager might ask. In effect, the computer is a gigantic filing cabinet and furthermore the 'files' are separate from the applications which use them. For example, all information about an employee, be it for payroll, pension, career development, expenses claims or any other purpose, could be held on a single file. Each application would then access the file as appropriate.

1.7.7   Cost factors

As a trainee accountant, this topic should always be close to your heart. Indeed accountants are often called upon to evaluate costs and benefits of MIS and computerisation. Cost factors to be considered would include:

(a)   design and development of systems;
(b)   installation and implementation;
(c)   equipment cost, if appropriate (purchase/lease/rent);
(d)   use of in-house computers or external bureaux;
(e)   running costs;
(f)   manufacturers' training service and support;
(g)   any (essential) software not included anywhere above.

The above factors often require extensive background research and the use of modern financial **evaluation** techniques such as discounted cashflow (DCF). Many organisations have failed to make any effort to quantify the likely costs before proceeding with computerisation. It is not only the 'out of pocket' costs such as equipment costs that can mount up. The cost of a firm's own staff is invariably ignored in the development work. Many systems require considerable initial clerical effort, for example, the setting up of the basic product files that might be used for a stock control system. You must also never overlook the question of 'cost-effectiveness' of MIS and the possibilities of cost reduction techniques, for example, by the use of more efficient methods of processing.

1.7.8   Summary

Finally, there is no one 'ideal' approach to MIS design but the most satisfactory one would appear to include the following steps:

(a)   agree at top management level the basic characteristics of the business, its patterns of ownership, style of management, objectives and organisation structure;

(b)   establish the information groups and levels and define in broad terms their requirements for information frequency and content;

(c)   ensure that any proposed systems are sufficiently flexible and adaptable;

(d)   consider the various alternatives for data collection and processing, both manual and computerised;

(e)   evaluate the costs and benefits of MIS.

This 'high level' type approach can now be turned into a more practical consideration of how to develop and install an MIS and these subjects are described in the next section.

1.8   Development and installation of MIS

1.8.1   Appraisal of existing information and determining future requirements

The first steps in any development are to appraise the existing information and systems and then to determine future information needs and desires. It is therefore necessary to collect information and this can be done in one of five principal ways:

(a)   by interviewing;

(b)   by issuing questionnaires;

(c)   by direct observation;

(d)   by selecting specific functional managers to specify needs for all jobs within their area of responsibility;

(e)   by the use of industry studies and literature in selected fields, usually to supplement the above methods.

Each of these methods is described in more detail in the session on basic systems analysis where it is discussed in the context of computerised procedures. It is virtually impossible to cover in great depth the entire field of management information, so by way of example, we are going to confine our attention to the financial and statistical information which might be used within a firm to justify and evaluate management's plans and to measure the firm's performance and its financial position.

When appraising the existing financial and relevant statistical information, particular attention should be given to:

(a)   titles of the returns and whether they accurately describe their contents;
(b)   comprehensiveness of the contents of each return;
(c)   structure, and layout of each return and the general presentation of information;
(d)   frequency and speed with which the information is published;
(e)   distribution of the returns to the various levels of management within the company;
(f)   existence of timetables for the preparation of the information;
(g)   methods of producing the information;
(h)   use made of the information provided, and, in particular, the discussions that take place on the returns, the action that may be taken thereon and the general management feedback that arises from the uses made of the information;
(i)   managers' attitudes to the information provided;
(j)   accuracy of the information;
(k)   existence of any plans for the development of the management information systems;
(l)   information required.

1.8.2   Management's attitudes

No system can work unless top management backs it. This means that there must be complete management involvement from the top down to the lowest level. Any MIS system must be designed and operated with some understanding of human behaviour and attitudes. Ascertain whether they:

(a)   feel that their effectiveness is limited by lack of key information in a form in which it can be of real use;
(b)   think the present information is reasonably satisfactory and whether they are able to suggest any real improvements;
(c)   think that all financial information is of little value and that they can manage without it or with statistical information alone;
(d)   feel that the information is presented too late or is too inaccurate to be of real value;
(e)   use the accountants' reports in preparing their own reports to higher management.

Management that is receptive to improved information can considerably shorten the time required to get a new system implemented successfully.

1.8.3   Planning development

It is recommended that a 'master plan' for the developing MIS is prepared and approved by top management. The master plan approach has several advantages for systems work including:

(a)   the company-wide approach is used from the start thus avoiding the problems of fragmented efforts;
(b)   the master plan can highlight and correct problem areas before extensive work is performed;
(c)   the master plan can rank projects in order of urgency and also ensure that a sequence of applications is followed, each of which can be properly integrated with different interfaces;

(d)   the time allowed to prepare the master plan can be used to consider the basic fundamental objectives of the MIS and the direction of development effort;

(e)   more effective utilisation of equipment and resources will be achieved since total volumes, timings, frequencies and specialised needs can be forecasted, thereby facilitating the selection and choice of future equipment needs;

(f)   top management generally prefer to be presented with a planned development programme rather than a series of 'one off' projects, each of which needs special evaluation on its own merits often without the background of longer term objectives;

(g)   the work involved in the master plan often identifies weaknesses in present organisational arrangements.

The master plan should be prepared for a reasonably long period of time, say 5-10 years, and should be updated and reviewed in the light of progress on implementation and changing requirements for information.

1.8.4   MIS project team

It is normal to set up a small project team which might comprise:

(a)   a team leader;
(b)   a computer systems analyst;
(c)   a management accountant;
(d)   one or two representatives from the principal functional areas such as production and marketing.

The team would probably be engaged full-time on the MIS project, although the composition of the team might change from time to time depending on the stage of development, and the particular areas being considered. The team leader should report at a high level, for example, to the financial director and many companies often set up a steering group to monitor the overall development of MIS. Representatives of the various information groups can attend and thus be consulted on key aspects. The project team should be issued with clear terms of reference and be given a financial budget together with agreed timetables and programmes for each stage of development and installation work. Many organisations consider that the resources required for such a project team are beyond their capacity or that they have insufficient technical expertise and in such cases it may be convenient to utilise outside assistance in the form of management consultants. Before using consultants, it is essential to ensure that the selected firm has some experience in the field of MIS and computerisation and it is always useful to talk to their past customers.

1.8.5   Documentation

By this we mean all the master plans, timetables, outline proposals, detailed specifications, input forms, output forms, output reports, computer programs and system operating instructions and clerical procedures. Far too many systems are poorly documented with the result that they are difficult to maintain and amend because often those staff who designed the system have subsequently left the firm. Ideally a detailed procedures manual should be prepared by the project team.

Many organisations have recognised the importance of documentation and have developed 'minimum standards' which must be adhered to by all systems designers. This is particularly important in relation to computer aspects and the National Computer

Centre (NCC) has been in the forefront of developing various standards for use in respect of systems. Documentation standards are tools which allow the systems designers to set down their ideas quickly, accurately, completely and unambiguously.

Typical documentation for a system might include:

(a) background information on the company, terms of reference and requirements;

(b) meetings, implications;

(c) procedures;

  (i)   system outlines;
  (ii) clerical procedures;
  (iii) system operating instructions;
  (iv) program details;

(d) data:

  (i)   clerical files and documents;
  (ii) computer files, input, output, master and transfer files;
  (iii) computer records, input, output and stored;

(e) test documents and results of checking;

(f) performance requirements in terms of growth, timings and volume and operating instructions for the equipment;

(g) costs and benefits;

(h) minimum requirements for hardware, software and systems.

You need not at this stage worry about some of the technical terms used above, as these will be defined in later sessions.

1.8.6 Implementation

The implementation of an MIS requires careful planning and tight control. There are two principal tasks:

(a) *preparatory work*, which will include:

  (i)   preparing an implementation timetable;
  (ii) specifying clerical resources required;
  (iii) identifying accommodation, equipment, stationery and suppliers;
  (iv) preparing documentation;
  (v)   other considerations such as possible organisational changes;

(b) *conversion work*, which will include:

  (i)   gathering master data;
  (ii) setting up files;
  (iii) setting up the system;

(iv)   conversion to the new system;

(v)   other considerations such as interim arrangements during the transition stage.

As an example, the introduction of a computer-based financial and management accounting system might involve the following stages:

(a)   *Financial and management accounting system*

     (a)   preparation of outline specification of management requirements;
     (b)   preparation of detailed specification including proposed use of computers;
     (c)   development of an accounts code system;
     (d)   development and documentation of clerical procedures;
     (e)   development of staff training courses;
     (f)   introduction of accounts codes;
     (g)   preparation of test data;
     (h)   checking of systems test data and parallel running;
     (i)   implementation of computer system;
     (j)   instructions on the interpretation of management reports.

(b)   *Computer systems*

     (a)   detailed systems design including writing detailed computer program specifications;
     (b)   writing and testing computer programs;
     (c)   preparing computer documentation including instructions for the operation of the equipment;
     (d)   systems testing;
     (e)   parallel running;
     (f)   implementation.

Several of the above aspects are dealt with in more depth in the sessions relating to the introduction of computer systems.

(c)   *Maintenance*

It is normal for the project team to hand over the system to the user and the computer operations department during the latter stages of implementation. This ensures that each can operate the system and that it meets their requirements. The task of future maintenance is an important one and, as with any system, MIS must be properly maintained.

It is useful to carry out a 'post-implementation review' perhaps one year after implementation in order to ensure that the system is satisfactory and that the actual benefits and costs are in line with those originally proposed. The task of maintenance is made considerably easier if good documentation has been prepared. Inevitably changes will be required in the future and specific responsibility will need to be defined for the task of maintenance and amendment of the MIS.

1.9   Organisational aspects

1.9.1   Changes in the collection and use of data

The principal effect of an improved MIS should be better decisions and increased managerial efficiency. The introduction of MIS often requires modifications in the organisation structure and the responsibilities for inputting data.

Developments at the input points of an MIS are perhaps the most fundamental. Many organisations are 'decentralising' where it is now possible to install a mini-computer or an input device (terminal) in every small department or location of a company, and staff who had previously never heard of computers, let alone used them, are now often in daily contact with a central computer.

Responsibility for the quality of input needs to be defined - quality control checks are advisable. In manual systems the data collection was handled by low grade clerical staff but they were at least involved in using the information. The 'collector' in a new system might have no direct use and could therefore be careless.

The elimination of duplication of data handling and input sources often occurs as a result of the introduction of MIS. Another factor is the standardisation of systems and procedures. One firm with seven different accounting locations discovered that each office had different style cash books, journals and purchase ledgers and these were standardised as a result of developing a new accounting system.

1.9.2   Changes in distribution of reports

Most MIS are designed with a view to improving the output of information produced. Futhermore it is likely that a greater number of managers will receive information than hitherto. While in the past, most managers could obtain information if they really wanted it, it was likely to be available in another department or could not be produced without massive clerical effort. The mere fact that information is now available and, more importantly, accessible, increases its demand and use. It is likely that managers will tend to spend more time on the decision-making duties because more detailed information is available.

One area in which changes and improvements resulting from MIS and system study occur is the format used to inform managers. Three principal types of reports are issued:

(a)   *Traditional reporting* - these summarise detailed transactions, periodically evaluate the results of actions taken and provide a formal and standardised method of routine reporting.

(b)   *Exception reporting* - for example, budgetary control where only those items which reflect significant variation from plans are reported.

(c)   *Inquiry reporting* - where routine reports are not required but information is required to answer specific questions thus often replacing clerks searching through files in manual systems.

Another important factor is the increased speed of reporting. Most organisations find that the introduction of computerised MIS has reduced the time lag between activities and the reporting of those activities in quantifiable terms.

1.9.3   Changes in management structure

While many changes are the result of the introduction of computer systems, the information system is perhaps the focal point. Nearly all organisations are changing from time to time and change is an essential part of the flexibility necessary to meet ever-changing business demands.

Improved communication facilities often remove the restraints placed on management framework by distance, volume, cost and time aspects. Various types of changes occur as a result of introducing MIS and these may be summarised as follows:

(a)   general organisational reviews;
(b)   minor realignment of functions;
(c)   effect of new control procedures;
(d)   increased co-ordination;
(d)   increased flexibility.

Several companies take the opportunity to reorganise functions at the same time as introducing MIS as this causes minimal extra disruption.

A typical example is a firm where two managers prepared sales forecasts, one for sales and the other for production, without consideration of each other's estimate. Coordination of these two estimates provided closer links between sales budgeting and production scheduling while reducing stock and customer inquiry problems.

1.9.4   Personnel and training

The human factors implicit in introducing MIS should never be underestimated. You should recognise that you are dealing with changes and most of us do not like changes. Furthermore, there is still a considerable amount of mystique attached to computers and many people are openly critical of the possible benefits to be achieved.

The three main reasons why many people do not like change and often become uncooperative are:

(a)   aversion to learning new skills;
(b)   fear of loss of job;
(c)   fear of loss of status or authority in the organisation.

It is essential to ensure that management and staff are kept fully informed of all MIS development. This can be done by meetings, progress reports and internal communication devices such as house journals. Another important aspect is involvement of user departments and it was suggested previously that all project teams should include suitable user representatives. A comprehensive training programme should always form part of any MIS implementation work.

Another problem affecting the progress of MIS development is the lack of trained and effective systems designers. After all there is not an abundance of people trained in general management functions, systems design and computer processing. Also the tremendous growth in the demand for such staff has not helped matters. Many systems staff change jobs at perhaps more frequent intervals than other disciplines. The use of inexperienced staff often causes more problems than it solves.

1.9.5 Centralisation - decentralisation

You will find these terms crop up in many discussions about management problems so it is not surprising to encounter them in the study of MIS. Opinions differ on what is the most suitable approach and it is dangerous to generalise. It all depends on the type of organisation, the style of management and the distance between locations.

In general computer users are often justified in centralising the routine processing of data. But the collection of data is a separate consideration. We have already mentioned the extensive use of terminals whereby data can be input from the most remote locations.

Factors which need to be considered include:

(a) the role of the head office - is it advisory or executive?
(b) the nature of the information flows between different sections;
(c) the degree of standardisation of procedures and reporting;
(d) costs and benefits;
(e) the speed of communication and the problems of recreating inaccurate input data;
(f) the ability of a central point to meet day-to-day local demands.

Finally, it is not always an 'either, or' situation. You might well find that different aspects require different solutions.

1.9.6 Responsibility for MIS

As in so many of the topics so far discussed, there is no right answer. Many smaller organisations would look to the financial and management accounting function as the principal provider of information. However, in larger organisations it is important to adopt an unbiased viewpoint. It could be argued that if a company-wide approach is being adopted to provide a total, integrated information service, then such a function should enjoy a similar independence as compared with any other major function.

Many organisations have a management services director whose functions might include:

(a) data processing/computer operations;
(b) systems design and programming;
(c) organisation and methods;
(d) operations research.

Where a computer facility is part of the system it is normal to have a specific manager such as a data processing manager. The technical complexities of the equipment together with the highly trained personnel required to implement systems often lead to the establishment of a separate function.

1.9.7 Summary: the qualities of good management information

(a) *Timely* - As stated earlier the frequency with which management information is produced is crucial in determining its quality. The value of information diminishes with the length of time that the recipient has to wait for its production. Timeliness, however, is relative to the needs and features of the individual business.

(b)   *Accurate* - Information which is inaccurate is of little use to management. An important attribute of management information is that it is credible and therefore reliable.

(c)   *Discriminatory* - An important attribute of management information is that it is discriminatory. This means that the reports produced are tailored to the levels of understanding of the recipients. The information needs of the persons within an organisation vary greatly. The degree of detail required by, say, the managing director varies from the detail required by, say, the credit controller.

(d)   *Economical* - Management information has no intrinsic value. Its value is represented by the benefit derived from the information by management. Any new scheme for installing and developing management information systems must be validated by considering the benefits that could be derived therefrom.

Management information systems should also economise management effort. A management information system that increases rather than reduces the drudgery of management tasks is not going to be popular with the people that use it.

1.10   Conclusion

This session has examined the essential elements of business systems. Objectives and control and feedback have been explained. Recall the type of loops which are possible.

Information is a vital ingredient in good management. We have examined the kinds of information which exist and outlined the attributes of good information. Finally MIS and its uses were set out.

1.11   Questions

Quick questions

(1)   What is the value of management information?

(2)   'You can't have a management information system without having a computer'. True or false?

(3)   For which level(s) of management would you design a management information system?

Written test question

1.1   Quality of management information

The quality of management information is directly related to its timing.

(a)   Discuss this statement with particular reference to:

(i)   the different purposes for which the information may be required; and
(ii)   the relative merits of speed versus accuracy in each case.

(b)   Explain in what ways the timing of information flows should be taken into account when designing information systems.   **(20 marks)**

SESSION 2

Data processing systems - an overview of non-computerised methods

Every data processing system has certain common features which are as follows:

- a section for input;
- a section for output;
- a section for storage;
- a section for processing;
- a section for control.

This generalisation applies to all data processing systems: manual, mechanical or electronic. In this session, we will review non-computer-based data processing systems as a prelude to looking at computerised systems.

2.1 Manual systems

The common features of all manual systems can be exemplified by a clerk at a desk (Figure 2.1).

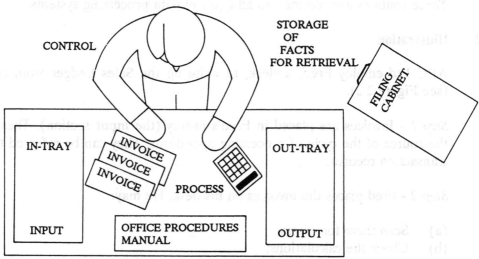

Figure 2.1: A clerk at a desk

In Figure 2.1, the clerk's in-tray becomes the **input** section where the raw facts (**data**) are collected.

The out-tray is the **output** section where the processed raw facts (**information**) are placed ready for distribution.

The filing cabinet becomes the repository for **storage**, ie facts which are required for future retrieval are stored therein.

The central area of the desk is for **processing** the new facts. You will observe that there is a calculator there for carrying out mathematical operations.

The **control** of the whole operation is by means of the clerk's brain. He can interpret his instructions set out in the office manual, and achieve an orderly and logical day-to-day routine.

However, this system suffers from the following drawbacks since it is

- expensive;
- erratic;
- prone to fits of boredom, temper and illness;
- incapable of handling large volumes of work.

Due to the lack of people available who are prepared to dedicate their lives to carrying out clerical routines, it is not surprising to find that they have been replaced by mechanical and later, electronic data processing methods.

2.1.1   The language of data processing

You have encountered a number of new terms peculiar to this subject in Session 1. Data processing is, unfortunately, a subject prone to the use of 'buzzwords'. It is important to learn the correct terminology and to avoid the use of colloquialisms (however fashionable) in dealing with examination questions. Some important terms are illustrated in the following example, which deals with the operations that are involved in a manual system of data processing.

These routines are common to all types of data processing systems.

2.1.2   Illustration

ABC Ltd employ Fred, a clerk, to write up the Sales Ledger from customers' invoices (see Figure 2.2).

Step 1 - Invoices are placed in Fred's in-tray (the **input** section). These invoices provide the source of the cycle of processing operations. They can be referred to as the source or transaction records.

Step 2 - Fred places the invoices on his desk. He may:

(a)   Scan them for errors;
(b)   Check the calculations;
(c)   Sort them into some sequence (possibly alphabetical).

Step 3 - Fred then enters the sales invoices into his sales day book so that he creates a permanent record of all the transactions for that day.

Step 4 - Fred posts the items from the sales day book to the sales ledger. He calculates the customer's new balance and balances his account.

From this routine, which is so familiar to accountancy students, we can derive some of the terms that will become familiar in the weeks of study ahead.

Step 1	*Step 2*	*Step 3*	*Step 4*
Sales invoice: Able	Douglas Charlie Baker	Able Sales day book	Sales Ledger
Sales invoices are placed in Fred's in-tray	Fred sorts them into alphabetical order	Fred posts the entry to the sales day book and then to the sales ledger.	

Figure 2.2: ABC Ltd, Fred's daily routine

(a)   The sales ledger is a collection of customer accounts - we can describe it as a data **file**.

(b)   Each customer account sheet in the sales ledger provides information about an entity called a customer. Each customer account sheet is called a **record**.

(c)   Each customer record contains units of related information about each entity. Each unit of information is called a **field**.

(d)   Each field of information is made up of letters of the alphabet, numbers or symbols like £, $ etc. Each field is said to be made up of **characters**.

Therefore information in any data processing system can be seen to be organised in a hierarchical form as shown in Figure 2.3.

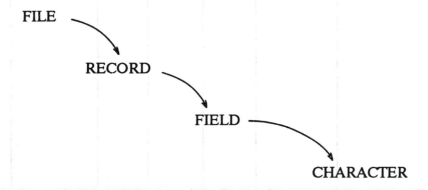

Figure 2.3: The hierarchy of information

Some of the data in the sales ledger file are always changing; other data are static. The sales ledger balance is changed by each system input of cash, invoice or journal entry. Data such as the customer's name, address and credit limit change infrequently, and such data are used for permanent reference. The sales ledger can be described as a master file, as it is a collection of records containing permanent, as well as variable data (Figure 2.4).

The sales day book contains details of the data that bring about change in a master file. Such a collection of data can be called the **transaction file** as it is created purely to update the data held in the master file.

33

ALPHA BETA LTD		A 1
1 TRADING ESTATE	**Sales ledger account**	Credit limit:
NOTTS		£200

DATE	DETAILS	Dr		Cr		BALANCE	
10/11/x3	SDB 40 Inv. 1130	£ 100	89			£ 100	89
12/12/x3	SDB 81 Inv. 1469	£ 25	60			£ 126	49

Figure 2.4: A sales ledger master file record

2.1.3   Manual systems in business

Most manual systems of data processing are essentially for the smaller business. However, certain proprietary systems can be obtained which attempt to offer a labour saving element to the user. An example of this type of system is the one sold under the proprietary brand of Kalamazoo and it is illustrated in Figure 2.5.

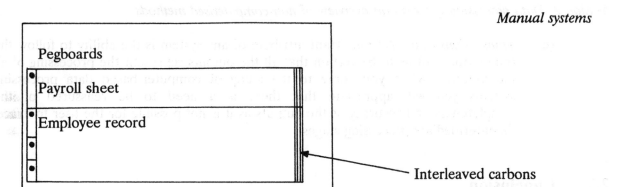

Figure 2.5: A pegboard and carbon record system

In this system, the prime entry record and the master record are processed by one clerical operation.

The documents are fixed to a pegboard and carbon paper is placed between the documents. As an entry is made on the top document, a carbon impression is made on the bottom copy. This system is used in the following applications:

- cheque payments / bought ledger systems;
- bought day book / bought ledger systems;
- wages sheet / payroll record systems (see Figure 2.5);
- sales day book / sales ledger systems;
- cash receipts / sales ledger systems.

2.1.4 Managerial controls in systems of data processing

It is useful to mention here the controls that are commonly encountered in data processing systems of every type. Many of the points stated here apply equally to computerised systems:

(a) *Sequential controls on documentation* - Source documents which originate transactions should be prenumbered serially and sequentially controlled. Spoilt documents should not be thrown away but retained.

(b) *Multipart documents* - An essential feature of any good paperwork system is that certain documents are produced in multipart formats. This is done by designing paperwork with carbon interleaves or with NCR (no carbon required) paper.

(c) *Batch controls* - The greater the degree of automation the greater the danger that records may be omitted or even duplicated. A useful discipline resorted to by many businesses is to collect homogeneous records in discrete units (batches) and to record both the number of documents in the batch as well as the aggregate money value of the transactions (if available).

(d) *Balancing and control accounts* - You are familiar with the concept of control accounts from Papers 1 and 5 (*Basic Accounting* and *Accounting*). Control accounts have an important part to play in data processing systems as they provide a way of validating the arithmetical accuracy of transactions. It does not matter if the sales ledger is loose leaf, kept on a bookkeeping machine or a VRC or maintained on a data file in a computer installation. Every user wants to be sure of the following equation:

Opening values + input transations = closing values

(e) *Transactions trail* - An important attribute of any system is the ability to follow the transaction trail ie, to be certain that all the outputs represent the processing of all the inputs. When you come to the study of computer-based data processing systems you will appreciate that there is a need to be reassured of the completeness and accuracy of the outputs as it is not possible for the user to 'trace' the intermediate processing stages.

2.2   Conclusion

It is important that you appreciate how computerised data processing systems work in the same way as manual systems. The only difference is the speed and accuracy of processing and the machinery used to do it.

Electronic data processing

We now turn our attention to the computer and the way that it works in order to appreciate its use in business as a management tool. Familiarity with manual methods of data processing will make the task of understanding easier, since many computer systems are, in fact, analogies of original manual systems.

3.1 Introduction

3.1.1 Features of a computer

The characteristics of a computer which distinguish it from other forms of data processing are:

(a) it has the capacity to store its programs of instructions;

(b) it has the capacity to store data and to act upon the data by means of stored instructions. It can also **modify** its stored program of instructions;

(c) it has the capacity to function with a high degree of automatic control.

There are broadly two types of computers:

Analog - these measure physical quantities as continuous variables, eg electric current, temperature, pressure etc.

Digital - these manipulate discrete numbers, letters and symbols as separate entities. The digital computer is used for commercial data processing.

To help you understand these terms, think of your wristwatch: if it has hands, it is an analog watch and by their position the hands can represent any time at all. If your watch has a display of numbers it is a digital watch and is only capable of showing a specific number at one time.

3.2   Main elements of a computer

3.2.1   Similarity with other systems

Figure 3.1 shows the main parts of any computer whether mini, micro or mainframe. All data processing consists of the computer reading in data (**input**), processing that data (central processing unit), often with reference to other data (backing store) and producing results (output).

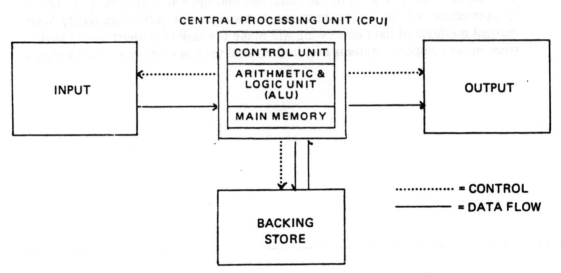

Figure 3.1: Computer - main components

3.2.2   The Control Unit

This consists of circuits and registers which carry out the following functions:

(a)   reading stored program instructions;
(b)   decoding stored program instructions;
(c)   causing the instructions to be executed;
(d)   obtaining the next instruction in sequence.

3.2.3   The Arithmetic Logic Unit (ALU)

This section has two main functions:

(a)   arithmetical functions
(b)   logical functions (ie, comparing two numbers to see which is larger).

The ability to perform different actions which are dependent upon the results of any processing step gives the computer its unique decision-making ability.

3.3   Data representation

3.3.1   Communicating with the computer

When we communicate among ourselves we use a bewildering number of conventions and methods. The written word is communicated using the Roman alphabet (26 states of representation from A-Z plus symbols of various types). Quantities are represented using the so-called decimal or denary system which uses ten states of representation which are absolute (from 0-9) and various positional states of representation by moving digits around a decimal point. A quantity such as 7936 is based upon the convention of a 'base of ten':

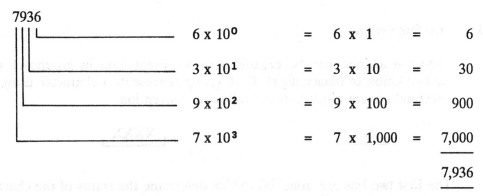

6 x 10^0	=	6 x 1	= 6
3 x 10^1	=	3 x 10	= 30
9 x 10^2	=	9 x 100	= 900
7 x 10^3	=	7 x 1,000	= 7,000
			7,936

The computer, however, cannot cope with these various states of representation. Computer memories are composed of tiny magnetisable devices which can be either positively or negatively charged. Computer memories are said, therefore, to be composed of two-state devices. It follows that the complex communication patterns that we use for the written word or for computations must be broken down into a two-state code so that they can be stored in the computer's memory and be manipulated for processing purposes.

3.3.2 The binary system

Denary or decimal notation consists of ten absolute values (from 0-9) and as many positional values as the user requires. The binary system uses two absolute states of representation, 0 and 1. The contrast between the binary and denary scale is shown hereunder:

	Denary	Binary	2^3 = 8	2^2 = 4	2^1 = 2	2^0 = 1
Zero	0	0	0	0	0	0
One	1	1	0	0	0	1
Two	2	10	0	0	1	0
Three	3	11	0	0	1	1
Four	4	100	0	1	0	0
Five	5	101	0	1	0	1
Six	6	110	0	1	1	0
Seven	7	111	0	1	1	1
Eight	8	1000	1	0	0	0
Nine	9	1001	1	0	0	1

You will notice that each time a binary digit moves to the left it increases in value by a multiple of 2. It is therefore a **two-state** form of notation. Binary notation is, therefore, used as the basis for computer codes. Each magnetisable device, when positively charged, can represent a binary 1 and when negatively charged a binary 0.

It is therefore natural to find that computer codes are based on binary notation where, by analogy, a positive state can be represented by a binary digit (1) and a negative state can be represented by a binary digit (0). The memory of a computer can be considered to be a collection of storage devices each capable of representing a binary digit. These binary digits can be grouped into individual areas or locations each of which can be separately identified by a unique serial number (the address). A character or a group of characters can be represented in each location whether they are alphabetic (a,b,z), numeric (0,2,4) or symbolic (£,*,/). This character representation can vary according to the particular machine.

3.3.3   Coding systems

Some machines may be organised to represent data in groups of six bits (bit is an abbreviation of binary digit). Each group represents a character using the **binary coded decimal system** which uses the following convention:

$$\underbrace{XX} \qquad\qquad\qquad \underbrace{XXXX}$$

The first two bits are 'zone' bits which determine the status of the character, ie, numeric, symbolic, alphameric.

The next four bits are used to represent a number, a letter or a symbol.

By varying the first two digits, it is possible to represent 26 letters of the alphabet as well as symbolic characters. This method of representation is a feature of older machines and offers 2^6, ie, 64 states of representation.

Other machines store data in groups of 8 bits each known as a byte. In a byte-based code such as EBCDIC (Extended Binary Coded Decimal Interchange Code) a maximum of 256 (2^8) characters/symbols can be encoded. Some small machines may use 8 bit groups to store data according to the ASCII Convention (**American Standard Code for Information Interchange**). This code uses seven bits (the eighth is for code checking purposes) and provides 2^7 or 128 possible states of representation. Figure 3.2 illustrates extracts from EBCDIC and ASCII codes.

Certain makes of computers may hold data in 16 bit or 32 bit formations. Such formations are known as *words* (as they hold more than one character) and they may also be used for storage of large 'pure' numbers.

Byte machines can offer a valuable facility of variable word length storage. A numeric field such as 121489 would normally require 6 bytes.

By removing the zone digits which are common to all numeric characters, this field could be accommodated in 3 bytes, each byte holding two numeric characters. This is known as **packed decimal storage**; machines that offer this facility are known as **variable word length machines**.

3.4   Physical characteristics of the hardware

3.4.1   The 'chip'

The constitution of the modern computer (regardless of size) is based on the development of minute pieces of metal oxide silicon (silicon chips). The ALU and Control Unit consists of complex logic circuits which are miniaturised on single chips. Such single chips are termed **microprocessors** when they embody the complete assembly of memory, ALU and Control Unit.

Character	EBCDIC Bit representation		ASCII Bit representation	
0	1111	0000	011	0000
1	1111	0001	011	0001
2	1111	0010	011	0010
3	1111	0011	011	0011
4	1111	0100	011	0100
5	1111	0101	011	0101
6	1111	0110	011	0110
7	1111	0111	011	0111
8	1111	1000	011	1000
9	1111	1001	011	1001
A	1100	0001	100	0001
B	1100	0010	100	0010
C	1100	0011	100	0011
D	1100	0100	100	0100
E	1100	0101	100	0101
F	1100	0110	100	0110
G	1100	0111	100	0111
H	1100	1000	100	1000
I	1100	1001	100	1001
J	1001	0001	100	1010
K	1001	0010	100	1111
L	1001	0011	100	1100
M	1001	0100	100	1101
N	1001	0101	100	1110
O	1001	0110	100	1111
P	1001	0111	101	0000
Q	1001	1000	101	0001
R	1001	1001	101	0010
S	1110	0010	101	0011
T	1110	0011	101	0100
U	1110	0100	101	0101
V	1110	0101	101	0110
W	1110	0110	101	0111
X	1110	0111	101	1000
Y	1110	1000	101	1001
Z	1110	1001	101	1010

Figure 3.2: An example of computer codes

In the 1960s and 1970s the memories of computers were composed of ferrite cores. Ferrite cores are now obsolete and have been replaced by the miniaturised chip memories. The principle of the storage of data using two state representation remains unchanged.

3.4.2 Memory size

The main memory of the computer is also composed of such silicon 'chips'. Each chip can hold a module of storage. The small personal computer sold in the shops today may hold between around 32,000 to around 64,000 addressable locations on one chip. This is often expressed as 32K or 64K (in this context K = 1,024). A large system which is engaged on continuous processing on a 7-day week with three shifts working may have a

0110z

memory size in excess of 1 million K in order to hold the large volumes of data and stored instructions which permit such a continuous mode of operation. The word 'system' was chosen instead of 'machine' as many large computer systems may consist of several processors arranged as one configuration. This is more fully explained in 3.5 dealing with system architecture.

3.4.3 RAM, ROM and PROM

The memory of a modern computer is generally divided into an immediate access store which is a working area of memory. This is termed **Random Access Memory (RAM)**. Part of the memory contains certain stored instructions which are permanently wired into the circuiting. This is stored in **Read Only Memory (ROM)**.

Certain machines may have areas of memory which are programmable; once programs are stored, they are not capable of erasure. This type of memory is called **Programme Read Only Memory (PROM)**.

The programmed instructions held in ROM are those which enable a computer to receive instructions and in some cases to translate or interpret instructions in a high level language like BASIC. This type of program is sometimes termed the monitor and is a fundamental part of making a computer work like a computer, ie, it controls the hardware. This matter is fully dealt with in Session 12. A brief explanation, however, might be useful at this point (Figure 3.3).

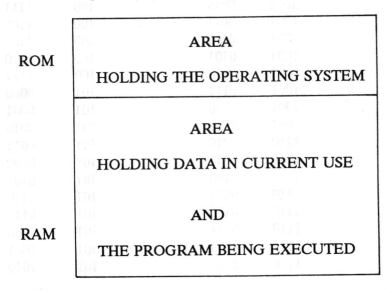

Figure 3.3: The division of computer memory

A significant part of the computer's memory is reserved for the storage of the **operating system**. This is a generic term to describe a number of control programs that enable the computer to carry out the functions listed below.

(a) Controlling input, output and storage peripherals.

(b) Output/stop/interrupt.

(c) Enabling various tasks to be done in some particular sequence.

(d) Carrying out a variety of tasks within a particular time scale.

0110z

(e) Producing a two-way conversational mode of operation between the user and the computer. This is known as interactive processing.

(f) Keeping a log of each action carried out by the computer. (This is not usually a feature of certain microcomputers.) On some machines the operating system (a part of it) is permanently resident in ROM.

On small machines the 'systems software' is read into the memory before commencing operation. On large computers a significant part is held on disk and this must be read into memory as and when required.

3.5 System architecture - small computers

3.5.1 Mini, micro or mainframe?

The advances in the development of computer technology have made it very difficult to classify computers into convenient categories. It is very difficult to discern the division between minicomputers and microcomputers or between minicomputers and mainframe-installations.

Let us start with the type of computer that everyone is aware of: the small computer that no accountant seems to do without!

3.5.2 Modular structure

Most small computers are built on a modular system whereby units of hardware can be combined into one configuration. This can be illustrated by Figure 3.4.

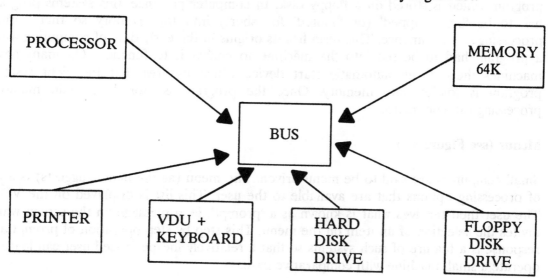

Figure 3.4: The modular structure of a small computer

3.5.3 Explanation

(a) *Processor* - The chip here would hold control unit and ALU.

(b) *Memory* - A typical 'chip' module would hold 64K of RAM.

(c) *VDU and keyboard* - A Visual Display Unit (like a TV screen) and a full typewriter keyboard would be provided. Data entered on the keyboard will be displayed on the VDU. An optional extra would be a calculator attachment for entering numeric data and similar options. Output can also be displayed on the screen.

(d) *Floppy disk* - A floppy disk or diskette is a commonly used storage medium. A floppy disk that is 5¼" in diameter can hold anything from 100K to 700K of storage (depending on the ingenuity of the manufacture).

(e) *BUS* - This term refers to the control organisation to which the various components can be wired. It may be possible to **enhance** the memory size by adding on an extra module of 64K of RAM. Similarly the user may wish to add an extra keyboard and VDU.

(f) *Printer* - The user of a small computer would not be satisfied with output that is flashed up on a screen. Hard copy output will be required for reference purposes. It is therefore common to find a printer linked to the system to provide permanent output. The commonest type of printer is a **fast** serial printer such as a daisy wheel printer (which provides high quality printing) or a dot matrix printer (where the quality of printing is somewhat inferior).

3.5.4   Methods of operation

As explained earlier, a computer requires certain stored instructions to enable it to be operated as a computer. A small computer **monitor**, therefore, requires to be augmented by certain specialist programs to enable the hardware to function. The typical small computer user therefore is required to read into the memory a systems program which is stored on a floppy disk. In computer parlance, this systems program has to be 'bootstrapped' (or 'booted' for short) into the memory so that normal processing can commence. This term has its origins in the early days of computing when a program had to be fed into the machine to enable it to function. On many small machines there is an automatic start device which ensures that the right systems program is loaded into memory. Once the program is stored in main memory, processing can commence.

3.5.5   Menus (see Figure 3.5)

Small computers are said to be menu driven. The menu (as the name suggests) is a list of processing options that are available to the user. This list is displayed on the VDU. The user then receives what is known as a 'prompt', ie, a message on the screen which invites the selection of an item on the menu. This step by step operation of prompt and response is a feature of such systems so that a relatively inexperienced user can learn to operate a small machine with comparative ease.

Unfortunately this type of operation presents drawbacks for high volumes of input or for repetitious operations on homogenous data which are more efficiently dealt with by other techniques.

Nectarine Model II

PROGRAM SELECTION

Module No	name		
1	SALES ORDER		
2	SALES LEDGER UPDATE	⎯	MENU
3	PAYROLL		
4	NOMINAL LEDGER		

KEY IN MODULE NO AND PRESS CR   'Prompt'

Figure 3.5: A menu in a small computer application

3.5.6   8 bit, 16 bit or 32 bit micros

You often hear comparison being made between 8 bit micros and 16 bit micros. You will now have realised that the difference relates to the number of binary digits allocated to individual addressable memory locations. The term 'word' is used in computer parlance to mean 'unit of addressable location' and word length can make a considerable difference to operating speeds and capabilities. The highest 'pure' value that can be stored in 8 bits is 2^8-1 = 255 and the highest 'pure' number for a 16 bit unit of storage is 2^{15}-1 = 32,767. The maximum number of addressable locations available, though, on a 16 bit micro without special programming is 65,535. 16 bit micros are faster in operation as fewer memory locations require to be manipulated. The computer's instructional ability is also greater with 16 bit memory architecture. 32 bit memories are a feature of the 'super micro'.

3.5.7   Categories of microcomputers

The microcomputer of the 1990s exists in several categories:

(a)   the **desktop** which is the largest of the three, and this may be a standalone version or a multi-user unit;

(b)   the **transportable** which can be transferred from one location to another; and

(c)   the **lap-portable which fits into a small carrying-case**, the smallest weighing 23.6 pounds (from Compaq) and costing around £2,700.

The lap-portable has an **acoustic coupler** which allows it to utilise a public telephone by linking to the handset. This allows data to be transmitted and received to and from, say, the HQ computer.

3.5.8   Minicomputers

It is difficult to determine where minicomputers and microcomputers divide. It is, however, fair to say that the typical minicomputer installation may have the following features which again (confusingly) may also be common to **some** microcomputer systems:

    (a)   internal storage capacity between 4 and 16 Megabytes
    (b)   hard disk storage
    (c)   tape storage facilities
    (d)   fast printers, eg, line printers
    (e)   supporting several keyboard and VDU workstations
    (f)   use of 16 bit/32 bit word lengths for storage purposes

In short, a minicomputer is very much like the large air conditioned monster of popular imagery that works all around the clock, but on a smaller scale.

There are also **superminicomputers**, offering high levels of performance at a price which is relatively low - something like 33% to 50% of the supercomputer (see 3.6.1) performance at around one twentieth of the price.

3.6   Systems architecture for the large business

3.6.1   Large or mainframe systems

The division between certain minicomputer systems and mainframes is difficult to discern. However, when we look at the computer systems used for large commercial users such as banks, insurance companies and the like we realise that the installation may comprise more than one machine and that some machines are 'slave' processors which are engaged on computational exercises while other machines act as controllers or regulators of the system. This type of architecture reflects the change of emphasis in the design of processing systems over the last fifteen years.

The computer user is no longer content to process large volumes of data on a historical basis, but requires prompt information in order to make the right decision. There is also a need to ensure reliability of function. Computers, like any other device, can malfunction. Dependence on one machine alone could be disastrous for an organisation.

In many systems satellite processors are used for input/output functions. Such **Front End Processors** as they are called free the main central processor from routine editing and input tasks.

The multi-machine type configuration is explained schematically in Figure 3.6.

This type of multi-machine configuration offers a form of protection against machine breakdown. If you consider the system for providing cash facilities to customers of UK clearing banks, you have an illustration of how the dispenser terminal at the branch can act as a front end processor to receive and validate input (ie, a withdrawal).

The system as operated by, say, Barclays Bank receives input from customers and dispenses cash and a registration of the customer's request as output (Figure 3.7). The withdrawal will not be debited to the customer's account until the next business day as the inputs will be processed at some time when the terminals are not likely to be used (usually in the early hours of the next day).

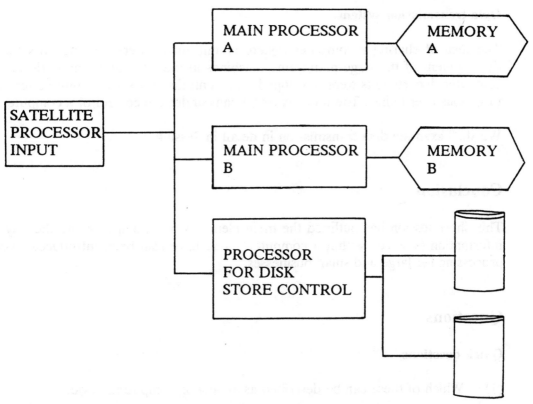

Figure 3.6: Multi-machine configuration

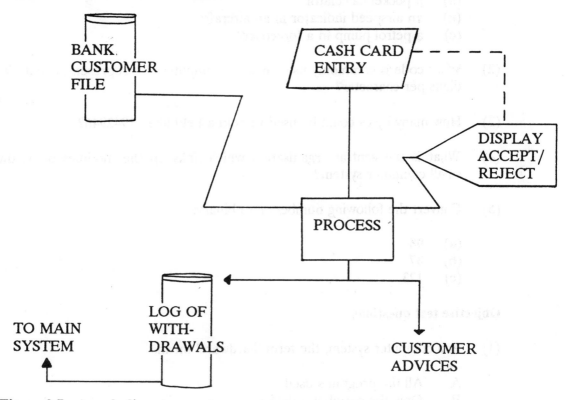

Figure 3.7: A cash dispenser system

In the 1990s we also have the **supercomputer**. There are over 25 of these in the UK at present. Used by companies like British Aerospace, these machines operate on the multiprocessing principle, having several processors which can be used simultaneously. The Cray Y-MP, for example, costs around $25 million and uses eight processors.

0110z

3.6.2   Data transmission systems

The idea of sharing a computer system among many users became possible with the development of the large mainframe machines in the late 1960s and early 1970s. Many computer departments were developed on a centralised basis with on-line terminal links to various user points. The term *on-line* means under the control of a computer.

We shall examine data transmission in detail in Session 7.

3.7   Conclusion

This short session has outlined the main elements of a computer and the way in which information is stored within a computer. You have also been introduced to computer processing for large and small businesses.

3.8   Questions

Quick questions

(1)   Which of these can be described as an analog computing device:

   (a)   a pocket calculator
   (b)   an airspeed indicator in an aircraft
   (c)   a petrol pump in a forecourt?

(2)   What code is commonly used in small computers for representing data in 7 binary digits per character?

(3)   How many bytes could be used to hold a field like 11942946?

(4)   What is the central organisation which links up the modules of hardware in a small computer system?

(5)   Convert the following numbers into binary:

   (a)   98
   (b)   37
   (c)   123

Objective test questions

(1)   In a computer system, the term 'hardware' means:

   A   All the programs used
   B   Only the peripheral devices
   C   All the physical devices
   D   Only the operating system

(2)   The initials 'ROM' mean:

A   Real-time, On-line, Microcomputer
B   Reactive, On-line, Machine
C   Read Only Memory
D   Randomly Organised Memory

(3)   A CPU consists of the main memory together with:

A   Control unit and backing store
B   Control unit, peripherals and arithmetic and logic unit
C   Peripherals, backing store and arithmetic and logic unit
D   Control unit and arithmetic and logic unit

(4)   CPU stands for:

A   Computer processing utility
B   Central processing unit
C   Computer peripheral unit
D   Central peripheral utility

Written test questions

3.1   Microcomputers

Identify and briefly explain **five** of the characteristics of the microcomputer which distinguish it from the larger mainframe.   **(10 marks)**

3.2   Micros in the office

'Microcomputers have helped to revolutionise office procedures.' Discuss with suitable examples.   **(20 marks)**

SESSION 4

Data capture techniques

In this session we shall concentrate on one important aspect of computer systems, namely that of data capture. The term 'data capture' will be used generally in this session to embrace the following areas of study:

(a) methods and media;
(b) business applications;
(c) advantages and possible disadvantages.

4.1 Introduction

4.1.1 The choice of hardware

The following matters determine the choice of data capture technique.

(a) financial constraints;
(b) volumes of data;
(c) technical skills possessed by staff;
(d) management information requirements;
(e) complexity of the data itself;
(f) availability or otherwise of manpower resources;
(g) cost minimisation.

These seven factors are useful pointers in arriving at the choice of a particular item of hardware or processing method.

4.2 Input devices

4.2.1 Initial considerations

When choosing input methods and media, most users are concerned with the following:

(a) how to economise on the use of manpower;
(b) how to prevent or detect errors in the source data;
(c) how to achieve data capture with the lowest possible cost.

4.2.2   Punched card input

The punched card remains a method of computer input despite its various drawbacks. The impact of small computers and advanced data conversion devices has meant a considerable reduction in the use of cards for large scale processing.

The punched card possesses the following advantages:

(a)   it is tried, tested and relatively uncomplicated;
(b)   it is man-understandable, and can be used as a dual purpose document.

The disadvantages of punched cards are that they are:

(a)   bulky to store;
(b)   slow to read and to write;
(c)   prone to error;
(d)   labour intensive to prepare and to correct;
(e)   their fixed format (ie, one character per frame) can inhibit systems design.

The card, once punched, must be verified by inserting the cards in a verifying machine and rekeying the data. Errors are notified by a flashing light on the verifier. The cards are read by a card reader.

Typical reading speeds are 1,000 cards per minute with a maximum of 2,000 cards per minute.

4.2.3   Paper tape

Paper tape is now almost obsolete. It is a continuous recording medium on which data are recorded by a pattern of punched holes, one character per column or frame. Paper tape possesses certain advantages over punched cards in that it is a continuous recording medium and is possibly more compact to store. It is largely used as a by-product of other systems; the commonest use is where on-line terminals are in use and the link to the computer is broken. In such cases, the paper tape is encoded as an alternative to allowing keyboard operations to build up a backlog of input data. The tape is then read when the system is 'live' again.

4.2.4   Magnetic tape encoding (key-to-tape)

Although magnetic tapes and disks will be covered in detail later there are several input devices, associated with these storage media, to be described here.

A magnetic tape encoder is an off-line device consisting of a keyboard, a magnetic tape drive and usually a visual display unit (VDU) for visual verification of data. An operator reads from a source document and enters the data via the keyboard. The hardware then records the data on the computer compatible magnetic tape.

On a unit without the VDU facility, verification must be performed by re-keying the data, although conscious errors can be corrected by back-spacing and re-keying. Verification is more efficient with a VDU available, since it allows the data to be checked visually as it is entered from the source documents. Usually a line (or a fixed number of characters) is entered, displayed on the screen and stored in a buffer to allow visual checking and correction of the complete line, before depression of a special key actually records the data on the tape.

In some sophisticated systems it is possible to display an image of the source document on the VDU. The operator then types in the information as if completing a form.

Magnetic tape encoders are used for collecting large volumes of data for use in what are known as batch processing systems, ie, systems where the emphasis is on processing large amounts of homogeneous data for historical recording purposes. Magnetic tape is a far more efficient recording medium than, say, punched cards, and the use of a VDU enables an operator to visually check items of data before it is stored on tape.

The format of the input record is controlled by means of a stored program (often held as a tape cassette), and errors in formatting are detected and rejected. In effect, this device is an 'intelligent' data system; ie, it is like a small computer in its own right.

An alternative name for this system is key-to-cassette.

4.2.5 Key-to-disk systems

These systems (Figure 4.1) have the following features;

(a)   various workstations consisting of keyboards with VDUs;
(b)   a small processor;
(c)   an area of disk storage;
(d)   magnetic tape units;
(e)   communication equipment (optional);
(f)   a supervisor's console.

The key stations are generally hard-wired to the small processor. They may be situated in a separate department for data conversion or sited at various strategic points in order to collect data at source.

The communication equipment mentioned above is used if it is desired to transmit information to a 'host' computer elsewhere, ie, the key-to-disk system functions act as a front end processor.

When data is entered via the keyboard, it is held in an area (temporary storage allocated to each workstation) which acts as a buffer. A resident program carries out logical checks on the data. If the data is accepted, it is written onto a designated area on the disk. Rejected data is identified by an audible signal so that the record may be amended.

Verification is possible by summoning the record for display in the key station buffer so that a record can be rekeyed.

Once the records have been verified, they can be copied onto magnetic tape which is then used as input to a main or host processor.

Advantages claimed for key-to-disk systems are:

(a)   greater control over the capture of input; operator errors are minimised and the need for verification is reduced;

(b)   a higher rate of productivity is achieved;

(c)   data is more portable;

(d)   the system is versatile in that it functions as a dedicated data entry system as well as a front-end processor for a host processor.

However, certain disadvantages are also perceived:

(a)   a breakdown in the processor immobilises all the key stations;
(b)   the system is costly to purchase and to maintain.

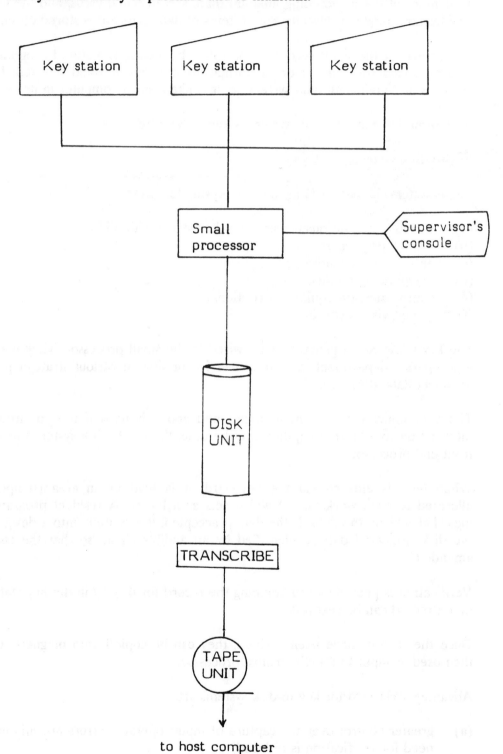

Figure 4.1: A key-to-disk system

4.2.6   Key-to-diskette

A floppy disk (or diskette), so called on account of the flexibility of the plastic material on which it is based, is a flimsy disk of roughly 5¼ or 8 inches in diameter which is held in a rigid square envelope for protection (Figure 4.2). There is only one key station to each floppy disk and the equipment would normally consist of a keyboard, a VDU and a disk drive. Verification is done by re-keying the data with the machinery set to 'verify' mode or by visual checking using the VDU.

After being recorded, the data on the diskettes is transferred to computer compatible magnetic tape by means of a data converter which can handle several diskettes at one time.

Other facilities are available on the more expensive systems. These include:

(a)   general validation checks (including check digit verification) using simple programs;

(b)   a printer attached to each data station to produce a printed copy of the diskette's contents if required.

Floppy disks are robust enough to be frequently handled and sent through the post without suffering any ill effects. They are also re-usable and inexpensive. Typically a 5.25" disk would cost about £3.00 and hold 120,000 characters of information.

Figure 4.2: A floppy disk

4.2.7   Optical mark reading (OMR)

This technique involves the use of standard preprinted documents on which horizontal marks are made with a black marker (pencil, ball-point pen, typewriter) in predetermined positions (Figure 4.3). The positioning of each mark is determined by dividing the form into areas or boxes printed in a distinctive colour. Each mark has a meaning which is dependent upon its position.

OMR is used widely by the following:

(a) utility companies, such as the gas and electricity boards, use OMR forms for meter reading purposes - each numeric digit on the electricity meter is represented by a mark on the form;

(b) certain educational establishments use OMR to evaluate examination papers of the multiple choice type.

ORDER FORM									
PRODUCT CODE				QUANTITY				UNITS	
0	0	0	0	0	●	●	●	0	singles
●	1	1	1	1	1	1	1	1	tens
2	●	2	2	2	2	2	2	●	dozens
3	3	3	3	●	3	3	3	3	hundreds
4	4	4	●	4	4	4	4	4	gross
5	5	5	5	5	5	5	5	5	
6	6	6	6	6	6	6	6	6	
7	7	7	7	7	7	7	7	7	
8	8	8	8	8	8	8	8	8	
9	9	●	9	9	9	9	9	9	

Figure 4.3: A form marked for use in an OMR application

A useful feature of OMR is the use of turnaround documentation which can be computer-produced output, which only requires marking with a black pen to transform it into computer-sensible input. For example, preprinted order forms can be generated by computers which in turn can be sensed by an OMR device after the user has indicated his preferences by marking the appropriate areas of the form.

It is important to cater for the correction of erroneous marks by ensuring that procedures exist which make the corrected form machine-sensible.

Advantages of OMR

(a) simple to use;
(b) less troublesome than hand produced OCR;
(c) can be marked with any medium;
(d) data is captured without labour intensive keyboarding and verification.

However:

(a) alphabetic characters cannot easily be identified;
(b) specialist form design is expensive.

4.2.8   Optical character recognition (OCR)

The idea of man-understandable characters which are also machine sensible is obviously attractive. The use of OCR is growing, but the practical drawbacks of the technique can inhibit potential users.

Typically, the use of OCR requires the use of two stylised fonts or typefaces which are in common use known as OCR-A (Figure 4.4) and OCR-B. The former is an American standard and the latter is designed for European use.

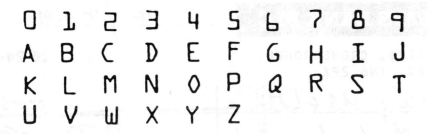

Figure 4.4: OCR-A typeface

More recently there has been a growth in the use of hand-printed OCR documents. A recent example of this in the UK is use, by the VISA credit card organisation, of sales vouchers which enable certain fields to be hand-printed so that they can be read by an optical reader.

A common use of OCR techniques is the remittance advices used by public utilities, eg, companies such as the gas and electricity boards. The consumer's cheque is despatched with the remittance advice when the bill is paid. The remittance advice provides computer-sensible input as the consumer's code number and amount are scanned by an optical reader.

A similar technique is used by hire-purchase companies who issue a book of payment vouchers encoded with the borrower's code number and amount. Each voucher is returned with the payment so that the borrower's account is correctly updated.

Advantages of OCR

(a)   Input is both man- and machine-sensible;
(b)   turnaround documents eliminate labour intensive keyboard preparation.

Disadvantages of OCR

Form design and stationery and printing costs are expensive.

2.9   Magnetic ink character recognition (MICR)

As with optical methods, a special typeface is used, but with the MICR system the printing ink contains a metallic substance in suspension which enables the print characters to be magnetised. The characters are recognised in the reader by the particular magnetic field pattern which they produce. The MICR technique is widely used by banks for the encoding of cheques where the sheer volume of documents would present an enormous punching problem. If you look at your cheque book you will see that along the bottom of each cheque, in computer numbers certain information (branch code, account number, cheque serial number) has already been printed in magnetic ink. When you issue a cheque and it is returned to the banking system for clearing, the amount of the cheque will also be encoded in the same way (Figure 4.5). All the necessary data is now encoded and the cheque can be read by the computer which automatically updates your account balance. It is no use trying to cheat by running a magnet across your cheques - they are all re-magnetised in the MICR reader immediately prior to being read!

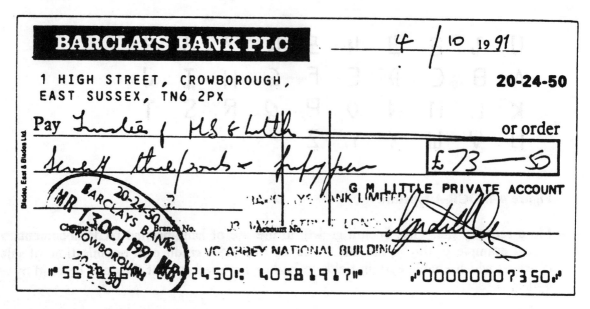

Figure 4.5: A cheque with the amount encoded in MICR (font E13b)

A similar system is used with luncheon vouchers. In both cases, the original documents are handled frequently before they reach the computer and can become dirty, crumpled or scribbled upon. The dirt and marks are not magnetic, so the underlying magnetic characters show through clearly to the reading device.

4.2.10 Kimball tags

These are small tickets having pre-printed numerical information and also pin-sized punched holes. The tickets are used as identification tags on goods, particularly in the retail clothing business, and are removed at the point of sale. The tags can be processed through a special converter and the coded information transferred to punched cards, paper tape or magentic tape for subsequent computer input. The system has the advantage of eliminating transcription from manually raised sales dockets which reduces the chances of error in subsequent computer-produced sales analysis.

4.2.11 Voice data entry (VDE)

This type of method is used where it is not possible to carry out any manipulative functions. For example, a common application quoted by some writers is the use of VDE in slaughterhouses where obviously it is convenient (and hygienic) to record data without handling any documents.

4.2.12 Electronic funds transfer (EFT)

This concept has been usefully applied to credit card transactions on an experimental basis with certain retailers. The customer's credit card is read by a badge reader which also provides a paper record of the transaction. The day's transactions which are so encoded are stored on some magnetic medium (like disk) and then transmitted to the accounts department of the credit card company. The banks are not overly enthusiastic about EFT as it could, when fully developed, make branch banking outlets obsolete.

2.13   Point-of-sale (POS) systems

Point-of-sale system is a generic term for various types of device used in retailing businesses. At their simplest they consist of cash registers which store data in computer-sensible form. They also provide a print-out/add-list and they also display the details of each transaction, the change required and a total.

The use of POS systems is widespread in chains of supermarkets or cash and carry warehouses where there is an acute need for regular information on stock positions as well as takings.

The working of a typical point-of-sale system is illustrated by Figure 4.6.

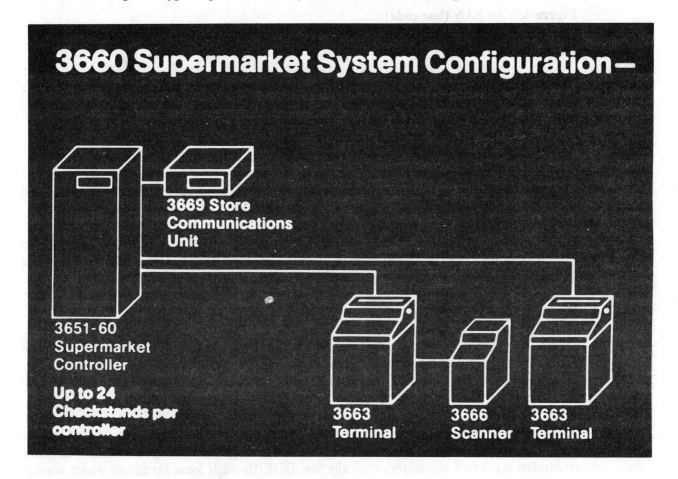

Figure 4.6: The IBM 3600 Supermarket System

Data can be entered via a keyboard or through the use of a light pen being passed over a bar code on a label.

A bar code may typically be of two types:

(a)   European article number (EAN);
(b)   uniform product code (UPC).

The bars (illustrated in Figure 4.7) are of various widths. The widths and spacing of the lines are used to represent numeric characters.

The typical EAN consists of thirteen digits; in order to ease identification of the EAN a human-readable sequence of numbers in the code is illustrated in an OCR typeface. This allows the code to be read by a light pen as well as an optical scanning device.

9 780273 024033

Figure 4.7: An EAN (bar code)

4.2.14 Badge readers

These devices are used in a variety of applications. The badge is a plastic card with a magnetic strip for data. The card is also embossed with data such as holder's name and number and expiry date. Badge readers can be used for:

(a)   recording times of production workers;

(b)   as part of cash dispensing systems to holders of credit cards. The card in this case acts as the badge.

The badges themselves can be embossed with an OCR character set so that they can be used to impress documents and create machine-sensible inputs. The credit card again is one obvious example of this type of application.

4.2.15 Direct data entry (DDE)

Direct data entry in this context refers to the transmission of data directly to the computer without any intermediate storage on any medium. A user of direct data entry obtains an immediate response from the computer acknowledging the data or rejecting it as invalid.

A typical method of DDE involves remote terminals using either duplex or half duplex lines linked to and controlled by a processor or processors (see section on data transmission). Small computers typically use DDE through local terminals which consist of a full QWERTY (typewriter) keyboard and a visual display unit (VDU).

A VDU looks very similar to a domestic television set. When used for commercial applications, the VDU displays data in the form of characters as opposed to diagrams. The cathode ray tube (which is an integral part of the device) is scanned to create a grid of horizontal lines.

The display of characters is made up of a pattern of dots of brightness on the tube. A typical VDU allows a full set of characters in ASCII.

The VDU display is in two modes:

(a)   **paging** is the display of a full screen which takes the form of a printed page;
(b)   **scrolling** is the display on a line-by-line basis.

Cursors are small symbols (dots, $ signs or arrows) which can be moved horizontally or vertically in order to edit the input. If 'J.Smith £99.36+' is entered as 'J.Smoth £9.93', the cursor will be moved to letter 'o' to aid its deletion and replacement by 'i', and then to '£9.93' to cause the alteration to be made.

Cursors can be used to direct the operator's attention to the editing of a record by such displays as 'correct Y/N'. Depressing the 'N' key will erase data from the screen.

VDUs are intelligent terminals, ie, they are microprocessor-based and can store data as well as a limited control program for the purposes of an editing function.

4.3 Conclusion

You now know the major input methods used in computer processing systems. Be able to describe each of them but also recall the practical circumstances in which they may be best suited.

4.4 Questions

Quick questions

(1) Name the *three* methods employed in document readers.

(2) Articles sold in a supermarket have their description encoded on them. What is this code called and how may it be used to eliminate human effort?

(3) Punched cards are readily man-understandable but paper tape is not. Explain.

(4) (a) A key-to-disk system is a computer controlled data capture system. True/False?

(b) A key-to-cassette system is not computer controlled but possesses a limited degree of artificial intelligence. True/False?

(5) Match the following applications with the most appropriate data capture technique:

(a)	Time-recording in a factory.	1	Punched cards.
(b)	Processing cash payments on a microcomputer.	2	Key-to-cassette.
(c)	Processing gas meter readings.	3	Direct data entry.
(d)	Cheque sorting and encoding	4	MICR.
(e)	Preparing weekly paid payroll records.	5	OCR.
		6	OMR.
		7	Badge reading.

(6) Kimball tags are most commonly used in (a) factory costing systems, (b) garment retailing, (c) pet shops.

(7) Processing credit card vouchers lends itself to OCR/OMR/punched cards input.

(8) OCR input must be in a special typeface to be machine-sensible. True/False?

(9) Name one business application for VDE systems.

(10) A chain of supermarkets could benefit from a __ __ __ system to control stocks and takings.

Objective test questions

(1) In computing terminology, POS normally stands for:

    A   Primary Operating System
    B   Point Of Sale
    C   Priority Oriented System
    D   Pilot Operation Schedule

(2) Which of the following input methods involves the use of a keyboard?

    A   Magnetic tape encoder
    B   MICR
    C   OCR
    D   Mark sensing

(3) Which of the following describes a key-to-disk system?

    A   An off-line method of output
    B   A method of interrogating the computer's disk files
    C   An on-line method of validating input data
    D   An off-line method of input

Written test questions

4.1 Data capture methods

Describe MICR, OCR and Kimball tags as methods of data capture and discuss their relative merits.   **(20 marks)**

4.2 Data capture in two different systems

Consider the following two separate situations:

(a) A TV rental company has several thousand customers who are expected to make monthly payments of rent at branch offices of the company. Records of all the customers are kept on a Head Office computer and these records require monthly updating with data relating to customer payments.

(b) An engineering company manufactures a wide range of standard products in large volumes. Products are made from a variety of components, each of which undergoes a series of manufacturing operations prior to final assembly. For input to computerised work-in-progress, stock control and operator bonus calculation systems, the company needs to capture data relating to the quantities of components passing through specified operations in the manufacturing departments.

Required

(a) Describe the method you would propose to capture data in each of the above systems. (10 marks)

(b) State what you consider to be the main merits of your proposals and briefly mention any possible disadvantages. (10 marks)

(Total 20 marks)

4.3 Alternative data capture methods

Your company employ seven key punch operators who prepare input data for mainstream accounting routines such as payroll, sales accounting and purchases accounting. It is suggested during a management meeting that 'It's no wonder you are always late with your reports if the data processing department insist on using such out-dated methods'. Stung by this remark your managing director has agreed to review alternative methods and has asked you to prepare a paper on two suitable alternative methods.

Draft your paper making whatever assumptions you consider realistic.

(20 marks)

Output methods and media

Output can be divided broadly into two categories:

- 'Soft' output which is the term given to output of an impermanent type such as voice simulation or visual displays.

- 'Hard' output which is the term given to output of a permanent type such as printed paper or microfiche.

It is also necessary to know something about the mechanical devices needed to handle output. A credit card company producing 40,000 billing statements ten times a month does not, obviously, rely on a battery of office staff to stuff statements into envelopes!

5.1 Introduction

5.1.1 Choosing the output methods

It is now common to refer to 'the output sub system' in order to describe the method, medium and the hardware. The choice of output method will be influenced by such factors as:

(a) *Cost and volumes* - A small business producing 200 invoices a day and processing payroll once a week is likely to want a relatively small, cheap printer to service this modest workload. A hire-purchase company producing 10,000 statements a month, together with reminder letters and default notices, will require a fast printer capable of producing multipart documents of good quality at speed, as well as visual displays for quick and easy reference.

(b) *Handling requirements* - Some output is long-lived and required for reference (eg, a printout of balances in the financial ledger); some output is required to be multipart for legal reasons eg invoices (for VAT purposes) and hiring arrangements (under current consumer credit legislation). Certain output requires to be printed but is used for a limited period of time eg, daily balance listings prepared by a clearing bank in the high street.

(c) *Speed of system response* - A customer interrogating his bank's computer requires a swift response. A telephone clerk employed by a credit card company wants to be able to give an instant validation or rejection of a transaction. There is not the same degree of urgency for producing, say, an aged list of balances for control purposes.

We can categorise output methods as **machine comprehensible** and **human comprehensible**.

In this session we have referred exclusively to **human comprehensible**, but in the case of machine comprehensible output we mean that the computer has created output on punched cards, disk or tape - usually for transfer to another system, or for storage.

5.2   Soft copy output

5.2.1   Voice systems

These systems are growing in popularity and are used in a variety of ways from the 'speaking clock' to the voice synthesisers in certain makes of motor car. There are two main ways of producing voice response:

(a)   by storing words converted into bit patterns, recalling them and converting the digital patterns to analogue wave forms transmitted via an amplifier;

(b)   by generating speech electronically from phonetic units. The sound produced is artificial as opposed to the synthesised speech in (a).

5.2.2   Visual displays

Visual display units (VDUs) can be either text or graphic display.

(a)   *Text displays*

The standard display of text on most screens is a total of 1,920 characters in an arrangement of 24 rows by 80 columns.

Displays can appear in two ways:

(i)   the **scrolling** mode, which allows lines to appear at the bottom of the screen and then move upwards; and

(ii)   the **paging** mode when the whole page is replaced by another.

Output on the screen may, with certain models, be altered by a light pen, or alternatively it may appear in the form of a dialogue; in the latter case, the user will be 'prompted' as to what to do next. Output on a VDU can be altered or erased by a keyed command such as CLS (clear screen).

(b)   *Graphics*

Graphic displays are a feature of many business applications. The component parts of the display are formatted by means of special software into a number of individual picture cells (pixels) in order to produce the required pattern.

Graphics possess the following advantages:

(i)   they emphasise relationships;
(ii)   they uncover previously hidden facts;
(iii)   they focus interest.

Graphics can be used in three ways:

- information graphics
- report graphics
- presentation graphics.

Information graphics are used, essentially, to present information to the computer user on the VDU.

Report graphics are used for the presentation of information in the form of a printed page.

Presentation graphics are used when it is desired to present information by projection onto a screen or a TV monitor. It is possible to print output directly onto a transparency and use these in a slide projection presentation.

5.3   Hard copy output

5.3.1   Printed output

The production of printed output can be achieved by a variety of devices. For convenience we can divide them into two categories:

(a)   impact printers;
(b)   non-impact printers.

Impact printers, as their name suggests, are those that produce output by the pressure of print characters on paper. They are, therefore, suitable for the production of multipart output such as invoices or payroll/payslip preparation.

5.3.2   Types of impact printer

The following types of impact printer are found in common use:

(a)   line-at-a-time printers - usually known as line printers;
(b)   daisy wheel printers;
(c)   matrix printers.

5.3.3   Line printers

When computers first entered the commercial scene, businessmen demanded that the results of their processing should appear in conventional **typed** form on paper.

To satisfy this demand, the manufacturers attached line printers to their computers and these remain today as the work-horses of all output devices. Almost every computer from minicomputers up has one, and it is used for the majority of printed output which the machine produces.

The printers in current use have a line of small hammers, one to each character position and some means of forming the characters to be printed - usually by type bars as on a typewriter. A wide carbon ribbon passes over the typeface and is reeled backwards and forwards onto take-up spools so as to present fresh carbon before the type which will form the printed letters on the paper. The paper is positioned between the carbon ribbon and print hammers. To print a line of characters, normally between 120-160 letters in length, the printer flicks each print hammer against the paper and carbon at the precise moment that the character required is flying past. In this way the typeface leaves its impression on the paper through the carbon and allows a complete line to be printed. This operation is performed so fast that to the naked eye it seems as though the whole line of print is being produced at one time - hence the origin of the name line printers. Typical operating speeds are between 750 and 2,000 lines of print per minute.

The various kinds of line printer are distinguished by the arrangement used for the type itself. Methods used include the following.

(a) *Chain printers* - The type characters are embossed on the outer edge of a closed metal chain which revolves continuously.

(b) *Barrel printers* - Similar to the above, but the type characters are embossed around a solid barrel.

(c) *Bar printers* - These contain a complete character set on a vertical bar. The bars move up and down to form the complete line of print and the paper is struck in one stroke agains the type.

(d) *Wheel printers* - Similar in action to the bar printers, but the vertical bars are replaced by wheels which turn on a common axis to form up the required line of type. Each wheel contains all the characters in the set.

(e) *Stylus or matrix printers* - At each printing position is a matrix of small pins arranged as a rectangle of say, seven pins by five. Characters are formed by moving the pins slightly forward to outline the figure or letter required. The resulting printed image is made up of small dots.

The first two methods are the most common. They are useful for high volume multipart printing eg, invoice sets.

5.3.4   Character printers

As may be guessed from their name, character printers only print one character at a time - like a conventional typewriter. The main types of character printer are:

(a) *Daisy wheel* - The character set is embossed at the end of the spokes of a wheel or, to relate the mechanism to its botanical name, at the ends of the petals of a daisy. The wheel spins round and each character is activated as required as the print head moves across the page.

(b) *Matrix printer* - Operation as described below, relying on any character being formed from a 7 x 5 matrix, eg, letter A as in Figure 5.1.

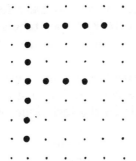

Figure 5.1: Matrix printer

5.3.5 Non-impact printers

(a) *Page printers* - Non-impact printers are only suitable for the production of single part output. For large volumes of output, optical printers or xerographic printers are used. There are no type bars or devices to be impressed against the paper. Instead an image is produced on a cathode ray tube (CRT) and a xerographic copy is made (as in a photocopier). A complete page of output can be captured at a single operation. The process is fast and silent with an output speed of around 18,000 lines per minute.

(b) *Ink-jet and bubble printers* - The ink-jet approach is to eject a special kind of ink from a nozzle under the control of a variable electric field. The paper receiving the jet does not need to be special in any way. There is a 'bubble jet printer' (produced by Canon), which sprays the ink in bubbles which are thermally generated. It uses 40cc ink-cartridges.

(c) *Electrothermal* - Using a collection of elements which are heated electrically to modify the chemical composition of the special paper, thereby creating specific characters.

(d) *Electrostatic* - This produces on special paper an electrostatic charge through a collection of wires and in turn this deposits carbon particles in the shape of characters. This is normally used for graph plotters rather than daily printing requirements.

5.4 Specialised methods

5.4.1 Graph plotter

Typical applications are:

(a) weather forecasting - for drawing isobars on weather maps;
(b) map making - for drawing contour lines;
(c) statistical work - for producing graphs of complicated mathematical formulae.

5.4.2 COM (Computer output on microfilm)

In certain business situations there is a need for high volumes of hard copy output at frequent intervals. An example of this type of application is the UK clearing banks who require a list of customers' balances on a daily basis for monitoring purposes. Formerly this information was provided by a bulky paper tabulation which required storage and, ultimately, destruction because of its sensitive nature.

Nowadays the information is prepared by a single microfiche which can be scanned with a microfilm reader. The microfiche is not bulky to store and preserves confidentiality as well. This advance is made possible by the technique of Computer Output in Microform (using microfiche or microfilm).

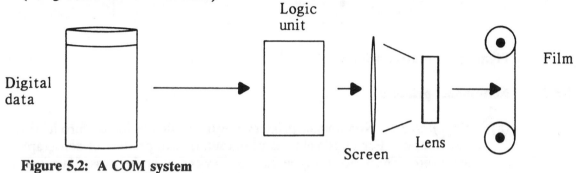

Figure 5.2: A COM system

The output which is collected on some convenient medium like magnetic tape is read by a **logic unit** which converts the binary data into character images. The images are displayed on a cathode ray tube (CRT). The images on the CRT are projected towards a camera lens and captured on a spool of microfilm.

The COM approach is assisted by a CAR (computer assisted retrieval) system which allows the contents of the fiche/film to be read onscreen or printed out. COM is one of the technologies related to what has become known as **image processing**.

5.5   Conclusion

As in the previous session we have seen that there are a number of output devices available. Again, it is important that you can recall the practical applications for each.

5.6   Questions

Quick questions

(1)   Identify the following devices as impact (I) or non-impact (N) printers:

      (a)   Ink jet printers.
      (b)   Dot matrix printers.
      (c)   Daisy wheel printers.
      (d)   Xerographic printers.
      (e)   Line printers.

(2)   A pixel is (a) a bug in a computer program; (b) a cell used in making up graphical displays; (c) another word for a light pen; or (d) a magnetic charge in a CRT.

(3)   A VDU can display text in either a

      _____ mode or a _____ mode.

(4) The slowest form of character printer is the type knows as (a) 'daisy wheel'; (b) 'matrix'; or (c) 'golfball'.

(5) Graphs of complicated mathematical formulation may be conveniently printed out using (a) a pixel; (b) a light pen; or (c) a plotter.

(6) Computer output on microfilm is done by (a) a manual process where individual printed pages are exposed to a camera lens; (b) a special technique which produces a cathode ray display which is captured on microfilm; or (c) magnetic tape output printed very small and photocopied automatically.

(7) Voice output systems use (a) speech synthesisers to generate artificial speech from phonetic text; (b) computer aided selection of pre-recorded messages using a tape recorder; or (c) a library of standard words converted from analogue to digital format and stored on disc in binary digits thus allowing recall, reconversion and amplification by loud speaker.

(8) Match the device with the application:

    (a) Printing 20,000 multipart documents as output from a single run daily.
    (b) Updating an investor's building society passbook.
    (c) Validation of a holiday booking.
    (d) Producing theatre tickets in a computer controlled ticket allocation system.
    (e) Airline ticket seat enquiry.

    (1) Line printer.
    (2) Xerographic printer.
    (3) Dot matrix printer.
    (4) Ink jet printer.
    (5) Visual display.

(9) Computer output devices can produce turnaround documents: explain.

(10) Teletypewriters and VDUs are both input and output devices. True/False?

Objective test questions

(1) A daisy wheel printer would be used when:

    A   Low quality print is accepted
    B   A line printer is too slow
    C   High quality print is required
    D   A matrix printer is too expensive

(2) A matrix printer prints at approximately the rate per second of:

    A   150 characters
    B   750 characters
    C   1,500 characters
    D   2,500 characters

Written test questions

5.1   Line printer, incremental graph plotter, cathode ray display tube

Describe the characteristic features of the following output devices:

(a)	line printer;	(5 marks)
(b)	incremental graph plotter;	(5 marks)
(c)	cathode ray display tube (VDU).	(5 marks)

(Total 15 marks)

5.2   Graphics

The training officer of your company has asked for your opinion on the usefulness of 'graphics' for personal computers. Draft a memorandum to her setting out your views.

(20 marks)

5.3   Page printers, dialogues and COM

Write short notes on:

(a)	page printers;	(5 marks)
(b)	dialogues;	(5 marks)
(c)	COM.	(5 marks)

(Total 15 marks)

SESSION 6

Backing storage

In any data processing system, there is a need for the permanent storage of information for reference and for archive purposes. In a computer, the amount of information that the computer can hold in internal storage is strictly limited. There is, therefore, a need for some form of storage in computer-sensible form which is external to the CPU. In this session we look at types of backing storage.

6.1 Introduction

External storage or backing storage now consists of various types of magnetic media drawn from the list below. Unlike RAM, backing storage holds data in a non-volatile form. However, such storage can be **destructively overwritten** by the computer.

6.1.1 Backing storage media in use today

The following devices may be found in use at the present time:

(a)   magnetic drum (now almost obsolete);
(b)   magnetic tape;
(c)   magnetic disk;
(d)   diskette;
(e)   optical disks;
(f)   mass storage units.

The physical characteristics of these devices will be described in each of the following sections in this session.

6.2 Computer file concepts

6.2.1 Types of file

In order to understand the way in which backing storage is used, it is necessary to consider the various types of file that may be part of a processing routine.

0113z

Transaction files

These record the source data that evidence any business transactions, eg, sales orders, cash payments etc.

Transition or pipeline files

These are files which contain the intermediate results of processing.

Reference files

These are files which are used as a source of standby or static data, eg, a name and address file for customers.

Master file

These are files which contain both constant and variable data, eg, a sales ledger file contains static items of data (like names and addresses) as well as variable items of data such as balances.

6.2.2 File processing - a definition

File processing can be regarded as the sequence of events concerned with an item or items of data. The events are as follows.

(a) *Validation* - reading data and submitting each item to some form of logical check before capturing the data on a transition or pipeline file.

(b) *Sorting* - rearranging the data into some predetermined sequence, eg, sorting cash payments into customer number order. Advances in systems design and disk file usage have meant a reduction in the use of sorting routines in file processing.

(c) *Merging* - this refers to the function of combining two or more files into a single file, eg, merging a file of despatch notes with a file of names and addresses in order to produce invoices.

(d) *Referencing* - the routine to seek out an item of static data which is combined with other data items in order to produce a given output, eg, reading a price from a catalogue file in order to calculate the money value of the transaction.

(e) *Updating* - the routine whereby change or transaction data brings about a change in a master file or reference file, eg, entering a cash payment from a customer and changing the customer's balance as a result.

(f) *Interrogation or enquiry* - this routine is concerned with looking up a file record for some decision-making purpose, eg, 'How much do X PLC owe us?'

6.2.3 File maintenance

The term 'file maintenance' is used to describe the operation of creating, amending or deleting records on a reference or master file, eg, a change in the address of a customer on a sales ledger master file is an operation associated with file maintenance. In any system, file maintenance must be carried out under carefully controlled conditions in order to ensure the following:

(a)   all new records are suitably authorised;

(b)   all alterations are authorised and relate to existing records; and

(c)   code numbers are allocated correctly to each record (it would be most inconvenient to have two customers with the same account number!) by means of registration procedures.

6.2.4   Physical and logical records

The terms 'physical record' and 'logical record' should be distinguished. The 'physical record' is the term used to describe *how* data is stored and *where* it is stored. The 'logical record' is the term used to describe *what* the record contains.

6.2.5   The hierachy of information

It might be useful here to repeat certain definitions which relate to the processing of data.

-    A **file** is a collection of related records. Each record refers to an entity (which may be a person or an object, eg, a collection of employees will have their personnel **records** stored on a file).

-    A **record** is a collection of related fields containing facts about an entity, eg, a personnel record for John Smith will consist of various facts about him.

-    A **field** is a section of a record, eg, 'John Smith' is the field containing employee name. '07394' is the field containing employee number. The field that distinguishes one record from another is often styled the **key field** or **entity identifier**.

-    A **character** is a unit which is a letter, number or symbol making up a field. In more modern systems it is sometimes usual to refer not to **fields** but to **attributes**.

6.2.6   Type of record

Records are often designed to be of a *fixed length*. This is often convenient for systems design. Certain records may well have to be of variable length; for example, a sales order may have one transaction (10 engines type 42983 @ £189.27 each) or more then one (20 sub-assemblies 42238 @ £2,000 each; 40 mountings 72918 @ £17.33 each) and so on.

Fields may be allowed to vary in size within a fixed length record. Fixed length records may be easier to manipulate but often result in a waste of file storage space.

6.2.7   How does the computer recognise a particular file?

The processor requires some system of recognition so that data from the right file can be read for a particular process. The ability to recognise the correct file for the particular application is a function of the computer's operating system. The system will require the file to be given a file name so that the user can communicate with the computer. This recognition device is known as a **header label** and a typical label could contain:

(a)   some code to identify the label **as** the label - possibly the words HEDR;
(b)   file name;
(c)   date written;
(d)   purge date, ie, the date from which the information is no longer required.

If, for example, a payroll file were loaded when it is intended to run the debtors file, the header label will be read and the operating system will signal an error to the operator.

On some disk file systems, the equivalent record may be known as the variable table of contents (VTOC).

Trailer labels are placed at the end of the file and contain the following details:

(a)   an end-of-file marker or, if the file is continued onto another reel, an end-of-reel marker;

(b)   a total of the number of records on the file.

Control records will also be found on those files that contain numerical or financial data. These control records are also known as pseudo records or dummy records.

The arrangement is illustrated in Figure 6.1.

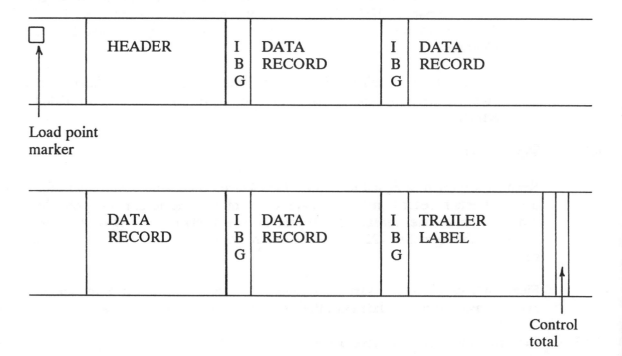

Figure 6.1: 'Header' and 'trailer' labels

6.3 Drum

6.3.1 Physical characteristics

The magnetic drum is contained within a unit which has a motor which rotates the drum at a constant speed. Read/write heads are situated close to but not touching the surface of the drum (Figure 6.2).

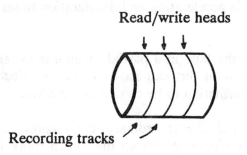

Read/write heads

Recording tracks

Figure 6.2: A magnetic drum

The drum is not removable and typically may store some 8m characters. The use of a drum is restricted to certain large machine installations.

6.4 Magnetic tape

6.4.1 Physical appearance

Imagine a domestic tape recorder on a much larger scale, operating in a partial vacuum, and you can picture a magnetic tape unit as a computer peripheral (Figure 6.3).

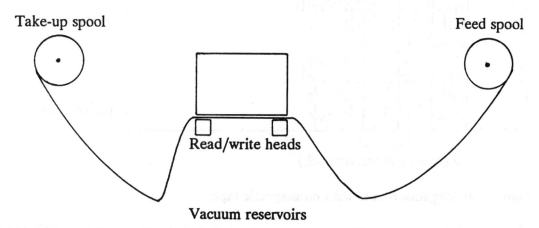

Take-up spool

Feed spool

Read/write heads

Vacuum reservoirs

Figure 6.3: A magnetic tape unit

Tape is a very versatile recording medium; it is used for input and output as well as storage. Unfortunately, it is a form of storage that only offers **serial access**; ie, it is read from one end to another like a domestic tape cassette. It therefore lacks the flexibility of magnetic disk. Tape is said to be bulk non-addressable storage.

0113z

Tape is moved from the feed spool, past the read/write heads and onto the take-up spool by the tape drive motor. Between each reel and the read/write mechanism a slack loop of tape is held in a vacuum reservoir to act as a cushion against sudden starts and stops. Not only does this help to reduce wear and tear on the tape but it also reduces drag on the tape and hence lessens acceleration and deceleration times. As with an ordinary tape recorder, a computer tape unit will play (read) or record (write) a distorted version of the information unless the tape is travelling at a certain fixed speed past the read/write heads. Any portion of tape which passes by the read station while the tape is accelerating or decelerating cannot be used because the tape is not moving at the correct speed. A reduction in acceleration and deceleration times is therefore critical in minimising tape wastage.

A further reason for operating the tape in a partial vacuum is to remove as many dust particles as possible. Tiny specks of dirt can have disastrous effects on reading from tape, sometimes causing the information to be completely misread.

Computer magnetic tape is very similar to ordinary tape-recorder tape, being made of the same material but of a far higher quality so that much more information can be packed into a small length of tape. A typical packing density is 1,600 characters per inch but may be up to 6,250 characters per inch. Normally ½ inch wide with 2,400 feet of tape on one reel, the tape signals the beginning and the end of the reel to the hardware by small aluminium foil markers placed 20 feet from the physical ends of the tape.

6.4.2   Data storage

The method of data storage on magnetic tape is similar to that of punched paper tape but, of course, no holes are punched on magnetic tape. One character is stored in one column or frame by a certain pattern of magnetised spots representing 0s and 1s which are equivalent to the presence or absence of holes on punched paper tape (Figure 6.4).

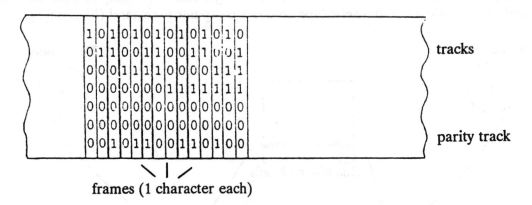

frames (1 character each)

Figure 6.4: Organisation of data on magnetic tape

The equivalent of the channel on paper tape is called the track, on magnetic tape, and there is one read/write head for each track. The above diagram shows seven-track magnetic tape with the bottom track acting as a parity check. In this case odd parity is being used, which means that every character must be represented by a pattern containing an odd number of 1s. If the original character representation contains an even number of 1s, an extra 1 will be recorded in the parity track. Although we have referred to the packing density in terms of characters per inch, it is more often referred to as bits per inch. This refers to how many bits per inch there are on any one track and means precisely the same as characters per inch.

6.4.3   Blocking

It was mentioned in section 6.4.1 that a certain amount of the tape is wasted because it is passing the read/write heads during acceleration or deceleration. If only one data record is read at a time, there will be a gap of wasted tape between every record and, because the packing density is so great, it could be that the gap occupies as much tape as a record.   In other words, half the tape is unusable. To overcome this, data is gathered together into **blocks** and, on receipt of a read instruction, the tape deck grinds into motion, gets up speed and transfers a complete block (ie, several records) into core storage all at once. At the end of the block it puts the brakes on and slows down to rest rather than stopping abruptly which might cause the tape to stretch or break. A gap between each block of data is still necessary but the proportion of tape wasted will be greatly reduced (Figure 6.5).

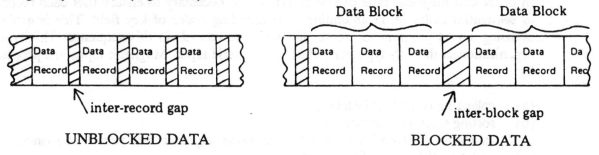

UNBLOCKED DATA   BLOCKED DATA

Figure 6.5: Blocks

The number of records in a block (the blocking factor) varies from machine to machine and is usually determined by the hardware circuitry, but may be selected through the software, ie, the programs.

A simple numerical example should help to show the advantages of blocking. Suppose the packing density is 1,600 characters per inch: we are dealing with records, each of 250 characters in length, and the inter-record gap (or inter-block gap) is 0.7" long. These are all fairly typical values and we will work out the percentage utilisation of the tape with:

(a)   no blocking;
(b)   a blocking factor of 10.

Case (a)

Each record will be followed by an inter-record gap so that a unit record (record + gap) will be:

$$0.7 \quad + \quad \frac{250}{1,600} \quad = \quad 0.7 + 0.156 = 0.856$$

The percentage utilisation of the tape, ie, the proportion used to hold data is therefore:

$$\frac{0.156}{0.856} \quad x \quad 100 = 18\%$$

Case (b)

Now, every group of 10 records will be followed by an inter-block gap so that a unit block (block + gap) will be:

$$0.7 \quad + \quad \frac{250 \times 10}{1,600} \quad = \quad 0.7 + 1.56 = 2.26$$

$$\text{Utilisation} \quad = \quad \frac{1.56}{2.26} \quad \times \quad 100 = 69\%$$

6.4.4 Tape file organisation

In order that magnetic tape can be updated, it is necessary to ensure that each record is in **sequential order** ie, in ascending or descending order of key field. This is achieved by using a **sort** program to create files with the records in this sequence. This type of organisation is the *only* type permitted by magnetic tape. Magnetic tapes are processed by:

(a)   collecting records in batches;
(b)   sorting them into sequence;
(c)   calling up master files arranged in the same sequence, one record at a time;
(d)   updating the master file record;
(e)   writing out the master file record onto a new tape.

This is explained schematically in the systems diagram (Figure 6.6).

6.4.5 File updating

Magnetic tape may only be updated (ie, the data changed in any way) by producing a **completely new tape** based on the information on the old tape and the amendments. This is for the following reasons:

(a)   Before the computer can erase or delete a piece of data, eg, an invoice on a debtors ledger which has been paid, it must have read that data from the tape to ensure that it is about to delete *precisely and only* that data. Similarly, if a piece of extra data is to be inserted, we must be certain that it is inserted in the right place.

(b)   Once the old data has been read, it has gone **past** the read/write heads.

(c)   There is no facility on tape to rewind for just one record (either to delete that record or in some way to insert extra data), although of course it can always be rewound in its entirety so that the reel may be removed for storage.

Therefore, each record is read from the brought-forward file, examined to see whether it is to be deleted, changed or have the new record inserted, and the result written out to a new tape.

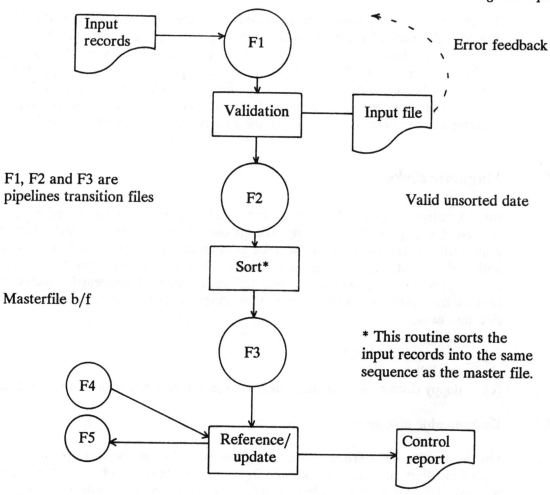

F1, F2 and F3 are
pipelines transition files

Valid unsorted date

Masterfile b/f

* This routine sorts the
input records into the same
sequence as the master file.

Masterfile c/f

Figure 6.6: Tape file organisation

6.4.6   **Security**

Any system which incorporates over-writing or erasing of data is potentially dangerous.
A small operating error could lead to important information being lost, eg, simply
writing to a record instead of reading it. Many security checks should be built into a
computer system during the design stage but magnetic tapes offer an extra security
check as part of their make-up. The equipment required is a simple ring of plastic,
known as a **write-permit** ring which can be clipped into a reel of tape by the computer
operator (Figure 6.7).

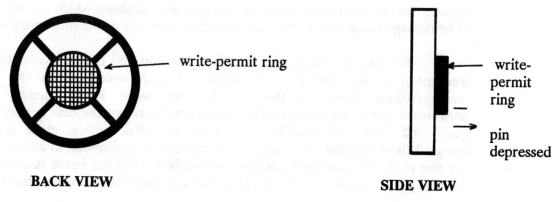

Figure 6.7: A write-permit ring

If a reel of tape is to have data recorded on it, the operator will clip the write-permit ring onto the back of the reel on its central spindle. The ring juts out from the surface of the reel, as shown in the diagram of the side view, so that when the reel is mounted on the tape drive unit, the ring depresses a metal pin. With the pin depressed, the tape may be written to; but without the ring the pin is not affected and an instruction to write to the tape will not be carried out. Instead, an error message will make the operator aware of the situation and allow a correction to be made, if possible.

6.5   Magnetic disks

An alternative method of file storage is to hold magnetically encoded information on the surface of a large disk, something like an outsize gramophone record, which has been coated with magnetisable material. Like gramophone records, disks hold information on both surfaces but, whereas a gramophone needle travels along a spiral path from edge to centre, here the information is recorded in a series of concentric circles or **tracks**. Disks were developed more recently than magnetic tape and at present three types of disk unit exist:

(a)   exchangeable disks;
(b)   fixed disks;
(c)   floppy disks (known as diskettes) - these will be dealt with in a separate section.

6.5.1   Exchangeable disk storage

On these units, disks are not used singly but in packs, several disks (commonly 6 or 11) joined together on a common spindle in such a way that the whole unit is fixed together and no disk may revolve independently. The name **exchangeable** is used because the packs work on the same principle as magnetic tape as far as the amount of information on-line at any one time is concerned. In other words a large number of packs may be are held in a disk library, and the operator selects the packs required for a particular run and loads them onto the disk drives before the program is started. In this way the packs are exchangeable, since, at the end of a run, they can be removed from the disk units and replaced by different packs.

6.5.2   Description

(a)   The physical appearance of a disk pack is most easily described by a simple diagram or by imagining several LPs held on a single spindle. A pack of six disks is illustrated in Figure 6.8.

Apart from the outer surfaces of the top and bottom disks, which are more likely to be damaged than the internal surfaces, both surfaces of the disks are used.

(b)   When a disk pack has been loaded onto a disk unit and the lid closed, the drive mechanism causes the pack to rotate at high speed. Once the correct reading/writing speed is attained, the read/write head assembly moves horizontally out of its casing and positions itself between the disk surfaces like a giant comb. The read/write heads, one for each disk surface, move in unison, being all fixed together on a single arm, and can be positioned to access data on any one of the 200 circular tracks on each surface. With the heads stationary, and the disk pack revolving, any one of 10 (for a 6 disk pack) circular tracks can be accessed. These tracks are vertically above each other in a cylindrical formation. Such a set of corresponding tracks is called a **cylinder**. The read/write heads do not touch the surface of the disk but **float** a fraction of an inch above it. Any contact, known as a **head crash**, causes damage to the disk.

Top
view

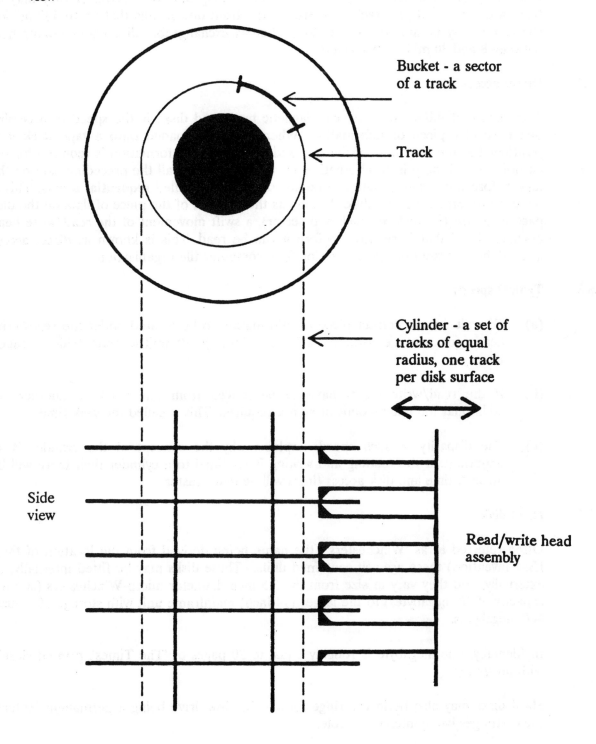

Bucket - a sector
of a track

Track

Cylinder - a set of
tracks of equal
radius, one track
per disk surface

Side
view

Read/write head
assembly

Figure 6.8: Magnetic disk pack

0113z

6.5.3 Fixed disks

The term **fixed** does not imply that the disk remains stationary - in fact a fixed disk rotates at a high speed in the same way as an exchangeable disk pack - but merely that the operator cannot remove the disk from the drive mechanism. Fixed disks, generally larger than exchangeable disks, may be as much as 3 feet in diameter. The read/write heads may be on a moveable arm as on the exchangeable disk drive, or they may be fixed with one head per track. The size of the fixed disk means that up to 400 million characters may be stored on one disk, whereas exchangeable disk packs usually hold between 8 and 30 million characters.

6.5.4 Direct access

The important difference between magnetic tapes and disks is the speed of accessing one particular piece of information. When a tape is loaded onto a tape deck it is positioned at the beginning of the reel and, if a piece of information is required for the end of the reel there is no alternative but to read through all the preceding data on the tape before the required data can be accessed. This is called **sequential access**. This is unnecessary on a magnetic disk. As long as the position of the piece of data on the disk pack is known (ie, surface, track and sector), a swift movement of the read/write head assembly is all that is required before it can be read. This is known as **direct access** and will be discussed further in Session 9 on computer file organisation.

6.5.5 Typical speeds

(a)   To wait for the correct piece of information to be rotated under the read/write heads (on average around half a revolution): 10 milliseconds. This is called **latency**.

(b)   If the read/write heads have to be moved from one track to another, an additional 100 milliseconds or so are required. This is called the **seek time**.

(c)   The disparity in such speeds explains why the concept of the cylinder is so important. If the reading and writing is confined to a cylinder then there will be no seek time and disk access times will be much faster.

6.5.6 Hard disk

Often referred to as 'Winchesters' (the name being derived from the location of their IBM invention) these are self-contained units. These disks may be fitted internally, or externally, and they vary in size from the 3.5 inch diameter micro-Winchesters (storage capacity of 10 megabytes) to the larger (14-inch) mainframe unit with storage of around 400 megabytes.

Incidentally, one megabyte is roughly equal to 30 pages of 'The Times', printed closely with no spaces!

Hard disks may also be in **cartridge** form - the disk drive being a permanent feature, the cartridges being interchangeable.

6.5.7 Bulk addressable storage

A record on magnetic tape can only be recognised by an entity identifier or key field (eg, an account number).

A magnetic disk, on the other hand, can be divided into areas, each of which can be identified by a unique number. In order to understand this, it is necessary to refer to the diagram of a disk surface and discuss the concept of the 'cylinder'.

6.5.8   The cylinder concept

In Figure 6.8, we assumed that the disk platter has 200 tracks and the pack has ten recording surfaces. Let us assume that the tracks are numbered from 0 to 199 with the outermost track starting at 0. The recording surfaces are numbered from 0 - 9. Therefore, when data is recorded on the disk, it will be stored as follows:

Track		Surface
0		0
0		1
0		2
↓	until	↓
0		9

This assembly of data is known as a cylinder.

Records will be stored on the next track as follows:

Track	Surface
1	0
1	1
1	2
↓	↓
1	9

A cylinder therefore can be described as a collection of common tracks. Therefore in our example the disk pack will contain 200 cylinders (from 0 - 199), each cylinder containing ten tracks (from 0 - 9).

6.5.9   The hierarchical nature of disk storage.

It was stated earlier that disks provided bulk addressable storage. It would be prudent here firstly to state the principles of how addressability can be achieved and secondly to give some common synonyms for terms that are used in this context.

Assume that a disk cartridge consisted of 10 platters offering 20 recording surfaces. Assume also that the disk had 200 concentric data tracks and that each track was further divided into ten sections. The address of each storage location on the disk would be made up of a hierarchical code consisting of:

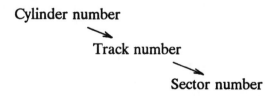

Cylinder number

Track number

Sector number

A disk address of 1020408 would mean sector 8 on track 4 on cylinder 102.

6.5.10   Using client access files in transaction or real time processing

It is possible to use a disk file in exactly the same way as a tape file, ie, to organise it with records placed one after another in **serial sequential** order. However, the physical properties of the disk (ie, the accessibility of its recording surfaces to read/write heads) and the property of addressability, allow the disk to be organised as a **Direct Access Storage Device** (or **DASD** for short). It is possible to select a single record on a disk, read it and alter it without extensive searching of the entire file. By analogy, you can select a track on a long playing record by carefully placing the arm in the required position without the 'trial and error' operations that you carry out when attempting to hear a selected part of a tape cassette.

This property of direct access allows the computer to process single transactions as they arise and provide an almost instantaneous result. This type of processing is known as real time or transaction processing and is only possible with direct access storage devices. If such a system is in operation, the steps that will be carried out are these:

(a)   Input the record's identifying number.

(b)   Select the desired record by reference to the disk address. (The techniques for doing this are described in the next session).

(c)   Read the record into the memory.

(d)   Amend it with the relevant transaction data.

(e)   Write the record back to the disk.

6.5.11   Destructive overwriting - the security aspects

This type of updating is known as updating by overlay or updating 'in situ'. However, if this updating is carried out erroneously the file is permanently corrupted. In order to protect the system from the consequences of error, security copies of the disk are made on magnetic tape as a cheap dense form of archival storage (Figure 6.9). This may be done by:

(a)   copying the disk onto tape at some specified time of day. This is commonly known as a tape dump;

(b)   copying the alterations onto tape during the process in a continuous stream. This is known as tape streaming;

(c)   copying the record *before* the change and *after* the change, onto magnetic tape.

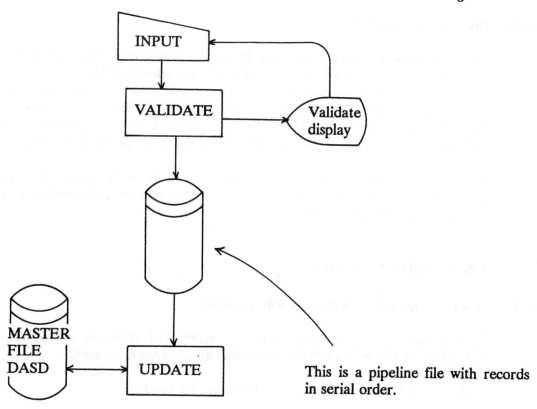

This is a pipeline file with records in serial order.

Figure 6.9: Updating 'in situ' using direct data entry

6.5.12 Overflows

The process of updating *in situ* can present a problem if records of variable length are maintained. If a record before updating consisted of 600 bytes and after updating consisted of 800 bytes, it may well have grown too large for its home track. In such cases the system software in use could create a special overflow area on the disk for such records. The record stored in the overflow area would have a cross reference to its home track so that it could be accessed directly if need be. Periodically the disk will be re-sorted and the records in the overflow area will be inserted into the relevant sequence. Complex mathematical formulae using statistical models are utilised for determining the need for overflow areas and the probability of this occurrence. The detail of these formulae are outside the scope of our syllabus.

6.5.13 Hard and soft sectors

Each recording track on a disk is divided into smaller units called sectors. (This term is often used synonymously with block or bucket.) Disks can be **soft-sectored** or **hard sectored**. A soft-sectored disk is one where the user can define the sector size and therefore can determine the number of sectors in each track. A hard-sectored disk is one where the number of sectors is determined by the manufacturer. This concept applies equally to floppy disks.

A hard-sectored disk or diskette will have the start of each track and sector delineated by a notch or similar mark. A soft-sectored disk or diskette will have the start of each track similarly marked, but each sector is marked by special data to indicate the boundary of the unit of storage. Some diskettes have a pattern of holes punched around the centre of the disk to indicate sector boundaries.

6.5.14   Diskettes (floppy disks)

Diskettes are widely used as backing storage on microcomputers. They have much slower access times than hard disks. Their physical characteristics have been described earlier and a brief recapitulation will serve for our purposes. Diskettes are capable of being used as bulk addressable storage. However, the address will be composed of a reference to track number and sector number within track number. As the diskettes are single entities (unlike disk cartridges) the concept of the cylinder is not appropriate here.

Diskettes are stored in envelopes in order to facilitate handling. They can be 'write protected' (ie, overwriting can be suppressed) by a notch which serves the same purpose as a 'write permit ring' on tape.

6.6   Laser (optical) storage

6.6.1   Optical disks/digital optical recording (DOR)

Laser stands for 'light amplification by stimulated emission of radiation'. In this technology, the laser beam burns holes into areas of sensitive metal.

Basically, we have three categories of optical disk product:

(a)   The **CD-ROM** (compact disk, read only memory): this evolved from the audio-compact disk player and is popular for PC access. A single CD-ROM, with a diameter of 4.75 inches is actually capable of storing the equivalent of well over a quarter of a million pages of text.

(b)   The **WORM** disk (write once, read many - indicating that no amendments may be made once data is on disk).

(c)   **Erasable optical disks** are now available (eg, from the American 3M supplier) which can be returned to their unrecorded form when necessary. Incidentally, the usual storage capacity is around 1,000 times greater than the standard magnetic hard disk. The entire text of a 31 volume encyclopedia (about 450,000,000 characters) can be stored on a single 5.25 inch disk.

6.7   Additional storage media

We are including under this heading three methods which differ in principle from the other versions we have been looking at.

6.7.1   Bubble memory

Although this unit does not move at all it is magnetic with tiny magnetised areas. Each unit is a 'chip' of around 10 mm (capacity one megabyte). This storage unit now has an improved access time and the latest Hitachi version is tough to withstand much handling.

6.7.2 Solid-state

Unlike the magnetic disk, this semi-conductor method does not possess any moving parts and, although expensive, allows very rapid access. This storage is normally used as *peripheral storage*, often as a buffer to hold frequently-accessed data.

There is also a card version (looking like a credit card) usually associated with PCs to store both programs and data. The card is not affected by scratching or by heat/cold.

6.8 Conclusion

Of the early sessions, this is perhaps the most important. We have looked at the principal methods of storing data. Recall the relative merits of each with regard to capacity and speed of access.

6.9 Questions

Quick questions

(1) Name *three* media which can be used to store files externally to the main memory of a computer.

(2) Individual records on magnetic tape are arranged in blocks. What is the name given to the space between these on which no information is recorded?

(3) In a magnetic disk file, which of the following is termed a 'cylinder'?

    (a) A set of corresponding surfaces.
    (b) A set of corresponding tracks.
    (c) A set of corresponding sectors.

(4) How are records on magnetic tape identified?

(5) Sectors on a disk are always engineered by the manufacturer. True/false?

(6) Magnetic tapes are updated by overlay. True/false?

(7) What is the name given to the type of storage which uses minute burn marks on a disk surface to encode data?

(8) The storage described in 7 above is volatile/non volatile.

(9) The first identifying item on a magnetic tape is called a ____ ____.

(10) Writing on a magnetic tape can be suppressed by means of:

    (a) A plastic write permit ring.
    (b) A load point marker.
    (c) A dummy record.

Objective test questions

(1)   Which of the following terms cannot relate to a tape file?

    A   Sequential
    B   Indexed sequential
    C   Serial
    D   Reference

(2)   On a header label, the purge date is the date:

    A   On which the file was updated
    B   Of the last transaction
    C   Before which no overwriting is possible
    D   The file was initially created

Written test questions

6.1   Interblock gaps, cylinder concept, tape cycling

Write short notes on:

(a)   interblock gaps on tape;   (5 marks)
(b)   cylinder concept;   (5 marks)
(c)   3-generation system of tape cycling.   (5 marks)
                                                                  (Total 15 marks)

6.2   Magnetic tape versus magnetic disk

Compare and contrast the attributes and uses of magnetic tape and magnetic disk as methods of backing storage.   **(20 marks)**

6.3   Sectored diskettes, header and trailer labels

Explain the following terms:

(a)   hard and soft sectored diskettes;   (5 marks)
(b)   header label;   (5 marks)
(c)   trailer label.   (5 marks)
                                                                  (Total 15 marks)

SESSION 7

Data communication systems

The combination of computing power in harness with high speed data communication has had a powerful influence on information processing systems.

In this session we shall look at the following methods of data communications:

- data transmission using remote terminals;
- distributed data processing;
- local area networks (LAN);
- packet switching systems (PSS).

PSS will be considered again in Session 9, which deals with 'office automation'.

7.1 Introduction

In recent years, there has been a considerable growth in the use of techniques of data communication from on-line ticket booking systems to on-line credit card validation, electronic funds transfer and similar applications. The early systems where on-line tele-typewriters were connected to computer systems have now given place to satellite computer systems in distributed data processing networks as well as to the automation of office services through applications like facsimile reproduction (faxing) and electronic mail box.

7.2 Data transmission using remote terminals

7.2.1 General concepts

We have already discussed the concept of data transmission using terminals. A terminal in this context is any input/output device. This topic is regularly examined and a student should be able to demonstrate an understanding of the principles involved, the hardware in use and the applications for business purposes.

Consider the following situation. X plc has centralised its data processing function in Milton Keynes. Several divisions and branches require the use of the computer. Each branch or division is equipped with data transmission/receiving devices so that computer power is readily available. These terminals are **on-line**, ie, they are linked to and controlled by the central computer.

Such terminals can also be used in a local mode or 'off line' if, for example, the computer system is out of service. Data can be captured on tape cassette or even paper tape 'off line' and transmitted to the computer when communication lines are restored.

7.2.2 Connections to the computer

Various means of transmitting data exist:

(a) For long distances, we have **satellite transmission** and **optical fibres** (eg, British Telecom provide these in Central London).

(b) Coaxial cables are used for short distances.

(c) Twisted pair (two wires wound around to form a single cable) are used for short and longer distances.

(d) In the UK telecommunication lines are used. British Telecom is the monopoly supplier of telecommunication services. Other suppliers exist such as Mercury Communications and the city of Kingston-upon-Hull. These bodies are licensed by government legislation to act as carriers for voice and data traffic.

British Telecom offers a number of services under the name of DATEL which are distinguished by various numbers as suffixes. These numbers refer to the speed of transmission. For example DATEL 400 means a circuit capable of transmitting at 400 bits per second (bps). Data can be transmitted over the ordinary public telephone circuits or on a private line. Transmission is possible in three modes:

(i) simplex: transmission is possible in one direction only;
(ii) half duplex: transmission is possible in two directions but not at once;
(iii) duplex: transmission is possible in two directions simultaneously.

7.2.3 The hardware

Terminals

Each terminal will consist of a keyboard and VDU. The keyboard will be a full QWERTY keyboard with certain special control keys. Most keyboards offer the full ASC II character set with the exception of IBM equipment which offers an EBCDIC character set.

Transmission devices

Where public telephone services exist, it is necessary to use an encoder/decoder device called a modem. This term is a contraction of **modulator-demodulator**. The modem takes the signals in computer understandable or digital form and converts them to pulses or frequencies (analogue) for transmission. Another modem decodes the pulses into digital data so that they can be understood by the computer (Figure 7.1).

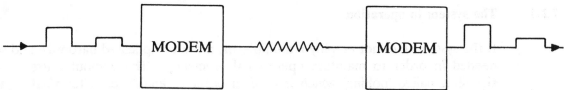

Figure 7.1: Turning digital signals into analogue and analogue signals into digital using modems

The central computer

The central computer should have a large area of RAM capable of holding a complex operating system which will allow

(a)   multiple access from a number of on-line terminals;

(b)   management of disk storage to enable a large amount of DASD to be capable of being accessed seemingly at once.

Multiplexors

Where there are several terminal devices connected to a processor it is usual to find a multiplexor in use (Figure 7.2). A multiplexor is a hardware device which handles incoming and outgoing messages and otherwise relieves the central computer from a number of time-consuming operations.   Where a multiplexor handles several data streams in one channel it is known as a **multidrop** multiplexor.

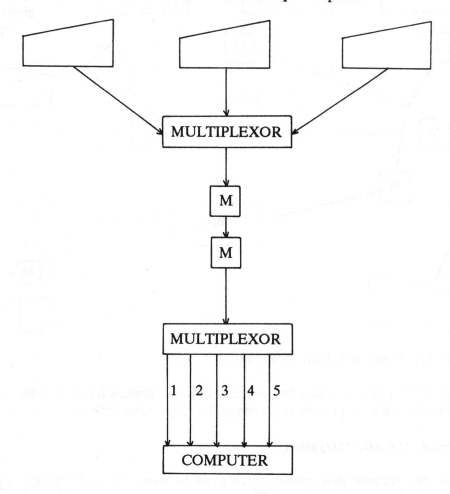

Figure 7.2: Terminals 'managed' by multiplexors

7.2.4   The system in operation

If the system does not employ a multiplexor, more complicated hardware and software is needed in order to maintain operational efficiency. The computer uses a system of signalling called 'polling' which is used in order to enable each terminal to access the computer. 'Polling' consists of the computer sending out messages to see if a terminal has a message to send. Polling can be done in two ways: half polling is where the signals go from the nearest terminal to the most distant; roll call polling is where each terminal receives a signal in turn.

7.2.5   Time sharing

When a large number of users wish to use a computer, it is necessary to impose some sort of control over the time taken for each processing task. Many systems operate different grades of work. Single file enquiries which are done in a conversational mode could be performed in 'fast' grade. The input transaction is held in a 'batch reservoir' or disk executed seemingly at once. In reality a slice of computer time is shared out to that user in order of priority. A slow processing task - such as converting a batch of sales orders into invoices - will often be done in 'slow' grade, leaving the communication channels free for more urgent work. These individual slices of processing time are made available by a sophisticated clock device which is part of the computer's mechanism.

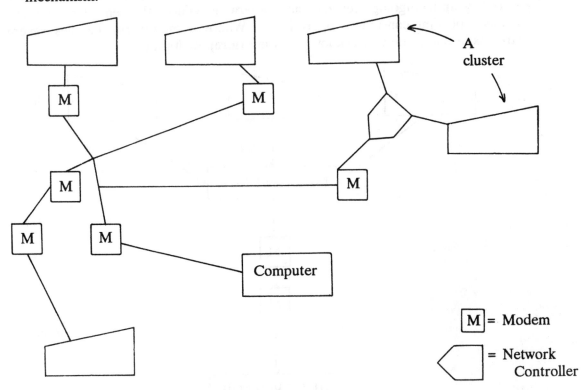

Figure 7.3: Polled terminals in a network

In Figure 7.3 a cluster means two or more terminal devices linked together by a cluster or network controller to provide one channel for data transmission.

7.2.6   Passwords and data encryption

In any data transmission system, there must be some form of control to guard against unauthorised access to the data. The most common control for this purpose is the use of

0114z

a password. This is a unique call sign which identifies the terminal and/or the terminal user on receipt of which the system will allow access to program or data files. Data transmitted on telephone lines is vulnerable to interception. *Data encryption* is the name given to the technique which scrambles all the data in the course of transmission and descrambles it at the receiving end.

7.2.7 Asynchronous/synchronous transmission

Asynchronous mode of transmission refers to the process of encoding data in a continuous stream. In order that the receiver can make sense of the transmission and to ensure that no data is lost, each character is encoded with a start bit (to indicate a new character) and a 'stop' bit (to indicate the end of the character).

Synchronous mode, however, means that the receiver expects certain bits to arrive at predetermined intervals by means of internal clock pulses. This method is faster than asynchronous transmission and is to be favoured when long transmissions of data take place such as 'remote job entry' (see 7.2.8).

7.2.8 Remote job entry (RJE)

A term often used in data communications is *remote job entry*. It refers to the collection of data in batches at a number of points local and remote. This data is then transmitted to the computer. This is one area where simplex communication lines would be used as the transmission is only required in one direction.

7.2.9 Alternatives to modems

The cheap alternative to the use of a modem is an acoustic coupler which makes it possible to use an ordinary telephone handset for transmission. This is only suitable for low speed processing. It is expected that the use of digital telephone exchange, pioneered by British Telecom under the name of System X will make modems obsolete.

7.2.10 Intelligent terminals

The power of such systems as described earlier has been considerably increased by the use of terminals which are in effect microcomputers. These devices are programmable and are capable of carrying out various checking operations on the data. Their use is more fully described in section 7.3.

7.2.11 Gateways

These form links (or routes) between two data communication systems by converting the protocol (see section 7.6.3). This allows connection between, say, LANs or between a modem and a PC and so on.

7.2.12 Servers

Servers are necessary for LANs in particular, but they have a purpose in all systems. They assign and offer resources for sharing. For instance, a file server utilises a hard disk to record information which is to be shared and a printer server is linked to a printer which is available for shared services.

0114z

7.3 Distributed data processing

We cannot refer to the distributed systems without first pointing out that there are also two other versions:

(a) The **centralised** systems, the first kind of computer approach to organisational needs. The central computer received all input and sent all output at and from the installation. In time, terminals were used for input and output (ultimately called 'teleprocessing').

(b) The **decentralised** system which consists of independent (standalone) computer units to carry out local requirements. Nowadays this is very likely to be a collection of PCs. In any case, it is very unlikely today that they would all be totally unconnected.

7.3.1 Distributed data processing systems - the concepts

The National Computer Centre (NCC) describes distributed data processing (DDP) as a system 'in which there are several autonomous but interacting processors and/or data stores at different geographical locations'.

7.3.2 The case for distributed data processing

The points in favour of distributed data processing can be listed as follows:

(a) end users of the facilities have control over their own data;

(b) end users have responsibility for their own data;

(c) there is much greater freedom allowed to the end user in order to determine processing requirements;

(d) the data processing systems that make up the total system can cooperate on common problems or can function independently.

7.3.3 The case against distributed data processing

The following points are often cited as disadvantages of the distributed data processing concept:

(a) the economies of scale associated with large-scale systems are lost;

(b) there is a lack of control over the definition of information requirements;

(c) costs and effort are often duplicated;

(d) the concept is a step backwards to precomputer days where each section of the enterprise had its own data processing system.

7.3.4 Types of distributed system

Hierarchical systems

These systems have several levels of computing power. At the highest level, there is a mainframe computer which is capable of carrying out a number of different functions such as local batch processing or file interrogation on a line-sharing basis. The next level may consist of powerful small computers which act as support for the mainframe. These machines may control a network of terminals, as well as carrying out certain processing tasks. The third level might consist of intelligent terminals or work stations; (ie, terminals with their own programmable facilities). This is illustrated in Figure 7.4.

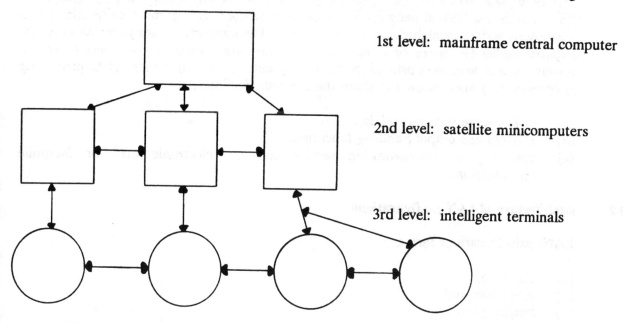

1st level: mainframe central computer

2nd level: satellite minicomputers

3rd level: intelligent terminals

Figure 7.4: Hierarchical distributed data processing

Lateral systems

In lateral systems of distributed data processing the main differences from hierarchical systems are that there are no central computers and each computer acts as an autonomous system. They are, however, capable of communicating with one another and operating as standby facilities for each other (Figure 7.5).

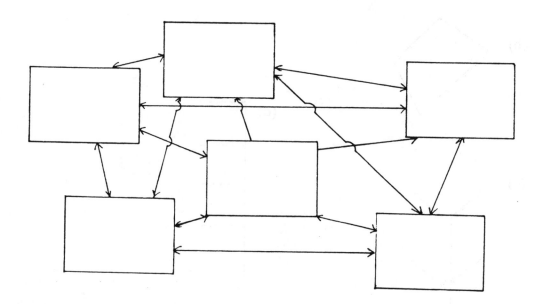

Figure 7.5: A lateral system of distributed data processing

0114z

7.4   Local area networks (LANs)

7.4.1   Definition

The term 'local area network' (LAN) is used to describe any arrangement of computing devices within a limited geographical area. LANs connect a number of terminals and computers, with very high data transfer speeds. The connections are generally made by physical media (ie, wires or coaxial cables) which are owned by the operator of the system. Local area networks differ from fully autonomous distributed data processing systems as they are designed to **share** the following facilities:

(a)   disk storage systems and data files;
(b)   printers and output handling functions;
(c)   operating a communication service such as electronic mail or facsimile reproduction.

7.4.2   Architecture of LAN configurations

LANs exist in various forms:

(a)   star form;
(b)   ring form; and
(c)   bus/tree form.

These are illustrated schematically in Figure 7.6.

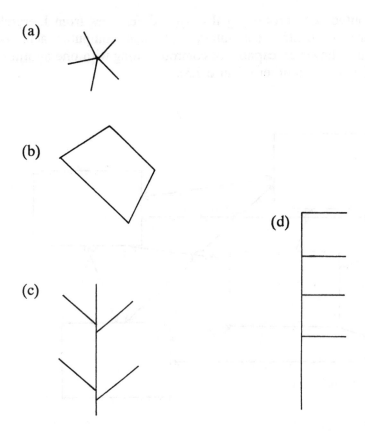

Figure 7.6: Types of LAN - (a) star; (b) ring; (c) tree; (d) bus

Obviously there must be systems to control networks, and these should be noted.

Some LANs use a private automatic branch exchange (PABX) switchboard to control the processes of switching messages and data between devices in the network.

Various attempts have been made by manufacturers of computer equipment to introduce standardised methods in LAN design. These standardised methods cover the following:

(a)   physical medium of transference;

(b)   speed of transmission;

(c)   conventions for sending and receiving messages without the hazard of 'message collision' which occurs if two devices which are connected start to transmit simultaneously. (Try talking to someone who insists on talking to you at the same time!)

7.5   Wide(r) area networks (WANs)

The WAN covers transmissions outside the frontiers of the LAN, linking organisational units on a worldwide or a wide national scale. Often, satellite transmission is adopted.

It is the WAN to which the modem is essential, although signals will be provided which, sometime in the future, do not actually need conversion (modulating/demodulating).

For WAN operations there are private telecommunication lines available for leasing, and public telephone lines may also be utilised using the ordinary telephone-dialling procedure to access.

For the typical WAN operation, the role of both the modem and the mux (multiplexor) are given in this diagram.

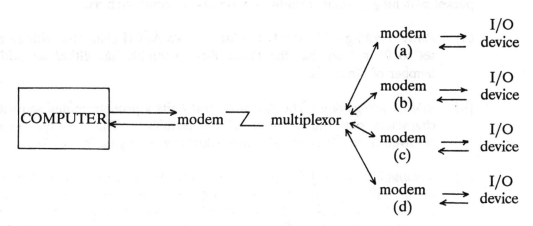

Figure 7.7

Notes

(1)   I/O signifies 'input/output'.
(2)   The mux (a kind of **concentrator**) can also allocate priority to a message.

7.6 Packet switching systems (PSSs)

7.6.1 What is a PSS?

This is regarded as an efficient method of data transmission and is based on the concept of a discrete 'packet' of data (typically 128 bytes) which is used in the communication of messages. The formatting of the message includes certain control data; this consists of the identity of the sender and an address for the recipient. The PSS is generally in the form of a computer network in which each computer redirects the message onto the next one. When the messages arrive at their destination they are reassembled and the recipient is left with a copy of the original message. The hardware used in a PSS is often styled 'store and forward', as each computer is equipped with a storage buffer for capturing the message before retransmission. A PSS can also copy or replicate packets of information, which can be redirected to other recipients.

7.6.2 Hardware types for PSS

Hardware for PSS can vary in intelligence and speed of operation.

(a) *Character devices* - These are keyboard operated terminals which transfer characters at slow speed.

(b) *Packet devices* - These are processers such as mainframes or micros which can format their own packets for insertion into the system. If semi-intelligent terminals are used, they must be installed in conjunction with a packet assembler/disassembler (PAD) which can format a packet as required. Apart from British Telecom's PSS System there are SWIFT (used by clearing banks) and SITA (used by airlines) as further examples of systems.

7.6.3 Protocols

This term means 'a set of rules governing the flow of information in a communication system'. The term is synonymous with **data link control**. Protocols associated with packet switching systems include very simple concepts such as:

(a) *Parity checking* - Seven bits are used for an ASCII character with an additional bit set to 0 or 1 so that the entire 8-bit assembly has either an odd or an even number of binary 1s.

(b) *Address recognition* - The computer transmits a predetermined sequence of control characters plus the 'address' of the terminal. The message response is only received from the terminal whose address was originally signalled.

(c) *Automatic repeat request (ARQ)* - This system guards against errors in transmission by the following process. The message is broken down into blocks of a convenient number of characters. A check character computed by a special algorithm is then added to each block. The check characters are then recomputed at the receiving end and it can be determined to a certain level of probability if an error has occurred. The receiving terminal can then send a message to the effect that the block is error-free or that an error has occurred. If the latter, a re-transmission is arranged. These two responses are often designated as ACK (acknowledgement) or NAK (no acknowledgement). NAK means that an error has been detected.

7.7 Value added and data network services (VANs)

7.7.1 The nature of VANs

VANs (strictly speaking this would be VADNs, but it would be less easy to say!) are actually services of various kinds which are available to users of system networks, the oldest of all being Prestel.

Basically, particular services can be provided for particular purposes, leased lines can be provided and transmission lines can be managed by a public network operator (such as Mercury).

It is far less expensive to accept the provision of a VAN than to establish a leased lines network on a private basis.

7.8 Conclusion

The wealth of data communication methods available has led to such developments as DDP, LANs and PSS. It is important that you can appreciate the benefits these systems have for business.

7.9 Questions

Quick questions

(1)   What do the following stand for?

LAN
PSS
ARQ

(2)   What is the name of the device that converts digital signals to analogue and vice versa?

(3)   Which is a faster mode of transmission?

(a)   Synchronous
(b)   Asynchronous

(4)   A password is:

(a)   an instruction to get the computer to repeat messages sent by transmitter;
(b)   a special message to the computer to start transmitting;
(c)   a special code entered by the user to access the system.

(5)   What is meant by the following terms in the context of telecommunications circuits?

(a)   Simplex
(b)   Duplex
(c)   Half duplex

0114z

(6) What is the name for the signalling system used to communicate with a terminal network?

(7) SWIFT is:

    (a) an aerial datapost system;
    (b) a high speed data terminal; or
    (c) a packet switching system used by banks.

(8) What is the name given to the type of distributed DP system which consists of mainframes, minis and micros and intelligent terminals?

(9) When transmitting data between terminals and computers on leased telephone circuits the security of the messages can be ensured by a system of _____ _____.

Objective test questions

(1) Which of the following is NOT a standard form of a local area network?

    A   Bus
    B   Star
    C   Ring
    D   Pyramidal

(2) Prestel is:

    A   Transmitted by the BBC and IBA. Interaction is not possible.
    B   Transmitted over telephone lines. Interaction is not possible.
    C   Transmitted over telephone lines. Interaction is possible.
    D   Transmitted over special communications links only. Interaction is possible.

(3) How would you describe the following system?

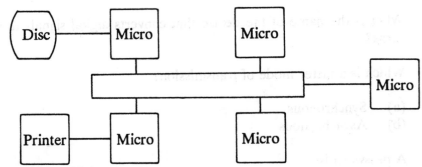

    A   Hierarchial system
    B   Local area network system
    C   Star system
    D   Multiprogramming system

Written test questions

7.1 Data transmission

(a) Describe with the aid of a diagram the main features of a data transmission system.

(8 marks)

(b) Define the terms:

(i) Synchronous transmission
(ii) Half-duplex transmission
(iii) Polling

(12 marks)
(Total 20 marks)

7.2 Distributed processing

Define the term **distributed processing** and examine the case for and against the use of distributed processing as a means of organising information systems.

(20 marks)

7.3 LANs, password controls, protocols

Write short notes on:

(a) Local Area Networks (5 marks)
(b) Password Controls (5 marks)
(c) Protocols (5 marks)
(Total 15 marks)

Written test questions

7.1   Data transmission

(a)   Describe with the aid of a diagram the main features of a data transmission system.

(8 marks)

(b)   Define the terms:

(i)   Synchronous transmission
(ii)   Half-duplex transmission
(iii)   Polling

(7 marks)
(Total 24 marks)

7.2   Distributed processing

Define the term distributed processing and examine the case for and against the use of distributed processing as a means of organising information systems.

(20 marks)

7.3   LANs, password controls, protocols

Write short notes on:

(a)   Local Area Networks
(b)   Password Controls
(c)   Protocols

(5 marks)
(5 marks)
(5 marks)
(Total 15 marks)

SESSION 8

The electronic office

In this session we consider the ultimate development in information technology - the electronic office.

8.1 Introduction

The electronic office is often loosely called the 'automated office', but the name does conjure up the false impression of science fiction robots!

We shall be looking at the major devices which constitute the typical electronic office. These are word processors, desktop publishing and database publishing devices, electronic mail, facsimile, television text systems, document image processors, workstations.

8.2 Word processing (WP)

8.2.1 What is word processing?

The need to reduce office overheads as well as to produce more typed documents has resulted in the use of microprocessor-based systems for such traditional office tasks as typewriting. The reduction in cost of hardware and the increased cost of office wages has led to the development of a variety of techniques designed to alleviate the shortage of good typists while coping with the need for good quality printed output. At its simplest, word processing is a superior form of typing which produces printed text as well as storing text in magnetic form. At its most sophisticated, word processing embraces the following activities:

(a) entering text;
(b) editing text;
(c) recording text;
(d) retrieving documents;
(e) transcribing and communicating text;
(f) controlling a printer to produce the required format/style.

The advocates of WP techniques claim a considerable improvement in throughput while detractors claim the opposite. There is no doubt that a well organised WP system can produce considerable savings in manpower.

8.2.2 Word processing applications

Word processing applications can be divided into the following tasks:

(a) preparing individual 'one-off' letters and similar communications;
(b) preparing replicated reports, or legal documents;
(c) preparing text which requires regular updating such as price lists, brochures etc.

Applications (b) and (c) have the most appeal for word processing applications and considerable improvements in quality and accuracy can be achieved together with greater productivity as well as economy of effort.

8.2.3 Hardware and software

Stand alone word processors, as they are called, consist of a full QWERTY keyboard, a VDU, a printer and a magnetic storage facility. The printer is generally a fast serial printer, such as a daisy wheel printer. The magnetic storage holds:

(a) the systems software that enables the word processor to function **as** a word processor;

(b) the text being prepared or retrieved or re-arranged. The most common storage medium is floppy disk.

A stand alone word processor can be **dedicated**; ie, it is sold with an operating system specially designed for word processing applications. Desktop microcomputers are normally able to run generalised word processing packages such as WORDSTAR WORD, WORD PERFECT AND 1ST WORD PLUS.

Shared logic word processors are those suitable for business where a large volume of text processing would make it cost-effective to invest in several terminals/work stations linked to a central processor. The processor is generally more powerful with a larger memory size than is normally found with most stand-alone processors. Shared logic installations permit a variety of printing devices to be used as well as using hard disk storage to increase library facilities. Input need not be local but can be done from terminals situated some distance away. They are particularly suitable for certain types of business such as educational establishments, solicitors' offices, accountancy firms and the like where large amounts of text are prepared or retrieved from day to day.

Mainframe word processors are those with an intelligent terminal linked to a mainframe. The text is stored as mainframe file records and retrieved and transmitted as and when required.

Communicating word processors consist of several WPs linked together and controlled by a communications controller so that a document typed by one WP can be communicated to and reproduced by another WP. This is similar to the concept of electronic mailbox, which is described later in this session.

8.2.4 How word processing works

The WP operator keys in text from source documents or from a dictaphone. The text is displayed on the VDU screen as well as being magnetically stored on diskette. Any errors of transcription can be corrected on the screen by the operator. It is also possible to use control information to determine the width of margins, the tabulation of columns of figures as well as full justification of text (ie, lining up text on both left and right hand sides of the page). When the operator is satisfied that the displayed text is free of error, the system copies the text from magnetic storage onto the page. Considerable time saving can be achieved by allowing the operator to input a fresh document while printing a file at the same time. Other facilities associated with word processing depend upon the individual model but most users would regard the following as essential facilities for WP applications.

Centring of text - The text is automatically centred or positioned between two margins.

Search and replace - Groups of words are replaced by others throughout the text.

Line spacing - This can be arranged to suit various documents.

Glossaries - Frequently used terms, words or phrases can be stored and retrieved as required.

Justification - The margins on each side of the page are said to be justified when the text is aligned. Compare this with conventional typewriting where the left-hand side of the text is aligned but the right-hand side is not.

Automatic carriage return - The operator can type at a steady pace without bothering to change to the next line.

Text editing - Words or phrases can be highlighted using a cursor; items can be deleted or inserted and the whole text is automatically re-positioned to give effect to the changes.

Page length control - The user can determine the number of lines per page.

Spelling checks and thesaurus functions.

8.3 Desktop publishing

8.3.1 The nature of DTP

This is usually explained as the professional production of documents, using desktop equipment, producing anything from basic reports to journals and advertisements. It permits graphics and text to be designed by using the computer screen. It thus allows documents to be standardised.

A typical DTP device is Rank Xerox's Documenter. This has a 10-megabyte Winchester disk, a 19-inch screen, the ability to read software (such as Wordstar mentioned earlier) and a laser printer. It has a range of keyboards available, including options for Chinese, Arabic and Hebrew languages. One interesting point is that, say, an electrical engineer can use the DTP's library of standard shapes relating to his or her specialist areas to create diagrams of circuits which would otherwise take technical drawers, paste-up artists and proof-readers several days.

Another interesting aspect is that the DTP device can be linked by network to other machines to receive what information they may have. However, the distinction between WP and DTP is becoming blurred!

8.4 Database publishing

8.4.1 The nature of DBP

This is virtually a linked DTP and DBMS system: new software, introduced at the end of the 1980s, which allows information from database to be read and formatted into a DTP page-design. The contents of database may be thus presented in a professional manner and may be simply updated on the pages by a simple amendment.

These database publishing results can be orientated to dictionaries, catalogues, annual reports, study texts and so on.

8.5 Electronic mail

8.5.1 The nature of electronic mail

Electronic mail (Email) facilities have been utilised for some years and some of the larger computers have generally incorporated some Email system. The contemporary Email is usually limited to transmitting types text.

Email consists, broadly speaking, of a terminal (possibly a word-processor or even a sophisticated electronic typewriter able to take WP programs), linked to a network. The device can be portable and could also have a screen for message displays. Sophisticated Email devices can transmit at a predetermined time (useful in the case of Emailing to USA or other country with different timing) when there is nobody in the office. A telex user can also receive a message formatted by Email.

The **mailboxing** technique is adopted, and this means that items of mail (notes, memos, etc) are deposited with a specific mailbox and the subscriber is only able to retrieve these if the address stated is appropriate. A password is usually adopted for security and encryption is also undertaken.

8.6 Facsimile

8.6.1 The nature of 'fax'

Contemporary fax has the same general principles as the original invention one hundred and fifty years ago of Alexander Bain, except that light is used and not Bain's pendulum.

Fax is simply described as 'photocopying down the telephone line' and, indeed, such a line is often used. It takes on average some 25 seconds to transmit an A4 page.

Encryption ('scrambling') is used, as in Email, for security protection.

An example of the contemporary sophisticated fax machine is the ITT 3533 which uses an in-built optical mark reader to peruse the transmission instructions (written in soft pencil or black ballpoint) from the user on a 'command card' placed in front of the pages to be faxed, in the document feeder. The fax then automatically dials the number at the time stated and transmits. It will also use its polling facility to contact other faxes and collect any documents awaiting transmission. It also produces a printout of transmission and receipt details (eg, document numbers, timings, identification of users and so on).

8.7 Television text systems

8.7.1 The nature of videotext

Videotext is the name given to television text systems which may be of the following types.

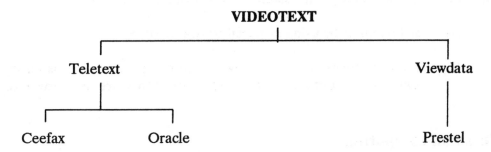

The teletext version relates to a one-way only system of information provision, the facts being presented on a TV/VDU screeen. The subjects range from weather reports to train timings. (By the way, if we use the term 'teletex' we are referring to an advanced form of telex.)

The 'viewdata' category allows interaction via telephone lines between the computer and the user. An additional service under this heading is 'Lawtel' which specialises in the latest law reports for members of the legal profession.

8.8 Document image processors

8.8.1 The nature of 'document management'

Here we are looking at the idea of tracing paper-based documentation by the computer and software which copes with documents stored on hard disk as computer files.

The systems link DTP with optical storage, as we observed earlier.

8.9 Electronic funds transfer

This term covers a variety of techniques and applications. EFT is based upon the following:

(a) financial transactions are encoded and transferred by electronic means instead of being physically handled as documents;

(b) the accounts of the parties are updated simultaneously, ie, a debit to a customer's bank account for purchases is made at the same time as the shop's bank account is credited.

0115z

Inter-account transfers between banks are growing in use through a special packet switching system for banking transactions operated by the Society for Worldwide Interbank Financial Telecommunications (SWIFT).

8.10 Telephone exchanges

Computerised systems are now used in telephone exchanges in two ways:

(a) as a monitoring system to record the destination and duration of all outgoing calls;

(b) as an automatic telephone dialling and switching system to:

   (i) dial numbers by using a special truncated code;

   (ii) 'hold' numbers while the switchboard operator is answering calls and 'switching' them back to the switchboard if they are not answered.

8.11 Personal computing

The growth in powerful cheap microprocessor-based personal computers has led to the development of advanced software, which has resulted in the personal computer being used in such a way as to make conventional office aids (like the electronic calculator) obsolete.

Personal computers are now used by a variety of business persons for such tasks as:

- cash budgeting
- financial modelling
- statistical analysis.

The users of personal computers have various types of software available which aid the production of routine accounts or statistical information. **Spreadsheet models** are the personal computer's answer to a sheet of analysis paper and a calculator. A spreadsheet consists of a matrix of lines and columns. Each coordinate comprises a cell and the contents of each cell can be manipulated in order to produce:

- columnar profit and loss accounts
- cash budget schedules
- five-year plans.

A useful feature of such spreadsheets is that a change in a variable (cell) will be executed so that the entire spreadsheet reflects the change, eg, a change in the cash inflows in year two of a five-year forecast will automatically be reflected in years three, four and five. Popular spreadsheet software models are those marketed under the names of **Visicalc, Supercalc, Lotus 1-2-3, Quatro** and **Excel.**

8.12   The workstation

8.12.1   The nature of the workstation

The important thing to understand is that the term *workstation* is a very general one and includes sophisticated ('intelligent') terminals and PCs - desktop category - which allow the use of various facilities including:

(a)   processing;
(b)   videotext;
(c)   graphics;
(d)   database access;
(e)   updating and extraction from files;
(f)   *teleconferencing;
(g)   **use of the electronic diary system.

* Teleconferencing allows VDUs and keyboards to connect individuals who may be situated in different rooms, or buildings, so that a 'meeting' may be held (the approach permits interaction).

** Electronic diaries allow users who are linked together to seek information from each other's diaries, relating to meetings, and so on, and may be maintained by the manager's secretary. (An example of an electronic diary software package is Tapestry T2, which is used for inserting an item in the diary of another; an Email message is generated to explain what has been done.)

8.13   Overview of the electronic office

8.13.1   Integrating the office

Every administrative centre/office has certain basic functions to carry out and these comprise:

(a)   **Input of data:**   transferring collected facts/figures to some kind of document-report, timesheet, etc.

(b)   **Data vetting, editing:** ensuring accuracy.

(c)   **Presentation of data:** converting facts/figures into the required form.

(d)   **Distribution of data:** ensuring that the information (converted data) is received by those who require it.

These functions can be supported in some way by IT, but the functions of creative thinking and of managing itself cannot be completely undertaken by any electronic device.

The 'office system' consists of persons, procedures to be followed and technology. It is the integration of this which is so vital.

8.14 Conclusion

There are a number of elements making up the electronic office from word processing to electronic mail and fax machines. Recall the obvious benefits of these facilities to the modern business.

8.15 Questions

Quick questions

(1) Centring of text, full justification and glossaries are all features of what sort of office system?

(2) Teletext offers interactive home computing. True/False?

(3) If you want to send a handwritten memo from Bristol to Cardiff without physically posting the relevant document, you can do so by what technique?

(4) An accounting technician intends to use the chief accountant's personal computer for the company five-year plan. What sort of software will be needed?

(5) Midland Bank PLC sends £10,000 to the Chase Manhattan Bank in New York without any paper documentation. What is the name of the technique that makes this possible?

(6) I want to store certain important telephone numbers without the effort of dialling the full code. What do I need?

(7) A sales manager wants to send a confidential report from London to branch offices at Newcastle, Carlisle and Edinburgh. What technique would he use?

(8) I want to change the words 'John Smith' in a legal document to 'Kevin Murphy'. The relevant words appear 35 times in the document. What word processing facility will I use?

(9) A publishing company has a microcomputer linked to ten workstations, 20MB of hard disk and two printers dedicated to word processing. What is the name normally given to such WP systems?

(10) It is not possible to type data into a word processor when the printing of documents is in progress. True/False?

Written test questions

8.1 Modernisation of typing pool

Your company has carried out a review of its operations. Scathing criticism has been made of the typing pool's efficiency. 'How can anyone in this day and age get by with 30 typists using superannuated electric typewriters?' roared the managing director.

Write a memorandum to her suggesting a feasible alternative.

(20 marks)

8.2 Processing of credit card vouchers

You are the accountant for a chain of garages who allow customers to pay using credit cards. 80% of all credit card transactions are done using 'PASSPORT CARD', a worldwide credit card organisation. Considerable effort is needed every day to batch and summarise the credit card vouchers for paying into the bank.

Outline a solution which may overcome this problem, indicating any advantages or disadvantages of the method chosen. Your answer should take the form of a memorandum to the managing director. **(20 marks)**

8.3 Viewdata, teletext, electronic mail

Write short notes on:

(a) viewdata;   (5 marks)
(b) teletext;   (5 marks)
(c) electronic mail.   (5 marks)
(Total 15 marks)

8.2   Processing of credit card vouchers

You are the accountant for a chain of garages who allow customers to pay using credit cards. 80% of all credit card transactions are done using PASSPORT CARD, a worldwide credit card organisation. Chris/emble chart is needed every day, to batch and summarise the credit card vouchers for paying into the bank.

Outline a solution which may overcome this problem, indicating any advantages or disadvantages of the method chosen. Your answer should take the form of a memorandum to the managing director. (20 marks)

8.3   Viewdata, teletext, electronic mail

Write short notes on:

(a)   viewdata;   (5 marks)
(b)   teletext;   (5 marks)
(c)   electronic mail.   (5 marks)
                                    (Total 15 marks)

Computer processing systems

The purpose of this session is to examine the various types of processing systems and consider how they are organised to serve management's needs.

9.1 Introduction

Let us briefly consider what management may want.

- Routine recording of accounts data, eg, payroll purchase ledger, sales ledger etc.

- Preparation of regular 'packages' of management information, eg, monthly management reports.

- Retrieval of facts for decision-making purposes, eg, 'Can we allow X Limited to exceed their credit limit?'

- Retrieval of facts for forward or strategic planning.

The processing system must also take into account the following:

(a) volumes of input;

(b) the urgency of management's information needs;

(c) the purpose to which information is put;

(d) the speed of system response, ie, the time that elapses between the collection of the source data and the processing of the results.

Although computers carry out their operations at very high speeds the way in which businesses organise themselves may mean that considerable delays exist within the flow of information. Many businesses process in a **batch mode**, eg, the clearing banks operate largely in such a mode by storing all transactions for a business day and then processing the transactions in the batch, one after the other in sequence. This type of processing system may not be appropriate for certain businesses. Some concerns cannot store up transactions in batches but need to process each individual transaction as it arises and produce an immediate result. Such *real time* systems operate in various types of business and often alongside batch processing systems. Many modern systems are, in effect, **hybrids** in that they incorporate real time and batch processing techniques within the same application area.

We shall first review traditional batch processing techniques before we go on to look at *real time* applications and the hybrid systems under interactive processing.

9.2   Batch processing systems

9.2.1   The elements of processing

In order to obtain **outputs** from a given process we must have transaction data and master file **inputs**.

Remember: TRANSACTION INPUT + MASTER FILE INPUT = OUTPUT

In batch processing we require each record to be processed in sequence. The master file must therefore have the logical records in sequential order; this means in ascending or descending order of the record identifier or **key field**, eg, account numbers.

9.2.2   The stages in batch processing

The computer applications developed in the 1960s and 1970s for the processing of applications with high transaction volumes were batch processing systems. Many routine accounts applications today are still batch processes. Batch processing implies the following:

(a)   Source data of a homogenous type are collected, authorised, and batched in lots of discrete size. Each batch is allocated a number for control purposes.

(b)   The items are transcribed into computer-sensible form possibly using either key-to-tape cassette or a dedicated data entry system as key to disk.

(c)   The items comprising the input to the system are each capable of being identified by some entry identifier like an account number.

(d)   The input file is read into the system. The first stage in processing is to submit each record to a series of logical tests. This is known as data validation. A hand copy printout is obtained which would:

(i)   identify any individual record in the batch which is invalid;
(ii)   confirm the number of valid records.

On some systems, such as payroll processing, the existence of a single error will cause the processing run to be aborted. It will be started again after the error(s) have been corrected.

(e)   The valid batch data is captured on a temporary pipeline file.

(f)   The next stage is to take the valid records and sort them into the sequence of the master file, ie, into ascending or descending order. This is done using a sort-generation program.

116   0116z

(g)   The sorted file of transactions is then matched with a master file. As each record is matched it is updated and eventually written out onto a new file.

(h)   The new file which has been brought up-to-date is printed in order to yield management information.

Illustration

X plc employs a computer for processing its factory payroll for its workforce who are remunerated weekly. Each worker is paid for a 40 hour attendance. Overtime is occasionally worked but never more than 10 hours per man per week. A worker records his time of arrival and departure by using a clock card which is inserted into a time recording clock. At the end of the week the clock card is examined by the works office who add up the attendance hours. The clock card has the employee's works number on it as well as the payweek (anything from 1 to 53) to which it relates.

The computer system is designed to:

(a)   validate the clock card data by checking the range of employee numbers, and that the hours of work are reasonable, ie, ≤ 50;

(b)   sort the records into master file order; and finally

(c)   indicate each transaction record by:

    (i)   reading the rate of pay, tax-free pay and national insurance;

    (ii)   computing gross pay, tax, national insurance deducted and net pay for the week;

    (iii)   creating a payroll record on magnetic tape which will be printed out to produce the payroll;

(d)   bring the master file totals up-to-date by adding on the data referred to in (ii) above;

(e)   print the payroll transaction file onto special payroll stationery.

Stage 1 - input and validation

Clock card data is passed to a key-to-disk operator who encodes the data on magnetic tape which is used as the input medium.

The payroll master file is loaded in the drive. Two blank tapes are loaded on other disks in order to store:

(a)   the 'new' updated payroll file;
(b)   the current week's payroll.

In addition, up to four tape files may be needed as temporary storage in order to allow the computer to sort the records on the input tape into ascending or descending order.

Stage 2 - sorting

The input file is sorted into a chosen sequence by a standard sorting program.

Stage 3 - matching

This sorted file is then used in the next stage in processing which is concerned with **matching** a master record from the payroll file with a transaction record from the file of sorted wage records. The matching is done by comparing the clock card/employee number. Once this matching is done, the program calculates the gross pay, tax and payroll deductions, updates the payroll record with the current pay data and writes it onto the output master file. The weekly payroll data is written onto the other blank tape together with the name and payroll number.

The logic used is explained stage by stage Figures 9.1 and 9.2. You should work through Figure 9.1 on a step-by-step basis.

Transaction file

1	2	4	7	9	13	15	19	26	28	31	32	99

Master file

1	2	4	5	7	9	13	15	17	19	26	28	31	32	99

Figure 9.1: Transaction file and master file records arranged in ascending order (sequential organisation)

INPUT RECORD

Employee	Wk	Hours worked
1	43	40

Transaction files

MASTER RECORD BEFORE UPDATING

		NO	Dept	Rate of Pay	TAX CODE
LEIGH J		1	A3	£4.000	278
Wk	Gross	PAYE	NI	NET	Employer's contn.
42	7148.00	2196.00	746.00	4206.00	1488.00

118

OUTPUT PAYROLL TRANSACTION RECORDS for week 43

Name	Hours	Gross	PAYE	NI	NET	EC
LEIGH J	40	160.00	31.00	16.00	113.00	24.00

MASTER RECORD AFTER UPDATING

	NO	Dept	Rate of Pay	TAX CODE
J LEIGH	1	A3	£4.000	278

Wk	Gross	PAYE	NI	NET	Employer's contn.
43	7308.00	2227.00	762.00	4319.00	1512.00

Figure 9.2: Layout of master and transaction records

Let us assume that the sorted records refer to employees as follows:

Key field	Name
1	Leigh J
2	Jobson A
4	Little M
7	West O
9	Dunlop R
13	Lock C
15	Long T
19	Reynolds J
26	Turpin H
28	Naik K
31	Abraham I
32	Boyd G

The records are arranged (for this illustration) in single record blocks on magnetic tape. In addition to these records there is a control record which contains various totals:

(i)   the total number of records;
(ii)   the totals of hours worked. It is identified with the code 99.

Let us assume that the master file include two records which did not get processed this week as the employees concerned have been suspended from work for disciplinary reasons!

Payroll number	Name
5	Goodboddie F X
17	Katzmeit A

The master file also has a control record; it is also identified with the code 99.

The logic is designed in such a way so that pairs of records are read into the memory and matched and the transaction record is used to compute the week's payroll figures and thus update the master file. The updated record is written out onto a new file. If a master file record is not matched with a transaction record it is written out unaltered. If a transaction file record has a number which does not match the master file record it is either:

(i)   an insertion to the master file; or
(ii) an illicit record requiring an error to be signalled.

If both control records are read then this indicates an end to the updating routine.

Using the arrangement of data depicted in Figure 9.2 we can explain the logic of the weekly process on a step-by-step basis.

Step 1. The program reads a master record and a transaction record into the memory. A test is made to see if the key fields match.

$$M \quad = \quad T?$$

As the key field is 1 in each case they match, the program evaluates the hours worked and increases the 'sterling' values on the master file. The weekly payroll output record is written onto tape and the master record is written out on tape. This is depicted in Figure 9.2. The program also increments the control totals on the master control record with the results of each update.

Step 2. The program now reads the next pair of records.

Records No 2 (M) and 2(T) are in the memory.

The test $M = T$ is positive and the transaction record is duly evaluated, the master file is updated and the new master file record is written out.

Step 3. Records No 4(M) and 4(T) are read in, evaluation is carried out and the master updated and written out.

Step 4. Records No 5(M) and 7(T) are in the memory. Clearly

M is not equal to T.

If $M < T$ this means that there is no matching T record for M. M is written out without updating.

Step 5. As the key fields did not match the program is directed to read the next M (record 7).

$$M \text{ (record 7)} = T(\text{record 7})$$

The process of updating and evaluation is carried out.

Step 6. The program reads M(9) and T(9) into the memory and the evaluation and updating routine proceeds normally.

Step 7. The program reads M(13) and T(13) into the memory and the evaluation and updating routine proceeds normally.

Step 8. The program reads M(15) and T(15) with no deviation for the evaluation and updating routine.

Step 9. The program reads M(17) and T(19). Clearly

$$M \neq T \text{ but rather } M < T.$$

The M record is written out unaltered.

Step 10. The program then reads the next T record.

$$M(19) = T(19)$$

and the evaluation and updating routine proceeds as normal.

Step 11. The program reads M(26) and T(26).

Step 12. The program reads M(28) and T(28).

Step 13. The program reads M(31) and T(31).

Step 14. The program reads M(32) and T(32).

Step 15. The program reads M(99) and T(99).

As the keys match and as they are the end condition the routine directs the computer to create a new control record in the new master file, print out totals from the control record and stop.

(d)   *Stage 4 - printing the output*

The weekly payroll data file is then printed out onto payroll stationery which is generally multipart stationery.

This can be illustrated in a systems overview (Figure 9.3).

Disadvantage of this method

You will readily appreciate that this routine is only suitable for applications where there is a high volume of homogeneous transactions and a significant number of records on the master file that require change. The principal drawback to the system of processing is that information is out of date as soon as it is processed.

The above system could have been operated using magnetic disks organised as sequential files. Magnetic disk sequential files are quicker to read and can be searched more selectively because of the disks' physical characteristics.

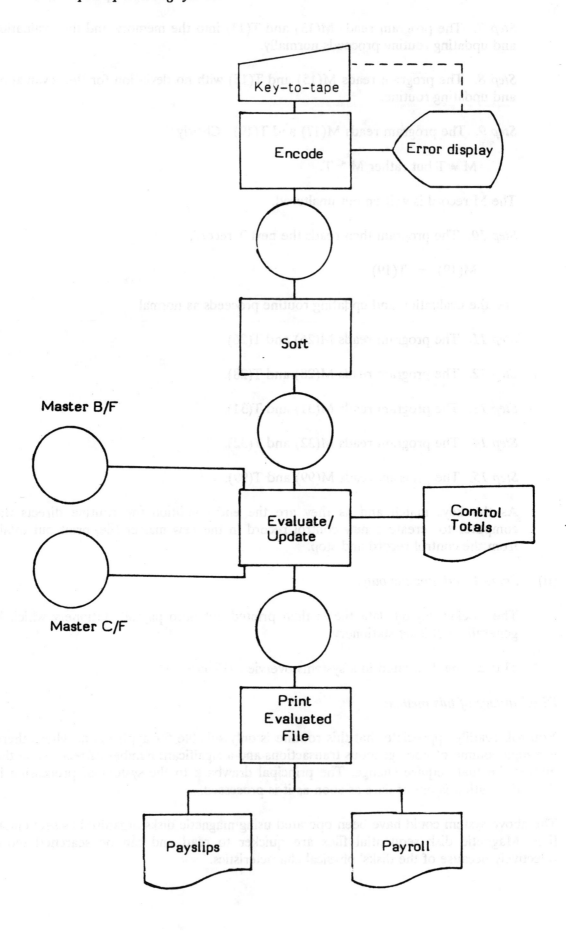

Figure 9.3: Overview systems chart for batch process-payroll

122

9.2.4   Systems control and security

The user of a batch processing system relies on various system controls as follows.

(a)   *Validation of input*

The user relies upon a data validation program. Each record is read and certain fields are subjected to logical tests. The detail of these are dealt with later in internal control. A report is produced as a by-product of the validation routine. A specimen of such a report is shown in Figure 9.4.

PURCHASE INVOICE SYSTEM		BATCH 1Ø2
VALIDATION REPORT		
REC NO	ERROR TYPE	AMOUNT
Ø34Ø	4	178.39
Ø644	1	26.78
TOTAL REJECTED	2	205.17
TOTAL ACCEPTED	198	17461.24
BATCH HEADER TOTAL		17666.41

Figure 9.4: Validation report printout

Error type 4 = invalid supplier code number.

Error type 1 = invalid record size.

(b)   *Control totals*

If a file is concerned with processing numeric data or money value data it is only natural to obtain confirmation that such totalling procedures are correct. The ability to provide control totals of the intermediate results of processing is part of **system audit** trail. If we assume that our system was concerned with posting cash receipts to the sales ledger we would wish for reassurance that the cash input agreed with the cash posted to the ledger.

This reassurance is provided by printing out the **control record** of the file. This is sometimes known as the dummy or pseudo record and is the last record in a sequential file. The report provided might look like the tabulation in Figure 9.5.

SALES LEDGER UPDATE	01/04/X4
OPENING POSITION SALESMASTER	1790431.00 +
CASH BATCH 32	90429.48 -
CLOSING POSITION SALES MASTER	1700001.52
1408 records on file	

Figure 9.5: File update control report

(c)   *File security*

In a sequential file processing system (whether maintained on tape or disk) the file is updated by copying. The security of the master file therefore is secured by the generation of a later copy. For security purposes three generations of the file are kept in order to preserve existence (Figure 9.6). The system user is also able to regenerate files if errors are found by re-running the transaction data with the previous generation of master file.

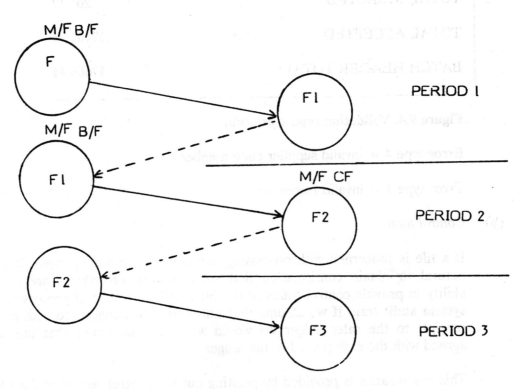

Figure 9.6: The three generation system of file security

If errors are found in F3, F2 will be reprocessed with the appropriate transaction data to produce an error-free version of F3. If errors are discovered in F2, F1 will be reprocessed to create a new F2.

9.3   Direct access file organisation

9.3.1   In contrast to the sequential processing systems discussed earlier, we can now examine direct access file organisation and the various processing methods that are available. Direct access files must be held on Direct Access Storage Devices (DASDs) - normally magnetic or optical disks.

124

9.3.2   Indexed sequential organisation

Indexed sequential organisation implies the use of a sequentially organised disk file. However, the disk file is equipped with an index in order to locate the desired record.

Data is stored on the file using the cylinder concept (see 6.5.8).

Let us assume a disk pack with 10 usable surfaces, each surface containing 200 tracks. As data is stored in each track, the highest key field is stored in order to create a track index within that track. As the cylinder is filled up with records, the highest key field in that cylinder is stored in a cylinder index.

When it is desired to find a record, the cylinder index is searched to find one where the highest key field is greater than or equal to the record key. The track index is then searched in a similar fashion in order to find the desired track. The track is then searched to find the relevant record.

9.3.3   Applications

An indexed sequential file can be used:

(a)   as a sequential file in a system of selective sequential processing;
(b)   as a direct access file processing a single transaction at a time. This is known as transaction processing.

These terms are explained below.

(a)   *Selective sequential*

With selective sequential processing, an input file of transactions is sorted into the sequence of the master file.

Each transaction record is read into the computer memory. The computer then searches for a matching key field in the cylinder and track indexes. When the record is found, it is read into the memory and updated. This record is then written back onto the disk. This is known as updating by overlay. There is no brought forward or carry forward file. This method may produce saving in machine time. Selective sequential updating is illustrated in Figure 9.7.

(b)   *Transaction processing*

In a transaction processing system, input records arrive in no set order and are processed as and when the results are required. There is no prior sorting of batches into sequence. Here again, the master record is updated by 'overlay'. This may also be known as 'real time processing' where the result is obtained instantly.

9.3.4   Random access

Where there is a large population of records on a master file and very few require change from day to day, the sequential updating systems that we have described earlier, are not suitable. The user would wish for a prompt response to any processing requirement without the need of prior sorting of input into batches arranged in sequence. Records may be stored and accessed by at least two possible methods.

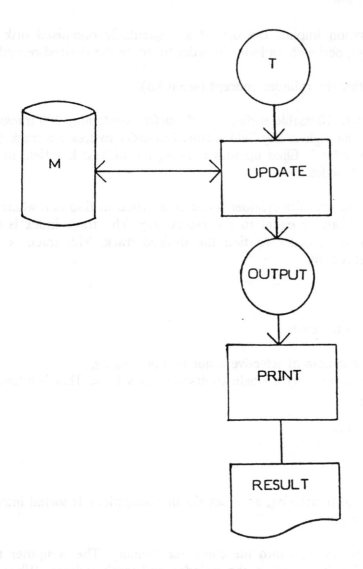

T

Sorted transaction records
the same order of the master
file.

M

UPDATE

OUTPUT

PRINT

RESULT

Figure 9.7: An indexed sequential file

(a)   *Self addressing*

Let us assume that we are creating a debtors file on disk. Two customers, A Smith and P Green open accounts with the firm.

A Smith is allocated a code number of: 110 0804
P Green is allocated a code number of: 110 0809

When A Smith's record is keyed into the computer, the program used for creating records writes in onto sector 4, track 8 of cylinder 110. P. Green's record is stored in a similar fashion on sector 9, track 8 of cylinder 110.

This method of file organisation is called 'Self Address Generation'.

There are certain drawbacks associated with self addressing, namely:

-        fixed length records must be used and there is often a good deal of wasted space;
-        code number design is constrained by the range of disk addresses.

Advantages include the following:

- the wanted record is found directly;
- no searching of an index is required;
- the concept is simple.

(b) *Randomising programmes*

This method of allocating and accessing records to disk addresses relies upon special mathematical techniques to compute a disk address from the record's key field. A simple example of how this works is shown below:

Mr Brown's record is assigned an account number of 8830. There are 1,000 sectors available for storage.

This number is squared giving 77968900.

The middle four digits 9689 are taken and divided by a factor in order to arrive at the range of sectors available, say, 9.

$$9689 \div 9 \quad = \quad 1076.5 \quad = \quad 1077$$

The sector number is   1077

The advantages of random accessing are as follows:

- an even spread of records is obtained
- no searching of an index is required.

Disadvantages:

- certain key fields may yield identical disk addresses.

9.3.5 Hit rates

The hit ratio refers to the number of records requiring amendment on a file compared to the total record population. In a payroll system for example the hit ratio is high eg,

$$\frac{\text{number of records requiring change}}{\text{total population}} \quad \frac{999}{1000} = .999$$

In a stock system the ratio is often low eg, $\quad \dfrac{100}{1000} = 0.1$

High hit rate files are most efficiently processed by batch methods; low hit rate files are often processed by direct access methods.

9.4 Security aspects of DASDs

9.4.1 Hazards of direct file accessing

Unlike sequential processing systems described earlier, the use of direct access systems for file updating poses particular problems of control and security.

9.4.2   Dumping

When a file is updated destructively, there is the ever present danger of corruption due to errors in the input. When such corruption occurs, it will be necessary to reconstruct the file at a point when the records were free from error. This is made possible by the use of periodic file copying onto tape. Tape is a cheap medium and admirably suited to the role of archival storage.

9.4.3   Overflow - a review

Updating disk files destructively poses another problem when variable length records are used.

- new records that are to be inserted may not always fit in the sequence of records on the file;

- records which are updated may become too large for their home sector.

In such cases, an overflow area is set aside within the file. Any records that grow too large for their home sector are placed there and cross referenced to their original track and sector. Periodically the file is re-sorted and the records correctly inserted in the appropriate sequence.

9.5   Real time and on-line systems

9.5.1   On-line systems

The growth in systems of data transmission has meant that more and more computer systems are described as **on-line systems**. This term implies that data is captured and conveyed to the machine using terminal devices which are under the control of the processor. The term *on-line* does not necessarily mean that the system is a real time system. It is quite possible to enter batches of data using some on-line device. Equally it is possible to have a **real time data entry** system without having a real time processing system. Most systems operated by mini- computers offer real time entry systems whereby each transaction is entered, validated and either instantly accepted or rejected. The batches of data once captured may be processed at some later stage.

9.5.2   Interactive processing

Interactive processing (also known as transaction-driven processing) may well encompass the use of remote terminals or local terminals or work stations. This processing mode describes the *modus operandi* of most microcomputer systems where the user enters data and operates the computer through a step-by-step routine using a menu which enables individual program options to be selected. Such user/machine dialogues as they are called enable even relatively inexperienced computer users to carry out a processing routine.

9.5.3   Real time systems

The term 'real time system' implies the following:

(a)   A computer capable of offering multiple access to a number of users linked to it by terminals or work stations.

(b)   A large memory capable of holding an operating system to manage a terminal network.

(c)   Dual access disk files.

(d)   Transactions are input in random order - they are validated, accepted or rejected and immediately processed.

9.5.4   Application of real time systems

The most popular example of a real time application is a seat reservation system operated by any major airline. Airline seat booking systems are expensive, sophisticated and in constant use as it would not be possible to function without them. A crucial factor which affects airlines, travel companies and others in similar fields is the very small margin of safety between making a profit or making a loss. An airliner carrying 130 people to Majorca may earn enough revenue to recover costs and make a profit. The same airliner carrying 115 to Majorca may not earn enough revenue to break even.

It follows that there is a need to have up-to-the-minute information on seat availability in order to maximise revenue. A good example of such a system is the one known as BABS (British Airways Booking System) which uses several thousand terminals linked to several computers in London. Passengers can enquire about seat bookings and make reservations on any flight in the forseeable future. The seat reservations are done by terminals in offices operating in an interactive mode, ie, with man/machine dialogue. The terminals can access centralised files and have a very swift response time.

Figure 9.8 shows a real time booking system using a DASD master file.

9.5.5   Real time systems - architecture and design considerations

There are various matters that the real time systems designer must take into consideration.

(a)   *Response time* - The speed at which a transaction is processed can be affected by the transmission time, query system for messages in transit and the speed at which files can be accessed.

(b)   *'Traffic pattern'* - The volume of messages will obviously affect the speed of response.

(c)   *System reliability* - Real time systems demand a higher degree of system reliability than traditional batch systems. The designer must cater for the contingency of system failure.

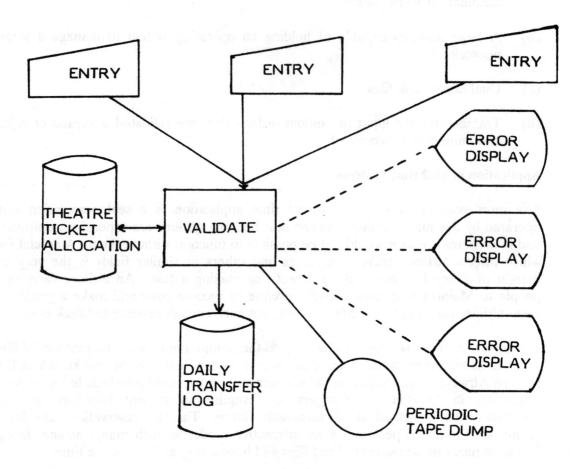

Figure 9.8: A real time ticket booking system using a DASD master file

It is common to use configurations of machines in order to preserve data security. Some design philosophies are outlined below.

(a)   *A duplicated configuration* (Figure 9.9) - If processor A fails, control switches to processor B.

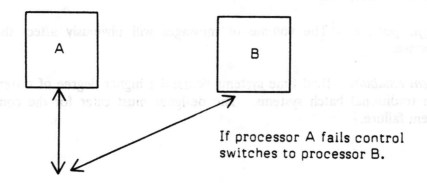

If processor A fails control switches to processor B.

Figure 9.9: A duplicated configuration

130

(b)   *A satellite configuration* (Figure 9.10) - A handles input/output of a real time nature while B handles large scale batch processing. If B breaks down, A will be able to handle the majority of messages.

Figure 9.10: A satellite configuration

(c)   *Shared file configuration* (Figure 9.11) - A and B are linked to a common bank of data. B is reserved for batch processing, while A is reserved for transaction processing.

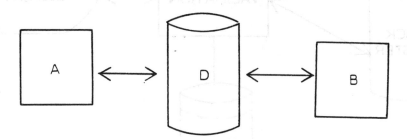

Figure 9.11: Shared file configuration

9.5.6   An illustration of interactive transaction processing

A plc has installed a computer to deal with a sales order processing/sales accounts/ stock recording system.

At daily intervals sales orders are captured on intelligent work stations. Each order is immediately validated and stored on an order file. At the end of the day the order file is printed out to produce picking notes so that goods are physically 'picked' and assembled into lots for despatch. The procedure is shown in Figure 9.12.

Once the picking notes have been used to assemble the lots these are then entered to the system; the names and addresses from the debtors master file are used to expand the picking note details and an invoice file is prepared. The picking note file is matched with the items on the invoice file and an error report is signalled if all items on the picking note list have not been re-entered. The procedure is shown in Figure 9.13.

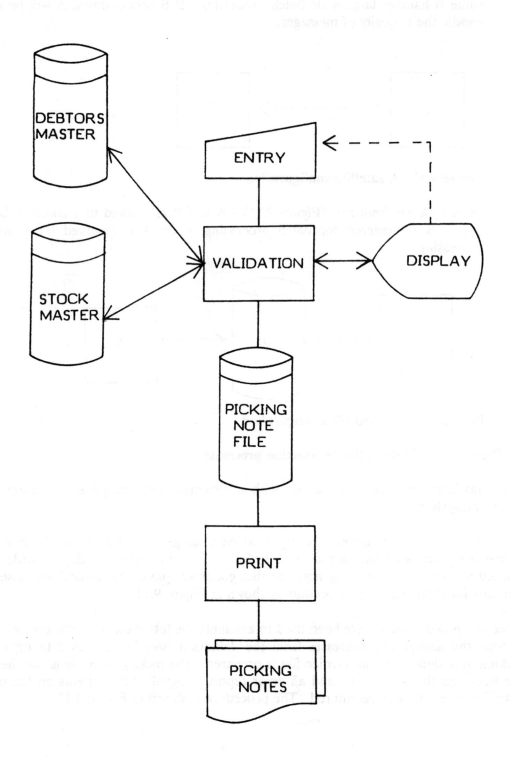

Figure 9.12: Interactive processing of sales orders

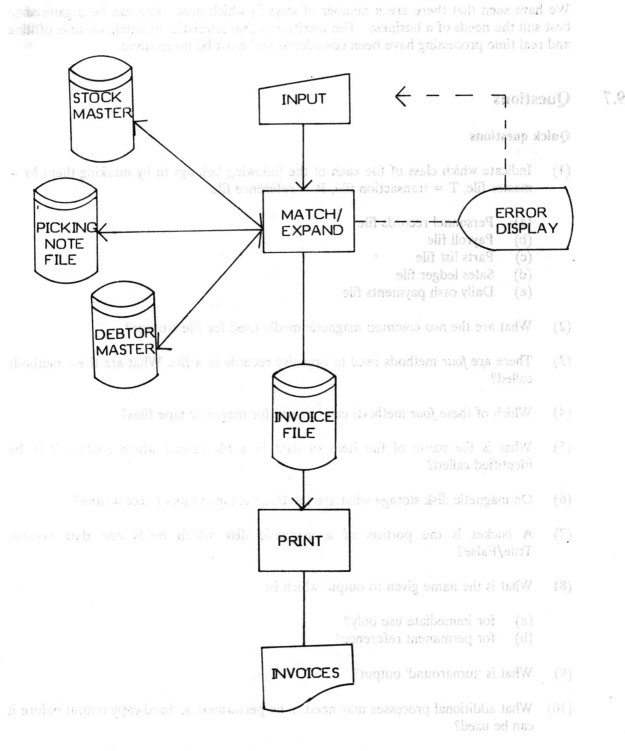

Figure 9.13: Interactive processing - invoice preparation

A feature of such a system is that although batches of data are processed there is no sorting routine; all master files are DASD and each transaction is accepted or rejected at the point of entry, ie, the system offers real time data entry. The real time data processing which is carried out might be limited to file enquiries in order to discover the amount owing from a particular debtor or the stock availability of a particular item.

0116z

9.6   Conclusion

We have seen that there are a number of ways in which processing can be organised to best suit the needs of a business. The merits and characteristics of batch, on-line, off-line and real time processing have been considered and must be understood.

9.7   Questions

Quick questions

(1)   Indicate which class of file each of the following belongs to by marking them M = master file, T = transaction file, R = reference file.

    (a)   Personnel records file
    (b)   Payroll file
    (c)   Parts list file   •
    (d)   Sales ledger file
    (e)   Daily cash payments file

(2)   What are the *two* common magnetic media used for file storage?

(3)   There are *four* methods used to organise records in a file. What are these methods called?

(4)   Which of these *four* methods can be used for magnetic tape files?

(5)   What is the name of the item of data in a file record which enables it to be identified called?

(6)   On magnetic disk storage what are the three components of access time?

(7)   A bucket is the portion of a magnetic disk which holds one data record. True/False?

(8)   What is the name given to output which is:

    (a)   for immediate use only?
    (b)   for permanent reference?

(9)   What is 'turnaround' output?

(10)   What additional processes may need to be performed on hard-copy output before it can be used?

Written test questions

9.1   Master file

What is meant by a 'master file'? Select an example of such a file and explain how it may be updated, illustrating your answer by a diagram.

(20 marks)

9.2   File organisation

Explain the basic principles relating to the organisation of data on a disk pack and describe the indexed sequential method of file organisation.

(20 marks)

9.3   Input techniques

Select three businesses which sell their products to customers but which differ radically in:

(a)   the number of customers supplied;   (5 marks)
(b)   the range of goods stocked;   (5 marks)
(c)   the volume of orders received.   (5 marks)

Suggest suitable techniques for inputting orders into a computer system appropriate to each example, giving your reasons.

(Total 15 marks)

9.1 File organisation

Explain the basic principles relating to the organisation of data on a disk pack and describe the indexed sequential method of file organisation.

(20 marks)

9.2 Input techniques

Select three businesses which sell their products to customers but which differ radically in:

(a) the number of customer supplied. (5 marks)
(b) the range of goods stocked? (5 marks)
(c) the volume of orders received. (5 marks)

Suggest suitable techniques for inputting orders into a computer system appropriate to each example, giving your reasons.

(Total 15 marks)

SESSION 10

Problem definition and analysis

In the preceding sessions, you have been introduced to processing techniques and methods. In this session, we are going to examine the ways in which a computer can be put to work.

10.1 Introduction

If we have a problem that we are trying to solve, we try to think about it logically and hopefully arrive at the right course of action. When we put our computer to work we cannot expect the computer to solve the problem for us. All that a computer will do is to carry out a course of action if we design a series of logical steps. A computer **program** is nothing more than a series of logical actions some of which are repetitious while others are not. The skill in putting a computer to work consists firstly in:

(a)   identifying the constituents of a problem;

(b)   designing an outline solution;

(c)   preparing a set of coded instructions that the computer can follow;

(d)   proving that the logic works by testing the logic with dummy data, correcting any faults and producing a workable program.

Of the four steps set out above, there is no doubt that the most demanding is (b). Once the logic has been analysed it is a comparatively simple matter to write a program for the computer, test it and amend the errors therein.

10.1.1   Program writing

As stated earlier, a computer can only understand information presented in some sort of binary code. All instructions that it is intended to carry out must be coded in binary. Any instruction that is given to a computer contains two elements:

(a)   an **operation** code, which describes the action to be performed;
(b)   an **operand**, which refers to the term of data affected by the instruction.

The operations and operands can be interpreted by the computer's control circuitry which can decode the binary formats. This is known as **machine code**. Unfortunately writing programs in machine code is extremely time-consuming and prone to error. Various aids were developed to help the process of program writing. These **programming languages** as they are called are more fully explored in the next session. In this session we will concentrate purely on problem definition and analysis.

10.1.2 The tools of analysis

The two commonest ways of analysing a problem for the computer are:

(a) flowcharts;
(b) decision tables.

The flowchart (also known as programmer's block diagram) can be drawn to various levels of detail and for various purposes. In the next section, we will consider the various types of flowchart and their relevance to the syllabus. The decision table is a useful alternative technique to the flowchart and has the advantage of making complex logic exceedingly simple. Certain types of decision table can also be proved by means of a mathematical rule which determines whether they are complete and logical.

10.2 Flowcharts

10.2.1 Types of chart

Flowcharts can be drawn in a variety of ways using various conventions. In this Study Pack, the conventions used are those of the International Standards Organisation. For convenience we can categorise flowcharts into three groups.

(a) *Clerical process charts*

These charts are designed to illustrate the steps and processes involved in any man-dominated system. This type of chart is illustrated in Figure 10.1, but it is not within the scope of this syllabus.

(b) *Systems overview charts*

These charts, also known as systems flowcharts, are designed to illustrate an overall view of a routine. A simple chart is illustrated in Figure 10.2.

You will, of course, recognise that this chart is familiar from earlier sessions in this Study Pack. These charts do not attempt a logical analysis but indicate (in outline) the various processing routines.

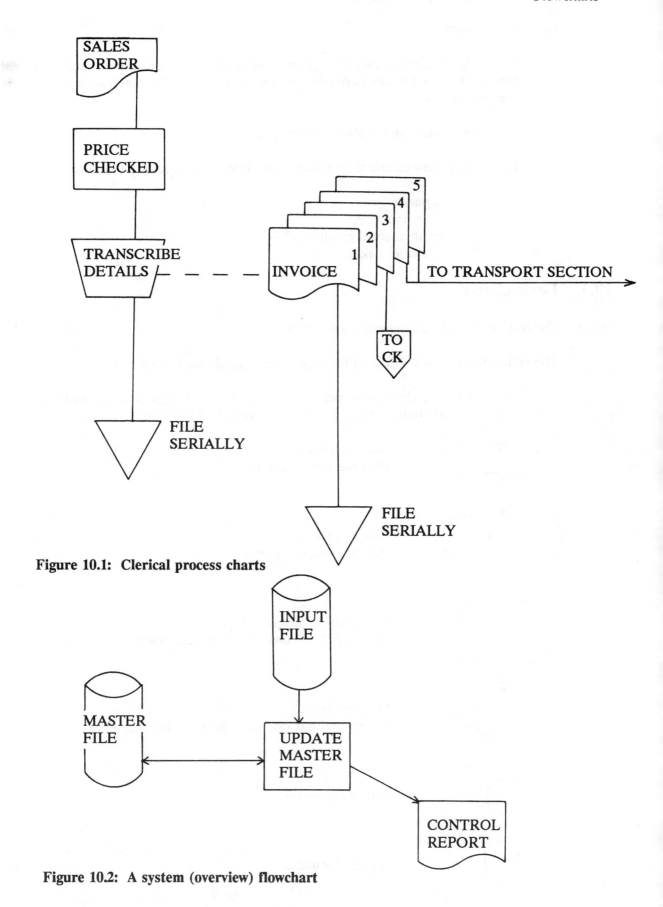

Figure 10.1: Clerical process charts

Figure 10.2: A system (overview) flowchart

(c)   *Logic charts*

These charts are also called program flowcharts as they indicate in detail the steps that are followed in any particular processing routine. The features of such charts are given below:

(i)   They must have a **start** and an **end**.

(ii)   They show clearly the various capabilities of computer processing:

> input/output;
> data handling;
> mathematical routines;
> decision-making.

10.3   Logic charts

10.3.1   Conventions (symbols) **and how to use them**

The conventions or symbols used for logic charts are shown in Figure 10.3.

It is important to use the symbol properly so that the examiner is in no doubt of your mastery of logical analysis. The tips shown in Figure 10.4 are useful to remember.

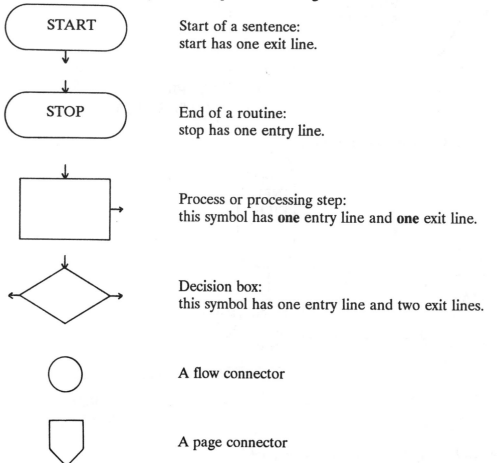

START — Start of a sentence: start has one exit line.

STOP — End of a routine: stop has one entry line.

Process or processing step: this symbol has **one** entry line and **one** exit line.

Decision box: this symbol has one entry line and two exit lines.

A flow connector

A page connector

Figure 10.3: Conventions when using logic chart symbols

10.3.2 Determining the level of detail

A question that is often asked by candidates is 'How far do I go in levels of detail?' This is a matter of judgement and the session contains copious examples of how to draw the flowcharts with sufficient detail to satisfy the examiner's requirements.

10.3.3 Tackling the problem

In order to draw a reasonable flowchart you need to remember a few things about computers that were covered in earlier sessions. Do remember that the memory is divided into a number of addressable locations, each of which is individually identifiable. It would be most inconvenient to try and remember where data is stored by memorising memory locations. It might be useful to give names to each term of data and refer to the data by this name in the course of our analysis.

Illustration

A magnetic tape file contains details of employees' pay for the 52 weeks ended 31 December 19X4. It is desired to prepare a simple average of employee pay for the year to 31 December.

If we wished to draw a systems flowchart to illustrate this, it could look like Figure 10.4.

This merely provides an overview of the problem. In order to break the problem down, it will be necessary to:

(a) open the file;
(b) read the record;
(c) store and accumulate each employee's pay;
(d) count the records;
(e) divide total by count;
(f) print average;
(g) close file.

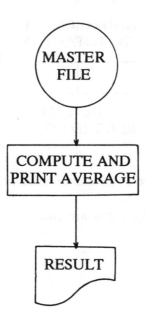

Figure 10.4: Systems overview chart

Now try to visualise a computer as a calculator with many memories. We will provide a 'map' of these memory areas (Figure 10.5). We will reserve a memory each for the workers' gross pay, the count of the records total pay and the average. These four items of data are knwon as the **variables** in this process.

Let us assume that there are only 5 pay records on the data file containing the following values: £7,498, £2,322, £3,612, £10,396, £4,389. When the computer gets to £4,389 it must receive some signal that there is no more data. We can insert a sixth record with £0 as the record total. Our logic flowchart can now be developed as in Figure 10.5.

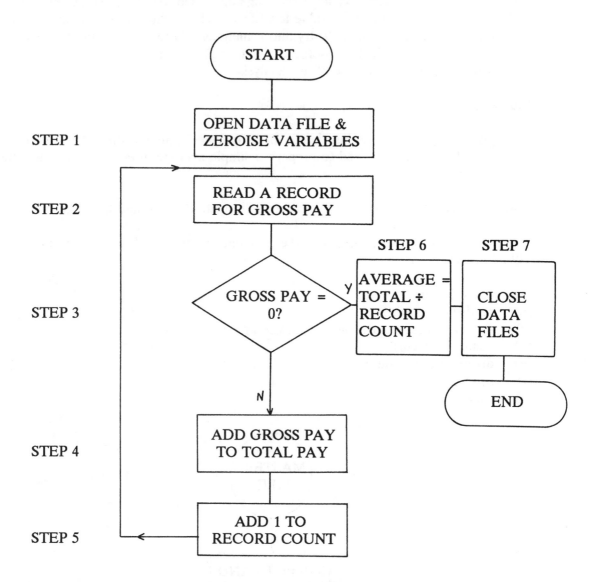

Figure 10.5: A logic chart used to illustrate calculation of an average

The contents of the memory locations are shown for each cycle of processing in Figure 10.6.

	GROSS PAY	TOTAL PAY	COUNT	AVERAGE
START	0	0	0	0
1	7498	7498	1	0
2	2322	9820	2	0
3	3612	13432	3	0
4	10396	23828	4	0
5	4389	28217	5	0
6	0000	28217	5	5643.4

Figure 10.6: Contents of memory locations

In the parlance of this subject, the flowchart illustrates certain fundamental programming techniques. The decision box creates a **conditional branch**, ie, the transfer of control in the program which is caused by some condition appearing in the data. There must always be two choices when a decision box is used. Step 5 is a return to the start and is an example of an unconditional branch. The ability to carry out a repetitive cycle of processing steps is known as **looping** and the escape from the loop is provided by the conditional branch. Occasionally, due to programming errors, no escape is provided in the logic; the program then continues to perform the same cycle of processing continuously. This is known as **permanent looping** and when this condition is identified, the operator must be alerted to stop the process.

Illustration

The construction of flowcharts need not present a problem for candidates who approach this question methodically and are prepared to test the logic of their diagrams with some data.

Consider this problem: a payroll file is maintained on magnetic tape. Each record contains name, sex, age last birthday and grading (1-5). It is desired to read the file and select all males who are not more than 25 last birthday who are grade 4 and above and all females who are at least 21 who are in grade 3. The selected names are to be printed out. The payroll file has an end-of-file marker which when read indicates the end of the routine. The end-of-file marker is a dummy record with age 99. You are required to devise the logic for achieving such a routine. (You are not required to worry about the print routine.)

Step 1   Work out the variables that you require. They are:

> (1)   name;
> (2)   sex;
> (3)   age;
> (4)   grade;
> (5)   total of males selected;
> (6)   total of females selected.

Step 2   You also require two values 25 and 21. These are not variables; they are constants, ie, they are fixed values.

Step 3   Now draft your chart. Do not look at the solution in Figure 10.7.

Suggested solution

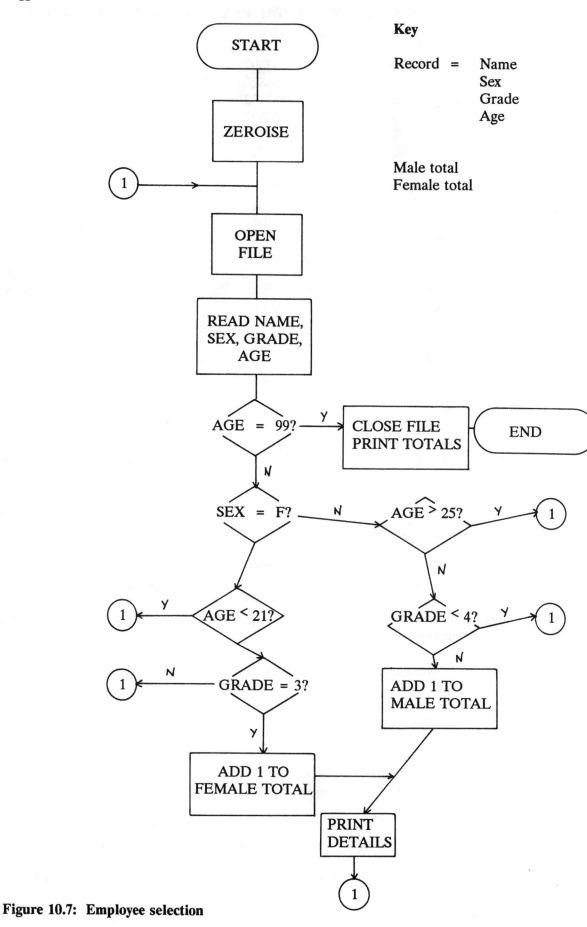

Figure 10.7: Employee selection

10.3.4   Nested loops

A nested loop is so called because it is contained within a larger loop. Nested loops invariably arise when one item of data is made up of individual parts each of which requires to be separately processed. A good example of a nested loop is given below.

Example 10.1

Data from a batch of customers' orders is held on magnetic tape and for each customer, consists of:

(a)   customer account number;
(b)   quantity of each product ordered;
(c)   price per unit of product.

Where a customer orders more than one product, quantity and price are repeated for each item until all his requirements have been included. The end of customer marker is '0' and the end of file marker is '-1'.

Required

Draft a program flowchart to print out:

(a)   the value of each separate product sale on each order;
(b)   the total amount to be charged to each customer;
(c)   the total value of the entire batch of orders.

You will note that the record is made up of a number of smaller units as represented in Figure 10.8.

		Customer account mumber
	(	Quantity
1st product	(	
	(	Price
	(	Quantity
2nd product	(	
	(	Price
	(	Quantity
	(	
3rd product	(	Price
		End marker '0'

Figure 10.8: The customer record containing subscripted variables

It is therefore necessary to have two loops; the inner loop deals with each transaction line (QTY X PRICE) and the outer loop then deals with the selection of the next record.

Try it: a suggested solution is shown in Figure 10.9.

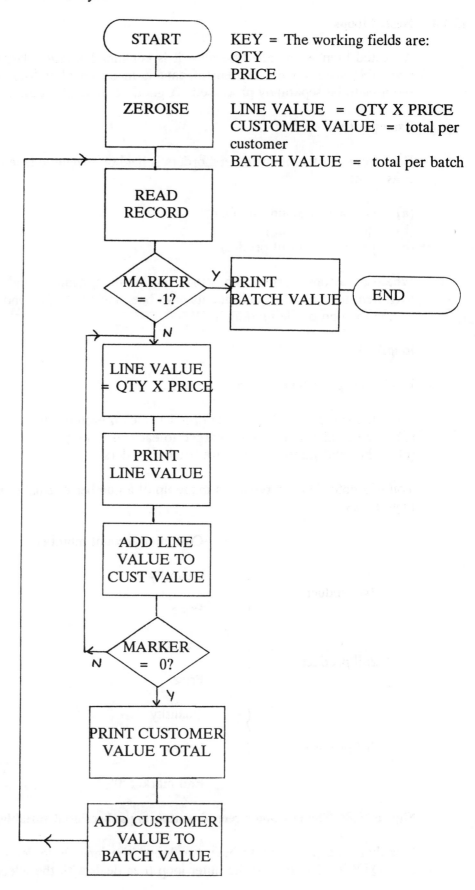

Figure 10.9: Nested loops illustrated

10.3.5 Sequential file processing

The concept of sequential file processing was dealt with in Session 6. Go back and revise the illustration of a payroll system. When you have revised it try this question.

Example 10.2

The main steps in the updating of a master file held on magnetic tape are as follows:

(a) A record is read from the master file brought forward. A record is read from the input file of transaction data. The keys of both records are compared.

(b) If the keys are equal, the input record is either an amendment or a deletion. If an amendment, the appropriate change is made and the updated record is written onto the master file carried forward. If a deletion, nothing is written onto the master file carried forward.

(c) If the key of the record on the master file brought forward is less than that on the transaction file, then this record is inactive, there are no transactions for it in this update run, and the record is written out unchanged onto the master file carried forward. Another record is now read from the master file.

(d) If the key of the record on the master file brought forward is greater than that on the transaction record then the transaction record is a new one for insertion and it is accordingly written out onto the master file carried forward.

Required

Draw a flowchart for a program to carry out the above procedures. (A dummy record numbered 9999 is held on both input and master files.) Ignore all error conditions.

Solution

(See Figure 10.10.)

10.3.6 Summary

Flowcharts should not present any real difficulties for you. Do remember that the examiner only wants you to explain (in outline) the mechanics of any particular process. *He will not expect considerable detail, merely the demonstration of logical thought.*

Do remember to:

(a) **plan** your answer;

(b) **test** a rough draft of your chart with dummy data;

(c) draft the fair version neatly, providing a key for any abbreviations and stating all assumptions clearly.

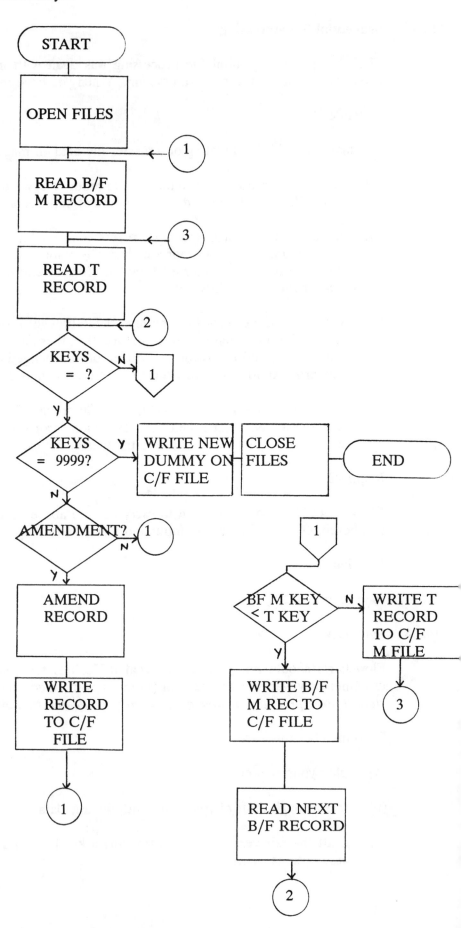

Figure 10.10: Logic chart for sequential file processing

10.4   Decision tables

10.4.1   Introduction

There are certain processes in business that require a series of decisions to be made. In some cases it may be more convenient to depict these in the form of a flowchart. In other cases the flowchart may become so complicated as to render the result completely unintelligible to all except the creator. Decision tables attempt to solve the problem of making complex logic easy to assimilate.

10.4.2   Format

The decision table is made up of four quadrants as illustrated in Figure 10.11.

CONDITION STUB	CONDITION ENTRIES
ACTION STUB	ACTION ENTRIES

Figure 10.11:   Format of a decision table

The terms are explained as follows:

(a)   *Condition stub* - This part of the table sets out the various conditions that might prevail in making a decision.

(b)   *Action stub* - This part of the table sets out the various actions that might be appropriate.

(c)   *Condition entries* - This part of the table sets out the various unique combinations of conditions that might arise. Their incidence may be indicated with a Y (yes) N (no) or - (not applicable).

(d)   *Action entries* - This part of the table sets out the appropriate action (or actions) that are to be taken for any set of unique conditions.

Illustration

A person unused to the unpredictable British weather may wish to construct a table for making a decision on what to wear.

He determines that the following conditions apply:

1   It rains.
2   It snows.

He has a choice of:

1   Using an umbrella.
2   Wearing wellington boots.

So he constructs a table as in Figure 10.12.

STUB	ENTRIES			
CONDITION	1	2	3	4
Raining	Y	Y	N	N
Snowing	Y	N	Y	N
ACTION				
Normal dress				X
Carry umbrella	X	X		
Wear wellington boots	X		X	

Figure 10.12: A simple decision table

Each of the columns on the 'ENTRIES' part of the table is known as a rule.

This table has two conditions, three actions and four rules.

10.4.3   How many 'rules' for the decision table

You will observe that there were **two** conditions in the table. Each condition could have had two possible answers yes (Y) or no (N). As a rough guide to determining the number of columns or rules, the formula 2^n (n = number of conditions in the conditions stub) is used. In our table $2^2 = 4$ ie, there were four rules.

Example 10.2

The following is a description of the procedure for dealing with delivery charges for goods bought from AB Ltd.

For the purpose of determining delivery charges, customers are divided into two categories: those whose Sales Region Code (SRC) is 50 or above, and those with an SRC of less than 50.

If the SRC is less than 50 and the invoice amount is less than £1,000, the delivery charge to be added to the invoice total is £30. If the invoice value is for £1,000 or more, the delivery charge is £15.

If the SRC is equal to or greater than 50 and the invoice total is less than £1,000, the delivery charge is £40. For invoices totalling £1,000 or more, however, the delivery charge is £20.

Construct a decision table to illustrate the procedure above.

Solution (see Figure 10.13)

You will observe that the table in Figure 10.13 has four rules; as there are two conditions in the condition stub we expected 2^2 = four rules.

Condition stub

	Condition entries			
	1	2	3	4
Sales Region Code < 50?	Y	Y	N	N
Invoice total < £1,000?	Y	N	Y	N

Action stub — Action entries

Delivery charge £15			X	
Delivery charge £20				X
Delivery charge £30	X			
Delivery charge £40				X

Figure 10.13: A simple illustration of a decision table

10.4.4 The relationship between decision tables and logic flowcharts

It is interesting to compare the logic of the previous example in decision table form with the equivalent presentation in flowchart form (which is shown in Figure 10.14).

You will see that each condition stub takes the form of a conditional branch and each condition entry is an alternate course of action. Each process box represents the individual action entries arising out of the condition entries.

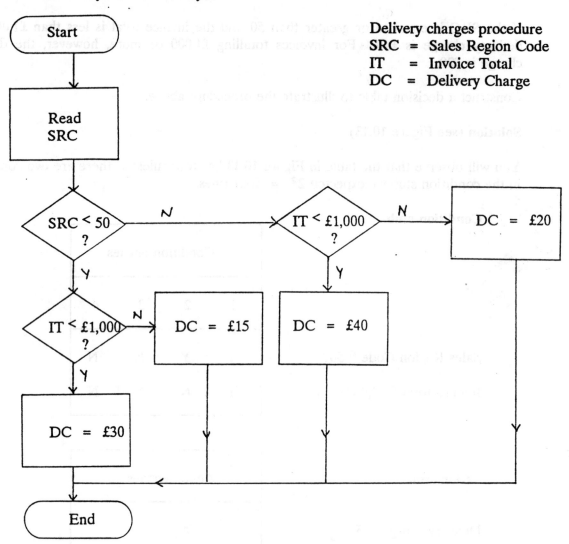

Figure 10.14: The logic of Figure 10.13 in flowchart form

10.4.5   Drawing up a decision table

The following note was taken at an interview while investigating the purchasing system at Cheap Frills Limited a wholesaler in ladies fashions.

'Bob Jones the buyer raises a purchase order when advised by stock control. They work on a system of reorder levels. When stock balance is less than or equal to the reorder quantity Bob goes into action. If we find that the reorder level has been passed and the minimum level reached Bob does one of two things: if an order is in progress he chases the supplier; if no order has been raised he makes out an urgent order ....'

Step 1. Draw up a proforma table containing the relevant number of conditions and the appropriate number of 'rules'.

There are three conditions:

Is stock balance $<$ reorder level?

Is stock balance $<$ minimum level?

Is order in progress?

There are therefore **eight** (2^3) rules.

We now draw up the table (Figure 10.15) and we complete it 'mechanically' without any regard for logic.

Step 2. We have now drawn up the table. If we work out through each rule we cannot help but notice that rule 5 needs amendment. It should read N Y Y (from the top down). It is clearly illogical. So it is amended below N - - as any other combination is illogical. This means therefore that rules 6, 7, 8 are also amended to read N, - , -. They are therefore redundant and the table is redrawn as in Figure 10.16.

10.4.6 Limited entry and extended entry tables

The table illustrated in Figure 10.15 is what is known as a **limited entry** table, ie, the entries require the simple two state logic of Ys or Ns in the condition entry part and an X in the action entry.

More complex logic is encountered in an extended entry table (Figure 10.17) where the decision-making demands more than simple two state logic.

Illogical rules

	1	2	3	4	5	6	7	8
Stock balance < reorder	Y	Y	Y	Y	N	N	N	N
Stock balance < minimum	Y	Y	N	N	Y	Y	N	N
Order in progress	Y	N	Y	N	Y	N	Y	N
NO ACTION			X		X	X	X	X
PLACE ORDER				X				
'CHASE' ORDER	X							
PLACE URGENT ORDER		X						

Figure 10.15: A decision table before eliminating redundant rules

	1	2	3	4	5
Stock reorder	Y	Y	Y	Y	N
Stock minimum level	Y	Y	N	N	-
Order in progress	Y	N	Y	N	-
NO ACTION			X		X
PLACE ORDER				X	
'CHASE' ORDER	X				
PLACE URGENT ORDER		X			

Figure 10.16: The decision table redrawn without redundant rules

The table has now been pruned of all its redundant rules.

Illustration

The Barnacle Building Society will offer mortgages to creditworthy men and women under the age of forty. Persons who have served in the Royal Navy get free life assurance. The amount of the mortgage advance is a function of the age of the borrower.

The decision table is shown in Figure 10.17.

10.4.7   The 'ELSE' rule

The ELSE rule in the condition entry part of a table is simply a catch-all rule inserted in order to make the table complete.

Illustration

Customers whose orders exceed £250 qualify for a 10% discount if they are in the London area, or 5% if they are not. Orders less than or equal to £250 pay 10% carriage charge if not in the London area.

The decision table is shown in Figure 10.18.

Occasionally the ELSE rule can be used to eliminate a number of rules with one common action entry. This has the advantage of making the table extremely concise.

Clean credit rating	N	Y	Y	Y	Y
Ex-Royal Navy	-	Y	Y	N	N
AGE	-	<30	<40	<30	<40
Reject application	X				
Free life assurance		X	X		
Grant mortgage		X	X	X	X
Proportion of advance		95%	90%	95%	90%

Figure 10.17: An extended entry table

					ELSE
Order value > £250	Y	Y	N	N	
London area customer	Y	N	Y	N	
10% discount	X				
5% discount		X			
Pay 10% carriage charge			X		
No Action				X	
EXIT FROM TABLE					X

Figure 10.18: The 'ELSE' rule applied

10.4.8   Advantages of decision tables

The following advantages are claimed for decision tables:

155

    (a)   They are easily understood by lay people.

    (b)   They express complex logic in a neat orderly format.

    (c)   In certain cases they can be proved by a simple mathematical rule.

    (d)   They can be used not only for systems investigation but also for program coding when used with a decision table processor. The software used by the processor turns the decision table into program language statements.

10.4.9 Disadvantages

    (a)   Simple logic becomes very complex when illustrated through a decision table.
    (b)   The table does not always indicate the correct sequence of actions.

10.5 Conclusion

Flowcharts and decision tables offer two techniques which may be successfully used to define the logic of a problem. By definition, as a problem-solving technique, the construction of a flowchart can be complicated and the decision table may be a simpler alternative. In the next session, we shall go on to examine the next stage in problem analysis - the writing and development of the computer program.

10.6 Questions

This session does not contain any quick questions as the subject matter is not suitable for short answers. Instead the questions have been extended to include questions on flow charts and decision tables.

10.1 Halls of residence

Five hundred students at a particular university have rooms in the McTavish halls of residence. One data card has been prepared for each student as follows:

Item	Columns	Narrative
Age	1-2	
Sex	5	(M or F)
Year	7	(1, 2, 3 or P = postgraduate)

A computer program is required to calculate and print out the following details:

(a)   average age of the students;
(b)   percentage of males and percentage of females;
(c)   percentages of 1st year, 2nd year, 3rd year and postgraduates.

Required

Draw a flowchart from which such a program may be coded. The cards should be counted as they are read in and this counter used to signal completion of input and hence the end of the program.   **(20 marks)**

10.2 West Ltd

West Ltd has, as part of its processing routines, input comprising 1,000 batches of records. The batches consist of a batch header which shows the number of records following in that batch, followed by the records themselves. These are followed by another batch header and so on for 1,000 batches.

The items are read in one at a time and processed so that the following amounts can be printed out:

(a) the average of each batch;
(b) at the end of the program, the highest and lowest average batch value found.

Required

Draw a program flowchart for the above process. **(20 marks)**

10.3 Gas invoices

A gas company produces invoices for its customers by reading in documents showing the current reading, the previous meter reading and personal details of the customer - name, address, etc.

The information is processed as follows:

(a) the first 100 units used are evaluated at £0.50 each;

(b) subsequent units are evaluated at £0.30 each;

(c) there is a standing charge of £20, but this will be limited so that it will never exceed one half of the total bill;

(d) there is no VAT.

Required

Draw a program flowchart which carries out the above processing and prints the invoices. Assume that the end of the run is signalled by a dummy record.

(20 marks)

10.4 Personnel

A personnel file, stored on magnetic tape, holds the following details for a company's employees:

>Employee name
>Department number
>Hourly rate of pay
>Hours worked
>Pension fund deduction code (A, B, C, D)
>Male/female

Management wishes to know how many male employees on the file satisfy all the following conditions:

(a)   work in department 47;
(b)   weekly hours not over 40;
(c)   have deduction code B or D.

They also require a printed list of all female employees satisfying all the following conditions:

(a)   work in department 48, 49 or 50;
(b)   weekly hours not over 40;
(c)   have deduction code C or an hourly rate of more than £2.

Required

Draw a logic flowchart to describe a computer program which would print the required list of female employees and the total of male employees satisfying the given conditions. The end of the file is marked by a dummy record with department number 999.

(20 marks)

10.5   Inequitable Life Assurance Company

The Inequitable Life Assurance Company offers insurance cover on the following terms.

If candidates are under 45 and in good health, normal premiums apply. If they are following a dangerous occupation or participate in dangerous sports, a 20% loading of the basic is applied. Candidates in poor health attract a 15% loading. Applicants over 45 and under 65 attract a 10% loading unless they follow dangerous occupations or play dangerous sports in which case the loading is 30%. Candidates over 45 and under 65 who are in poor health are rejected.

Required

Draw up a decision table in the most concise manner possible.

(20 marks)

10.6   Passport Card: credit vetting procedure

Passport Card, the worldwide credit card organisation, apply the following credit checks to candidates who apply for a card.

Candidates must be at least 21 and in full-time employment earning more than £8,000 per annum. A good reference from a banker is required. Persons who are not in full-time employment or who earn less than £8,000 will get a card provided they are married to an existing card holder. All others are rejected.

Required

Construct a decision table in the most concise form possible.

(20 marks)

SESSION 11

Programming principles

We stated earlier that a computer works under the control of an internally stored program. In this session, we shall be reviewing how a program is developed and the way in which program design is facilitated by the use of specialist programming aids, such as programming languages and language interpreters. In order to appreciate how program development is carried out it is necessary to explore, very briefly, other areas of work which are outside the scope of this syllabus.

11.1 Introduction

11.1.1 The task of systems development

If a business decides to develop a computer program (or suite of programs) for any particular business application, it is assumed that certain tasks have been carried out beforehand in order to provide a foundation for the programming task. These tasks are shown in Figure 11.1.

The **system specification** defines:

- the outputs from the system;
- the inputs to the system;
- the files maintained by the system; and
- the processes in the system.

The **systems specification** therefore is the **blueprint** of the system which must be accepted by management as a valid formulation of how the system will work.

The systems specification becomes the **terms of reference** for the task of programming. Program development is part of the very important phase of any new project; namely, that of implementation. In addition to producing a fully operational program it is also necessary to produce the program **documentation** which is an essential guide for the user on **how** the system works.

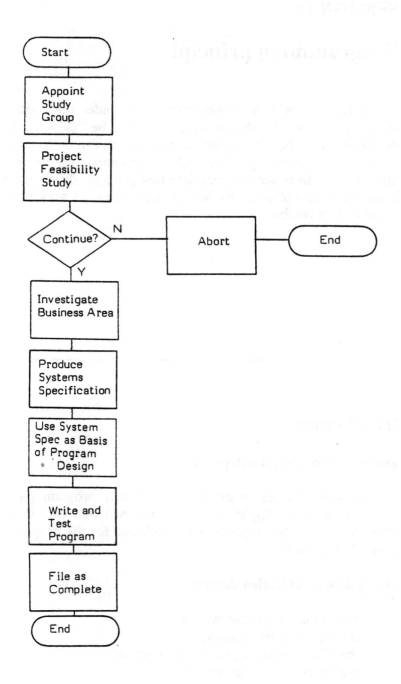

Figure 11.1: The development of programs in a project

11.1.2   Machine operations

The computer possesses the ability to do the following:

(a)   store a program;

(b)   decode the logical instructions contained therein;

(c)   execute the instructions and carry out the next step in sequence;

0118z

(d)   carry out a decision-making function by means of logical comparisons. The results of the comparison will determine the sequence of steps (this type of function is known as branching):

IF A > B   THEN PRINT A

(e)   carry out a repetitious cycle of events (looping) and where necessary modify its own instructions so that the same routine is carried out with different data.

The processor control unit is used to provide the computer with a finite number of operations that can be performed. These operations are known as the machine's instruction set. Details of these are set out in the manufacturer's user manual. Each instruction or operation code has a unique serial number. The instruction can be broken down broadly into the following groups:

● arithmetical and logical functions;

● input/output functions;

● data handling and transfer functions;

● branching functions, ie, the ability to transfer control from one part of a program to another as a result of some logical action.

11.1.3   Machine code

The computer will only understand a program if instructions are given in a binary code. Therefore each operation code has to be stored in binary. A computer also requires details of the data to be acted upon. The data must also be identified in binary. However, the data *per se* is of little consequence to the computer. It is necessary to identify the **address** of the location at which data is stored. If it were desired to add x to y in order to produce the value of z the computer would require logic (assuming that code 123 was the operation code for 'ADD AND STORE THE RESULT') as illustrated in Figure 11.2.

Operation	Operands		
Add	X	TO Y	GIVING Z
123	255	237	201

or to express this in binary (assuming one byte being used for each section of the instruction)

01111011	11111111	11101101	11001001

Figure 11.2: A program word

The figure shows a program word, which consists of two separate elements:

(a)   *Operation.* This is the action to be performed which is taken from the computer's instruction set.

(b)   *Operand.* This refers to the data affected by the operation.

In Figure 11.2, the program word had three addresses in the operand. Some machines have one operand whereas others may have two or more operands.

Obviously devising a logical series of instructions in binary notation is time-consuming and prone to error. Various methods have been devised to make the task of writing programs easier.

11.2   Programming languages and programming aids

11.2.1   Introduction

At the beginning of the computer's history there were only large mainframes which were the sole responsibility of the EDP department in the organisation.   Eventually the concept of distributed processing evolved and this meant that distributing power now placed itself on the desks of non-computer-specialist staff.   This, in turn, caused a revolution in that users had to learn to help themselves.

This was reinforced by the arrival of the PC.

11.2.2   The evolution of programming languages

(a)   *1st Generation:* These are **machine level languages** expressed in pure binary code - so the computer does not have to translate what the instruction means into its own machine language. These languages are machine dependent (meaning that there is a specific version for each make of computer). Few programs are today written in these languages, except in the case of very technical areas (eg, space research).   They make for very slow programming, error-prone and hard to amend later.

(b)   *2nd Generation:*   These are **low level languages** and allow assembler level programming. This used mnemonic coding (eg, MULT meaning 'multiply' or DIV meaning 'divide').   Use of such languages allows economy and efficiency in machine-use to be achieved. **Special instructions ('macros')** are used, each one conveying instructions for a number of activities under those headings. But the programmer has to have a detailed knowledge of the machine's working. Honeywell's Easycoder is an example of such a language.

(c)   *3rd Generation:* These are **high level languages** (eg, COBOL, PASCAL, PL/1, FORTRAN, ALGOL).   BASIC (Beginner's All-Purpose Symbolic Instruction Code) is a simple language used for educational purposes (but nowadays not used so much in business since it is found to have serious flaws).

This type may be used on more than one make of computer, and is easier to comprehend for people who did not write the actual program but who need to follow it. Also, they can adopt macro-instructions. However, these languages have to be converted to machine language by a **compiler program** and the languages are fairly limited to specific areas of activity (eg, for writing an application program for management accounting procedures, we would not use Fortran, which only copes with formulae).

(d) *4th Generation:* Here we have '4GLs' (although the term tends to be used very loosely and there are about 150 versions!).

Note that whilst other languages are aimed at instructing the computer as to **how** it should undertake the necessary activities, 4GLs are aimed at stating to the computer **what** is wanted. A generator is used to refer to a collection of templates (ie, a 'library' of specific commands relating to a specific task).

4GLs are not involved at all in procedures, as such - these have already been devised and grouped on the templates - and this does mean that users of 4GLs are constrained by what is on these templates. So 4GLs are 'non-procedural'.

So, we can say, that 4GLs allow the end-users to program their 'own' ('distributed') computer.

(e) *5th Generation:* These, being developed in the early 1990s, are founded on the principle of stating the processing needed by use of mathematical equations. This could ultimately mean that complicated processing may be undertaken as a result of a minimum extent of text.

11.2.3 Compilers

You will remember that the computer can only act upon binary code and a translation process is needed. This is performed by a compiler which is a computer program that will accept a program in a high-level language and translate it into machine code. It is performing the same task as an assembler but on a far more sophisticated level. As mentioned in the previous paragraph, the assembler's translation is usually one-to-one; with a compiler this is never the case. One statement in a high-level language may become twenty (or even more) machine code instructions after translation.

In addition a compiler will produce a copy of the translation on some storage medium (eg, magnetic tape or disk), produce a printed copy of both the original and the translation (known as program listing) and pick up simple errors of syntax, punctuation or spelling. Error messages (diagnostics) usually appear on the listing of the original program and if too many errors exist, the actual translation may not be attempted. These diagnostics do not help the programmer to produce correct logic but they do save a lot of time searching for careless mistakes where the rules of the language are broken.

The functions of a compiler can be said to be as follows:

(a) It translates statements in a high-level language (macro instructions) into machine instructions.

(b) It allocates areas of memory to each data field as well as identifying all peripheral devices.

(c)   It detects and reports syntax errors.

(d)   It provides a listing, in the programming language, of all program statements. This is known as the source program listing.

You should note that a compiler cannot identify logic errors. The programmer must identify logic errors in the course of testing the program, amend these and generally satisfy himself/herself that all such errors have been removed.

11.2.4   Source and object program

A source program is any program written by a programmer before entry to the machine. An object program is the program produced in the machine code by an assembler or a compiler after the translation process. Once tested, the object program will normally be copied onto a backing store to form a program library (see Figure 11.3).

Programs may then be called into the main store from there without the need for further compilation which is a rather time-consuming process.

11.2.5   Subroutines

Sometimes called *library procedures*, these are small independent sections of program which can be incorporated in a user's program to perform frequently required calculations or operations. Thus the program coding (and testing) is only done once and is then used by anybody who requires it. The subroutine coding must be easily accessible (eg, on magnetic disk) and may be incorporated into the main program by the compiler at the translation stage. Examples of typical subroutines are:

(a)   square root calculations;
(b)   statistical calculations such as determining the standard deviation;
(c)   calculating the number of days between two dates.

Subroutines will also exist for macro instructions which can be accessed from disk during a compiling process (see Figure 11.3).

11.2.6   Interpreters

On small computers (eg microcomputers) there is generally a translation routine which is permanently resident in the hardware. The usual name given to this translation routine is an **interpreter**. The difference between a compiler and an interpreter is that the latter operates in an interactive mode. The input of source programs on a microprocessor is achieved through direct data entry. Each program statement is keyed into the machine and receives an immediate validation for syntax purposes. Any syntax errors are rejected on entry and require to be amended before they can be entered and compiled.

11.2.7   Emulators and simulators

In the context of software programming aids, the use of simulators and emulators should be noted.

Simulation software is a specialist aid that translates programs in order to make program coding compatible between different makes of machines.

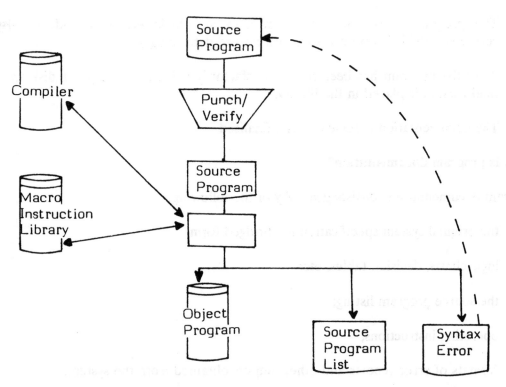

Figure 11.3: The compilation process

Suppose X Ltd were a Honeywell user who decided, after eight years, to convert his installation to IBM hardware. This would mean that programs would have to be written in order to modify them for the new machine. Time constraints may not allow rewriting the programs. Simulation software provides a temporary solution in that it will convert 'old' machine code to 'new' machine code without extensive recoding procedures. When a hardware device is used for this purpose to hold the simulation program it is known as an emulator.

11.2.8 The stages involved in developing a fully tested object program

These stages can be summarised as follows:

(a) The systems specification is obtained and given to the project leader who assesses the likely time to be taken to complete the assignment.

(b) The programming task is divided up into a number of modules and responsibility is assigned accordingly.

(c) The logic of the program is analysed using flowchart decision tables (structure charts or Pseudocode, which are alternative techniques and are described later in this session).

(d) The logic is reviewed and tested.

(e) The program is written out in source language.

(f) The source program is converted to computer-sensible form and fed into the system for translation. Syntax errors are detected and corrected.

(g)   The compiled program is obtained on tape/disk with a source program printout.

(h)   The programmer prepares test data with manually computed solutions.

(i)   The program is run with the test data and logic errors are identified and corrected. (This is referred to as testing and debugging.)

(j)   After the program has been tested satisfactorily it is filed on tape or disk and this final version is placed in the library.

(k)   The documentation is reviewed and finalised.

What is program documentation?

Program documentation consists generally of the following:

(a)   the original system specification in abridged form;

(b)   logic charts, decision tables, etc;

(c)   the source program listing;

(d)   operating instructions;

(e)   formats of error reports and other outputs obtained from the system;

(f)   details of running times and test data used;

(g)   amendments and any authorisations from management in respect of such amendments;

(h)   correspondence between interested parties.

Once the program documentation has been finalised, the systems specification can be amended into its final, feasible form. It then becomes a very valuable piece of information. It will provide a source of reference if the system is amended to suit changing circumstances or if the program is sold to other users as **application software**.

11.2.9   Structured programming

Various methods have been derived over the years in order to make the task of programming more efficient. Well known drawbacks that occur with the use of flow charts are:

-    lack of universality of language;
-    the level of detail may vary considerably from one chart to the next.

Some designers try to overcome this problem through the use of structure charts. This type of chart attempts to explain data processing requirements in detail but without the branching or algorithmic form of presentation which is sometimes confusing.

Structured programming is now used very loosely to describe any process of analysis which avoids the traditional branching and looping style of analysis. The methodology of the exponent of structured programming is to break the various operations down into:

-        sequences, ie, a step-by-step operation;
-        selections, ie, branching;
-        repetitions, ie, looping.

Structured diagrams are constructed from top to bottom in an attempt to break down the required level of detail.

Figure 11.4 shows a structure chart to prepare the payments advice printout.

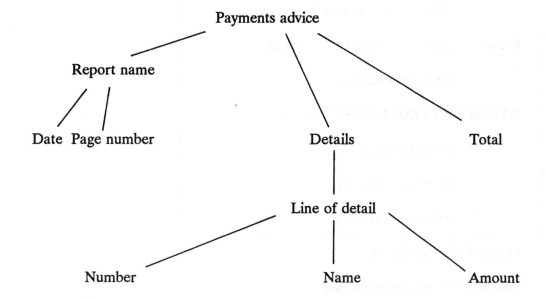

Figure 11.4:   Structure chart to prepare the payments advice printout

11.2.10   Pseudocode

Pseudocode is the term given to certain terms which fall between a programming language and English (also known as **structured English**).

The use of Pseudocode can be illustrated as shown in Figure 11.5 using the program to select suppliers for payment from the bought ledger master.

The programmer's tasks

It is no longer fashionable to regard the tasks of systems analysis and programming as being separate. In many cases programmer/analysts are engaged on project teams; a condition of employment being a degree of expertise in certain programming languages as well as skills in systems analysis.

A summary of the tasks expected of a programmer/analyst can be listed below:

(a)   Devising programming schemes and writing programs for new applications, testing these and developing fully tested systems.

(b)   Maintaining and amending systems and relevant documentation as required.

(c)   Carrying out reviews under the direction of management to ensure that programs operate with maximum efficiency.

(d)   Adhering to laid down programming standards on such matters as computer languages, programming methodology and conventions and control safeguards.

Print   report - name   date   page no.

IF   payment-code is current-month.

    Print number   name   amount

    Add   1 to line count

ELSE   Add   amount to sub total

    Read next record.

WHENEVER LINE COUNT   =   60

    Print sub total

    Increment page no

    Print page heading.

Figure 11.5: Pseudocode

Benchmarks and system tuning

Management are always concerned with the efficiency of computer operations. It is quite possible that a program written by A will take twice as long to run as a program written by B because of B's expertise in program design. Computer time has a considerable opportunity cost and management will be concerned with:

(a)   *Run times* - The time taken to operate a routine will be compared with a time standard or **benchmark**. If the variance is unacceptable, management may review the system to ascertain if run times can be improved.

(b)   *System tuning* - These are devices or methods that are used to streamline computer operations. They may consist of:

    (i)   minimising storage space used;

    (ii)   experimenting with the sizes of 'slabs' of data that are transferred between peripheral devices and CPU;

    (iii)   using software which provides simultaneity of peripheral operation thus minimising the effect of slow peripherals hampering the speed of computer operations.

11.3 Conclusion

There are three levels of programming language described here: machine code, low level and high level. Each one has its advantages and disadvantages. Practical examples of languages have also been given. In the next session we look at programs in more detail, but from the point of view of what they can do for us.

11.4 Questions

Quick questions

(1) A program written in machine-orientated low-level language is immediately understandable to a computer. True/false?

(2) An assembler is:

    (a)   a hardware device;
    (b)   a software device;
    (c)   another name for a programmer.

(3) A syntax error:

    (a)   is caused by logic errors;
    (b)   is caused by errors in the use of the programming language;
    (c)   both (a) and (b).

(4) Which are the odd men out:

    (a)   COBOL;
    (b)   FORTRAN;
    (c)   BASIC;
    (d)   SPOOL;
    (e)   ALGOL;
    (f)   MENU?

(5) Small computers only support low-level languages. True/False?

(6) A user who wishes to convert his programs from one type of machine code format to another can do so by using:

    (a)   a compiler;
    (b)   a text editor;
    (c)   a simulation program;
    (d)   an interpreter.

(7) If languages are classified from complex to simple in terms of coding effort on the part of the programmer, which of the following is the correct sequenced list?

    (a)   Low-level/machine code/high-level.
    (b)   High-level/machine code/low-level.
    (c)   Machine code/low-level/high-level.
    (d)   Machine code/high-level/low-level.
    (e)   High-level/low-level/machine code.
    (f)   Low-level/high-level/machine code.

(8)   A transfer of control from one part of the program to another which results from a condition in the data is known as:

(a)   a branch;
(b)   a conditional branch;
(c)   a loop;
(d)   an unconditional branch.

Objective test questions

(1)   An example of a microcomputer operating system is:

A   Lotus 1-2-3
B   CP/M
C   Cobol
D   dBASE IV

(2)   The main function of a compiler is to:

A   Check an existing program listing for errors
B   Translate a low level language to a high level language
C   Produce a detailed program flowchart
D   Translate a source program into an object program

(3)   BASIC is a:

A   High level language
B   Low level language
C   Machine code language
D   Binary language

(4)   Re-arrange the following operations into the order in which they would be carried out when developing a program:

(i)   Program written out in source languages.
(ii)   The logic is analysed using flowcharts.
(iii)   The compiled program is obtained.
(iv)   The programmer runs test data.

A   (i), (ii), (iii), (iv)
B   (ii), (i), (iii), (iv)
C   (i), (ii), (iv), (iii)
D   (ii), (i), (iv), (iii)

Written test questions

11.1 Assembler program, compiler program, syntax errors

Write explanatory notes on:

(a)   assembler program;   (5 marks)
(b)   compiler program;   (5 marks)
(c)   syntax errors.   (5 marks)

                                                                              (Total 15 marks)

11.2 Instruction format, branching

What do you understand by the following terms?

(a) instruction format; (5 marks)
(b) branching. (5 marks)
(Total 10 marks)

11.3 High-level language

A program has been written in a high-level language. Explain the steps involved in compilation and the use made by the programmer of the printed output.

(20 marks)

SESSION 12

Software - an appreciation

Software is a generic term used to describe all programs or programming expertise. In this session, we shall be dealing with two types of software:

- system or operating software;

- application software.

12.1 Introduction

12.1.1 System or operating software

The system or operating software is concerned with the control and performance of the computer system. It can be analysed into the following groups:

(a) operating systems;
(b) translation/program development aids;
(c) utilities, service programs;
(d) diagnostic programs;
(e) database management systems.

12.1.2 Application software

Application software can be divided into two main categories:

(a) Application packages are those complete packaged systems designed for a particular business application, eg, a payroll package.

(b) General purpose application packages are specialised systems which enable the user to carry out a variety of processing tasks of an allied nature. For example, the WORDSTAR package is a general purpose package for word processing which can be used to 'convert' an IBM-PC or similar machine to a word processing role.

12.2 Operating systems

12.2.1 Functions

The operating system is the term used to describe the suite of control programs that are used to regulate the operation of the computer. The functions of the operating system are:

(a)   to communicate with the operator;

(b)   to provide a record of all that takes place during processing (the log);

(c)   to identify errors and carry out correction routines;

(d)   to transfer programs into main storage;

(e)   to control input and output devices;

(f)   to schedule tasks to provide for continuous processing (not always a feature of small machines);

(g)   to open and close files and check that the file label identifies the file as appropriate to the processing task;

(h)   to manage the memory, altering word lengths for storage purposes (ie, storing numbers in packed decimal format);

(i)   to start/stop/interrupt;

(j)   to manipulate data;

(k)   to carry out multiprogramming;

(l)   to allocate processor time between programs according to some system of priority.

The operating system therefore determines to a large extent the capacity of the hardware.

Not all these functions are available on all machines. Small machines with limited memory size may not be able to accommodate complex operating systems.

12.2.2   Small machines

With small machines a **monitor** control program is present in the memory. This control program allows users to read into memory an operating system which is stored permanently on (say) diskette or hard disk.

On some machines part of the operating system may be hardwired into non- volatile memory called ROM (Read Only Memory). Other variations on a similar theme are areas of memory designated PROM (Programmable Read Only Memory) or EPROM (Erasable Programmable Read Only Memory). On small machines it is possible to transfer control from the operating system to, say, a general purpose system such as WORDSTAR if it is desired to change from a computational to a word processing mode, and then back to, say, processing in BASIC as the communicating language by appropriate typed system commands.

12.2.3   Large systems

The resident part of the operating system is often called the executive or supervisor. In large systems which offer both batch and real time processing modes, as well as communication systems, the operating system reduces the operator's role to that of a machine minder with a large number of operations carried out under automatic control. For example, organisations such as the Access credit card company are operational for 364 days a year on a 24-hour basis. It is useful to consider certain features of operating systems as they relate to the mainframe.

12.2.4 Multiprogramming

The earliest computers were only capable of carrying out the operations of input and output processing on each item of data in succession. Their mode of operation was effectively constrained by the speed of the slowest working peripheral device.

Later models of machine brought with them the concept of simultaneity in operations through the use of **buffered** devices so that input, output and processing could be overlapped.

A buffer is an area of memory allocated to a peripheral device. The buffer concept allows keyboard entry and printing to take place at the same time. This idea of simultaneity is taken further when tasks are run concurrently on the computer in order to utilise the processor's power to the maximum.

Certain tasks can be overlapped through **spooling**. This term requires a word of explanation. It is an acronym which stands for **simultaneous peripheral operation on line**. A problem that is encountered with large volumes of processing is the time spent by peripheral devices to either read in data or write out information.

Consider the design of a payroll system. The systems run diagram for producing the weekly payroll is shown in Figure 12.1.

The output of the processed payroll data onto disk will be done at the high speed associated with the transfer of data between memory and backing storage. The transfer from disk to printer will be a slow task which can be done as an ancillary task when another application program is being run. This arrangement whereby processor time is shared between peripheral devices minimises the differential in operating speeds.

12.2.5 Operator interface

With the large system the control of the operating system and the ordering of tasks is done by means of Job Control Language statements (JCL). Each task that is controlled by the operating system has its own job description and there are a number of control commands which are in use in order to activate a particular routine.

Some common JCL commands are given below:

      SORT   -   sort a disk file

      DELETE -   remove a file from storage

      ABORT   -   abandon current job

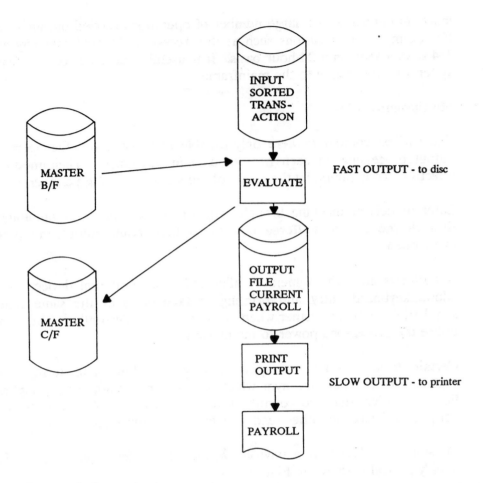

Figure 12.1: Fast and slow output

Small computer systems are often operated by people with limited data processing skills. The operating system control commands are set out on a visual display (a **menu**) and the user is guided by a series of 'prompts' which appear on the screen indicating the next course of action. (This type of conversational mode of operation is also a feature of those larger systems that operate in an interactive mode.)

Microcomputer users often use the operating system called MS-DOS (Microsoft Disk Operation System) which offers:

(a)   rapid access to disk;
(b)   an environment for developing programs;
(c)   a method for storing programs in different source and machine code;
(d)   a method of allocating space to new and old files.

12.2.6   Virtual storage

The concept of virtual storage is utilised to enable large programs to be accommodated in a machine with limited amounts of internal storage. For example, if 60000 bytes of storage were available and a program occupied 90000 bytes of storage, the technique of internal storage allows the program to be stored on disk and 'pages' or sections of the program are called into main memory as and when required. This process is called 'paging' or 'segmentation' and is controlled by a special program within the operating system.

12.3   Advanced operating systems

12.3.1   Database management systems (DBMS)

The term *database* has been defined as a file of structured data designed to serve a number of users and applications which is program-independent and substantially non-redundant. (The term 'redundant' in this context means 'without duplication'.)

The structure and use of databases will be dealt with in greater detail in Session 13. However, in this section we will briefly deal with the concept and talk about the software systems that are needed for this purpose.

The idea of a database is an attractive prospect; it is designed to be a common bank of data capable of being accessed interactively and used to supply information to a variety of users. It is important to emphasise here that a database does not just mean a system of on-line real time processing. Most systems developed around a database offer batch and real time processing as well as special interrogation routines.

For example, a student database operated by a polytechnic could offer the following applications:

(a)	Billing the students' sponsors.	(batch)
(b)	Entering cash received.	(batch)
(c)	Filing enquiries on attendance.	(real time)
(d)	Booking reservations on courses.	(real time)
(e)	Reporting on student examination results.	(data base)
(f)	Extraction of student details by geographical stratification.	(data base)

In order to manipulate data for these various purposes or **schemes** a complex software system is required. This is a database management system which is designed to:

(a)   create, amend or delete records;
(b)   manipulate records;
(c)   process input data;
(d)   retrieve information in various formats.

The DBMS also protects the system against risks such as unauthorised access, failure of hardware or corruption of data.

In order that the user can communicate with the system a data base generally requires a standardisation of all data descriptions through the use of a data description language (DDL). A data manipulation language (DML) may also be used to manipulate the data.

The DBMS is managed by an administrator whose task is to ensure that the data in the base matches the information needs of the users. This requires the administrator to liaise closely with programmers and analysts over the development of systems.

12.4 Utility programs

There are a number of programs which are written as utility or service programs and may be common to any number of applications. These are listed below:

(a) sorting programs;
(b) file copying;
(c) file reorganisation;
(d) file maintenance;
(e) diagnostic routines;
(f) housekeeping routines;
(g) audit enquiry packages;
(h) report writing software.

12.4.1 Sorting programs

Sorting is frequently required by systems specifications where it is desired to arrange records in some ordered sequence. In batch processing systems, sorting the records into ascending or descending order of key field is an essential part of the process.

12.4.2 File copying

It is frequently necessary to 'save' data for future retrieval by copying a file onto another storage medium.

12.4.3 File reorganisation

When variable length records are used on direct access disk files there is always the danger that a record will grow too large for its home track. Such records are placed in an 'overflow' area which is cross-referenced to its original track. Such files periodically require reorganisation in order to accommodate all records in their original tracks.

12.4.4 File maintenance

This term relates to the procedures necessary to:

(a) delete records from file;
(b) insert records on a file;
(c) amend records on a file.

12.4.5 Diagnostic routines

These are used by programmers in the course of program testing. A typical diagnostic routine is a **dump and trace** routine which transfers the contents of main store to backing storage and then to paper where the contents are printed out location by location with the contents by the side.

This is used in order to discover errors in program logic or to reaffirm that the logic was working according to the specification.

12.4.6 Housekeeping routines

These are tasks of a routine nature such as creating file identification labels and clearing storage areas.

12.4.7   Audit enquiry packages

Management often install special supervisory systems within the business which have the task of monitoring the systems of control and ensuring that the information produced for management purposes is reliable. It is not uncommon for such internal audit staff to want to examine files of data independently, ie, without relying on the services of the people normally engaged in operating the system. Such audit enquiry packages enable the user to:

(a)   read a file and extract information from it;
(b)   perform certain processing tasks such as control totals;
(c)   select samples of transactions for detailed testing with other records.

Such audit packages are also extensively used by external auditors (whose duties are regulated by statute) in order to verify independently the accuracy and completeness of recording systems.

12.4.8   Report writing software

Those systems which are not 'full blown' database systems offer users various methods to extract information and formulate reports using special software. Such report writing systems are often sold with small systems. No computer expertise is required by the user other than the ability to follow a series of command instructions which are used to formulate the user's needs.

12.5   Program development aids

You should now revise the various program development aids that were dealt with in the previous session, namely:

(a)   programming languages;
(b)   compilers, interpreters and assemblers;
(c)   simulators and emulators.

12.6   Software for specialised purposes

The growth of small machines on the market has led to a considerable increase in the various options that are made available to the users.

(a)   *Turtle graphics - Turtle* is a two-wheeled robot with a pin connected to the computer. Using the LOGO programming language, the turtle can be used to draw lines, squares or circles by giving a series of commands, eg, right 90 causes the turtle to trace a right angle; forward 10 causes the turtle to take ten steps forwards and so on.

(b)   *User-defined graphics and software* - The graphics characters contained within a computer's character set can be manipulated using an appropriate command to the operating system. (A POKE command allows a user to generate a character and place it in a specific location.)

12.7 Application packages

An application package is a suite of programs together with the appropriate systems documentation. The package is designed to meet the needs of a number of users and is modular in construction so that a limited amount of modification can be carried out to cater for the needs of individual businesses.

Packages can be obtained for a variety of applications and these are listed below:

- Payroll
- Purchase ledger
- Stock control
- Sales accounting
- Modelling.

There are also a number of packages which are specifically directed at the microcomputer market. Examples of these are word processing packages such as 'WORDSTAR' and 'MAILMERGE' as well as 'Spreadsheet' type packages for routines such as cash budgeting. These are very popular and offer powerful appeal to financial managers who may already use their microcomputers or mainframes but who require a more 'personal' office aid. Examples of spreadsheet packages are VISICALC and SUPERCALC.

As the name suggests they are the microcomputer's answer to the double sheet of analysis paper and the pencil beloved of accountants. The VDU displays a series of lines down the screen and columns across the screen. The operator can use a cursor to highlight each position on the spread sheet (or cell) to enter data, make alterations and obtain results.

12.7.1 Buying a package

A business often has to decide between developing its own application or purchasing a package from a consultant, software house or manufacturer.

There is a need therefore to ensure that any package that is purchased or acquired by other means (eg rent) is properly evaluated. The matters that must be considered in this context are listed below:

(a) Does the package meet the user's requirements and will it satisfy the user's objectives?

(b) What alternatives are offered by the market? Have these been examined?

(c) Is any member of staff fully conversant with the working of the package? Can the package be modified easily?

(d) How efficient is the package in terms of computer utilisation? What requirements are necessary for main storage and peripheral devices?

12.7.2 Advantages of packages

(a) A package represents tried and tested expertise and the user is spared the problems of the learning process.

(b) System documentation is provided with the package.

(c) The package can be adjusted if the user moves to another system.

(d) Systems investigation and design time is reduced to a minimum. Once the requirements of the system are known and the decision to purchase the package is made little extra work is required.

12.7.3 Disadvantages of packages

(a) The system that is tailored to the needs of the business is often regarded as the best system to have.

(b) Modifications may not be cost-effective.

(c) Packages may not be sufficiently flexible towards changes in the business situation.

12.8 Conclusion

'Software' is a general term covering all programs. As we have seen these programs can be of many kinds - operating systems, utilities and applications. Programs can be purchased off-the-peg or tailor-made. A company's choice will depend on the nature of its business (how specialised is it?) and the amount of money it has to spend.

One of the operating systems described deals with the management of a database system. In the next session, we shall look at databases more closely.

12.9 Questions

Quick questions

(1) What is the alternative name for an executive program?

(2) What is the difference between sorting software and a utility?

(3) Name *two* common types of sub-routine found as standard software.

(4) Fill in the blanks.

A compiler translates a .... program into an ....

(5) SPOOLING is a technique for:

   (a) fast rewind of magnetic tapes to save operator time;
   (b) fast production of paper tape;
   (c) operating peripheral devices with simultaneity to maximise use of the processor.

(6) MS-DOS is:

   (a) a programming language for microcomputers;
   (b) a programming language for remote terminals;
   (c) an operating system for microcomputers.

(7)   SuperCalc and VisiCalc are:

    (a)   brands of pocket calculator;
    (b)   diskette handling systems;
    (c)   spreadsheet systems for financial modelling.

(8)   Virtual storage is:

    (a)   plug-in compatible computer memory;

    (b)   a technique for segmenting programs that are too large to be held in main memory;

    (c)   a hardware device for storing programs.

(9)   A programmer who is testing his program may use diagnostic software at certain specific points in program execution. Name the software typically used.

(10)   Name three sources of application packages.

Objective test questions

(1)   A program which has been written to produce sales invoices is known as:

    A   an application program
    B   a spreadsheet program
    C   a utility program
    D   an operating system program

(2)   Multiprogramming is when:

    A   more than one program is in main memory and control is switched from one to another
    B   a number of programmers simultaneously develop different modules of the same program
    C   a large number of related application programs are stored on disc
    D   a number of users can simultaneously run the same program in a local area network

(3)   A program supplied by a computer manufacturer to sort data is known as:

    A   an edit program
    B   an object program
    C   a utility program
    D   a source program

(4)   In a computer system, the term 'software' means:

    A   only the utility programs
    B   all the operating system
    C   only package programs
    D   all the programs

Written test questions

12.1 Operating systems

In what ways do operating systems aid computer operations? **(10 marks)**

12.2 Compiler and interpreter programs, spreadsheet model

(a) Distinguish between a *compiler program* and an *interpreter program*. (10 marks)
(b) Briefly describe what you understand by a 'spreadsheet' model. (10 marks)

(Total 20 marks)

12.3 Programming languages

With the increasing use of microcomputers, one of the most widely used programming languages is BASIC (Beginners All-purpose Symbolic Instruction Code) which is a relatively simple example of a particular type of programming language.

Required

(a) State what type of programming language BASIC is and the main features of this type of language. (5 marks)

(b) Explain why languages of this type were developed and are being increasingly used today. (5 marks)

(c) State what other level of programming languages is available and the circumstances in which such languages are used. (5 marks)

(Total 15 marks)

Databases

In earlier sessions, we examined what are known as file-based systems, ie, for the purchasing system there are a group of files, similarly for the sales system, stock system, payroll etc.

In this session, we shall look at an alternative organisation - the database system.

13.1 Introduction

In the late 1960s, systems designers became dissatisfied with the piecemeal approach to data processing which was adopted by many users. A company would computerise its payroll system and then its purchase ledger system followed possibly by the sales ledger system and lastly by the general ledger. The need for an integrated management information system, IMIS, was recognised and this became the systems designer's goal. Integrated in this context could be taken to mean that the system would recognise the inter-dependence of all the various functions in business and would aim to provide a **total** service to the management. Every transaction would be processed so that its full effect on the business would be reflected in the recording process. For example, if a sales order were validated and processed it would affect:

(a)   orders in progress statistics;
(b)   debtors;
(c)   stocks;
(d)   sales;
(e)   agents' commissions;
(f)   royalties (if payable).

Many systems were designed in order to provide this integrated approach. However the evolution of the concept of the **database** further refined the way in which data recording and information processing is integrated by avoiding the major pitfalls of the integrated approach, ie, the duplication of data recording and the substantial redesigning of systems and programming which would occur every time systems were expanded or reorganised.

13.1.1   Definition of database

A database is a collection of data which supports the operations of the organisation. The data in a database must also be:

(a)   substantially non-redundant;

(b)   program-independent;

(c)   usable by all programs;

(d)   structured in such a way as to reflect the normal inter-relations between business functions;

(e)   subject to a common approach for insertion, amendment and retrieval.

Illustration

ABC (Wholesale) plc use a computerised sales order processing system for their customers. In order to construct a customer database, the following information is required:

1   Customer name
2   Customer number
3   Customer area code
4   Credit limit
5   Order values as follows

   •   input for the current period
   •   average normal orders for a twelve-month period
   •   value of orders unsatisfied

6   Total transactions this period
     Total transactions for the year
7   Total balance
     Current balance
     Balance + 30 days
     Balance + 60 days

In this context we can call the collection of customers on the file the **physical** database and the collection of fields comprising each data record the **logical** database.

13.1.2   Processing of transactions

Obviously, if a database is to be kept up-to-date, transactions have to be processed promptly. The system of processing that is usual is based on the concept of integrated systems.

Illustration

A sales order is received and logged on a transaction file.

(a)   It updates the order file so that the order input and orders on hand fields change.

(b)   It is entered on a picking list file used to produce despatch notes.

(c)   It updates the product file and reduces the amount of stock on hand.

(d) It also updates the invoice register (from which sales invoices are prepared) as well as updating the transactions history and balance fields on the customer database.

This is shown in the form of a diagram in Figure 13.1.

The management require periodic accounts to be prepared. These periodic accounts will be drawn from a number of sources (Figure 13.2).

13.1.3 Hardware required for a database system

The use of a database requires large volumes of disk store which can be directly accessed. Input is done on a transaction by transaction basis through on-line terminals (key stations and VDU).

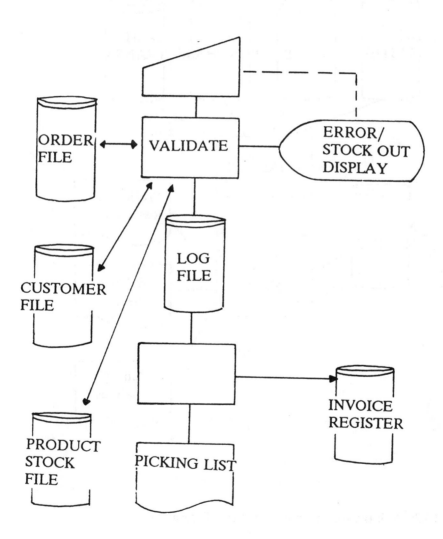

Figure 13.1: Systems diagram for an integrated stock/sales system

13.1.4 Software required for a database system

A special type of software is required in order to operate a data base. This software is known as the database management system (DBMS). In a large organisation the DBMS can control a variety of different processes; batch and real time processing can both be part of associated data processing systems. The whole point of a data base, after all, is that records are program-independent. In order to operate a DBMS, certain programming aids are essential. A data description language (DDL) is needed in order to render the data compatible with the DBMS. Certain languages such as COBOL have variants which contain instructions that are used for data base applications. The DBMS is capable of various **schemata** which are the programs used for extracting information in various report formats.

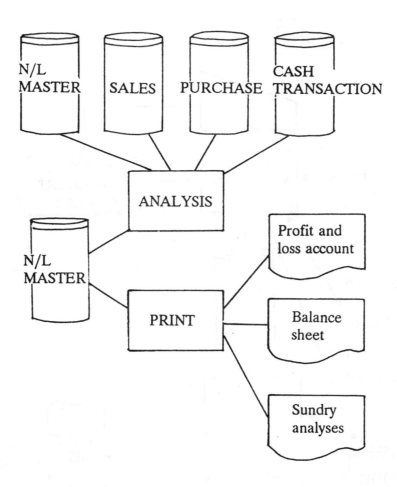

Figure 13.2: A database for management information

13.1.5 Using the database

The operations to use a typical database are set out as follows:

(a) Each user has a password which must be keyed in via a terminal. Once the system has signalled a response a menu is displayed showing the various options available.

(b) An option is selected from the menu; most retrieval systems offer a dialogue type approach which guides the user through various steps in order to access the relevant data in the appropriate formats.

(c) Data can be manipulated by the use of special commands which enable the user to specify:

(i) sorting by certain fields;
(ii) selection of records by certain fields/attributes;
(iii) print formats of the data selected.

(d) Once the system has confirmed that the records exist and there have been no mistakes of syntax in the interrogation language the results are printed out on paper.

13.2 Data and file structures

13.2.1 Types of data structure

The concept of the data base requires records to be structured in such a way as to facilitate the extraction of items to yield management information to the users. The student should be familiar with the main data structures.

13.2.2 Chains

A chain is a string of records each of which is connected to another record by means of a pointer. The pointer is held within the record and provides for the address of the next record in the chain. Chained record structures are usefully employed when the 'logical' record varies in length. Chains can consist of numbers of **fixed length** records. The access times may also be reduced as the system software can locate the whole group of chained records. A volatile file (where many record changes are made) may not be a viable proposition for chained record structures.

An example is given in Figure 13.3.

Record address	Customer number	Customer	Agent	Agent pointer
494	1771	Moon Fashions Ltd	H Roberts	496
495	1782	Golf Togs Ltd	A Silver	498
496	1794	Frills Ltd	H Roberts	530
497	1812	Topcoat Ltd	G Boddy	500
498	1814	Burnison Ltd	A Silver	499
499	1817	Capper Ltd	A Silver	513
500	1819	Bramley Ltd	G Boddy	509

Figure 13.3: Chained records; a customer file linked to an agent file

13.2.3 Rings

A ring is a string of records which are linked with pointers. The final record in the ring points back to the 'head' record.

Assume that there are four sales transactions that relate to J M White (Figure 13.4).

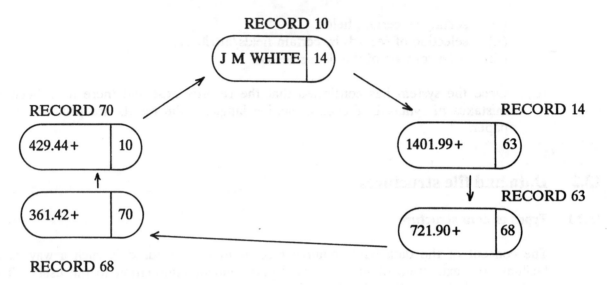

Figure 13.4: Ring data structure

13.2.4 Tree structure

A tree consists of a hierarchy of nodes the highest of which is the root. The node may be a single record or a number of records grouped together. The main characteristics of the tree structure are as follows:

(a) there is only one root;

(b) no node at one level has more than one linked node at the level immediately higher. By analogy a parent node may have many 'children'; a 'child' has only one parent.

Figure 13.5 illustrates the tree structure of data.

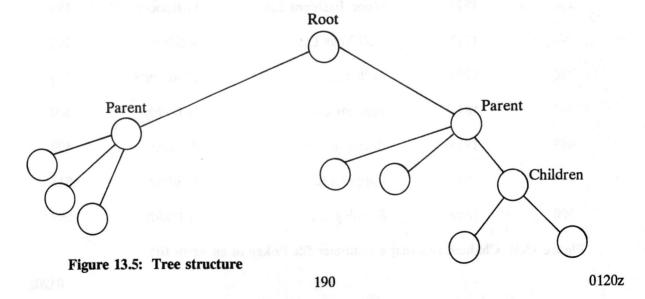

Figure 13.5: Tree structure

13.2.5   Networks

A network data structure has nodes linked to other elements at any level.

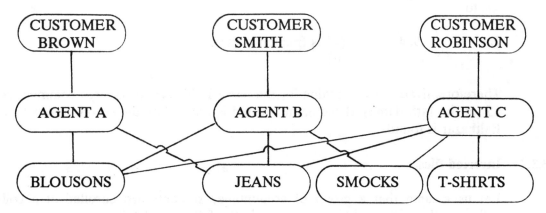

Figure 13.6: A network data structure

In the example shown in Figure 13.6, BROWN buys blousons and jeans through AGENT A.

13.3   Advanced file retrieval concepts

The system designer is constantly on the look-out for the most efficient method of retrieving data from a file. Some of the methods that you should be aware of are briefly discussed below.

13.3.1   Key position estimation

Assume that we had 65 students on a roster and the number of students' names beginning with each letter of the alphabet was as follows:

A	14
B	1
C	2
D	3
E	2
to	
Z	1

The fractions at **start** of the As would be as follows:

A	0	(as A is the first letter, the factor is 0/65)
B	.218	($\frac{14}{65}$ is fraction at start)

C   .234   ($\frac{15}{65}$ is fraction at start)

   to

Z   .984   ($\frac{64}{65}$ is fraction at start)

Therefore, if we were searching for the name Balthazar, the search commences at .218 x 65 (at the 14th name). If the name located is Bach, then the search moves forward until Balthazar is found.

13.3.2   Inverted files

Let us assume that a group of accountancy students are enrolled at a college. The college authorities would be interested in the following details:

-    name
-    course
-    country of origin
-    sponsor

Let us consider the following fictitious students:

03942	Tan J H	(Malaysian)	AAT L.3	Sabah Power Board
03117	Williams Mrs A	(British)	AAT L.3	Shamrock Investments plc
03417	Rahman A A	(Malaysian)	AAT L.2	Sabah Power Board
04212	Fox-Pitt J M	(British)	AAT L.1	Shamrock Investments plc
04219	Smith J R	(Trinidad)	AAT L.1	High Commission Trinidad & Tobago
02196	Wettimuny F X	(Sri Lanka)	AAT L.3	Tea Plantation Ltd
09129	Roberts P G	(Trinidad)	AAT L.2	High Commission Trinidad & Tobago

It is therefore advantageous to create the following lists of attributes on three files as shown in Figure 13.7.

Each attribute of the student can then be used to match entries from other lists. Therefore if it was desired to find all AAT Final students from Malaysia, it would be necessary to extract Tan, Wettimuny and Williams from the course list and compare with Rahman and Tan on the Country of Origin list. This would leave Tan as the only student with the desired attributes.

Country of Origin	Sponsor	Course
Britain	Sabah Power Board Rahman A A Tan J H	**AAT Level 1**
Fox-Pitt J M	Shamrock Investments plc Fox-Pitt J M Williams A	Fox-Pitt J M
Williams A	Tea Plantations Ltd Wettimuny F X	Smith J R
Malaysia	Trinidad & Tobago High Commission Smith J R Roberts P G	**AAT Level 2**
Rahman A A		Rahman A A
Tan J H		Roberts P G
Sri Lanka		**AAT Level 3**
Wettimuny F X		Wettimuny F X
Trinidad		Williams A
Smith J R		Tan J H
Roberts P G		

Figure 13.7: Inverted files

13.4   Conclusion

You should be able to list the advantages claimed for using a database.

(a)   Data is input once only.

(b)   Redundant data is eliminable as elements of data are stored in one location.

(c)   Data is retrieved very quickly.

(d)   The confidentiality of data and information is achieved using passwords which allow access to certain personnel.

(e)   Data can be sorted at high speed and searched in accordance with certain parameters.

(f)   Reports can be generated using data from various sources.

(g)   Data can be accessed and inspected by means of screen displays.

13.5   Questions

Quick questions (**Note:** Some questions have more than one answer.)

(1)   Which of the following attributes apply to a database system?

      (A)   non-redundant;
      (B)   program-independent;
      (C)   program-dependent;
      (D)   polymorphic;
      (E)   structured.

(2)   A database system does not support batch processing. True/False?

(3)   Binary chopping is a technique used for:

      (A)   disk files only;
      (B)   tape files only;
      (C)   both types.

(4)   In the context of tree structures, indicate which statements are true:

      (A)   A 'child' may have two 'parents'.
      (B)   A 'parent' may have only one 'child'.
      (C)   A 'parent' can have many 'children'.
      (D)   A 'child' may have one 'parent' only.

(5)   Systems which attempt to simulate the thought processes of humans in any particular field of activity are often known as _____ _____.

Fill in the blanks.

(6)   An inverted file requires each record to have a number of _____ which are stored on _____.

(7)   What do the initials DDL stand for?

(8)   A record is connected to another by means of a pointer held within the record giving the address of the next record. This is known as a _____ in the context of data structures.

(9)   A collection of records linked by pointers with the final record pointing back to the first record in the collection. This is known as a _____ in the context of data structures.

(10)   In a block searching system there are 625 record keys. How many keys would you expect to find in a block?

(11)   A college maintains its students records on disk. Each record contains the student number, name and course. The student number is the key field.

To list quickly all the students attending a specific course, the file organisation required is:

A Sequential
B Serial
C Inverted
D Variable length

(12) Which of the following cannot be performed if a write permit ring is fitted to a magnetic tape file?

A Reading the file
B Over-writing the file
C Copying the file
D Inverting the file

Written test questions

13.1 Inverted files, tree data structures

Write short notes on:

(a) inverted files;
(b) tree data structures.   (20 marks)

13.2 Schema

Briefly explain the term *schema*.   (10 marks)

13.3 Databases

Some computer installations, particularly the larger, more sophisticated ones, are using data bases in which to store the organisation's data.

Required

(a) Define a *database*.

(b) List and explain briefly *five* of the advantages claimed for a well designed database.

(c) Explain briefly *three* of the major problems associated with the implementation and operation of a comprehensive database.

(d) Distinguish between the *logical* and *physical* structure of data.

                                                               (20 marks)

SESSION 14

Controls and security in a computer-based system

In this session we shall deal with the organisation of the data processing function and the very important matter of controls and security.

In this session we will deal with controls in three key areas:

- organisational controls;
- controls over systems development;
- procedure controls.

14.1 Introduction

The introduction of computerised methods inevitably brings the problems of errors and fraud.

Any computer user has to become aware of the need for a good system of controls and security in order to be assured that the system produces reliable and accurate data. In a manual system it is always possible to follow the **audit trail** of a transaction, ie, to look at the visible evidence of transaction processing. In a computer system there is visible evidence of input and output only. Additionally computer systems bring with them a remoteness in human involvement with large volumes of transactions processed at speed. Errors that are made are difficult and costly to correct. Fraudulent use of computer facilities is becoming more common. Frauds can be committed by employees, senior management or other third parties. Data can be tampered with; files can be destroyed by accident or by malicious acts. Fraudsters can divert funds from an enterprise to their own pockets or can attempt to hold employing companies to ransom by the threat of sabotage to vital computer systems. No information processing system can afford not to install rigorous systems of control and security.

14.1.1 Internal control revisited

Any organisation which wishes to regulate its activities does so by designing a system of checks and controls normally called **internal controls**. The objectives of any such system of controls are generally perceived as follows:

- to safeguard assets;
- to follow stated policies instituted by management;
- to maintain reliable records;
- to carry on business activities in an orderly and efficient manner.

All of these objectives can be seen to be relevant to an information processing system.

It is useful here to consider briefly the features associated with a system of checks and controls. These are:

-    *Physical* controls over property - in this context controls are necessary over equipment, files, etc.

-    *Authorisation* of all actions.

-    *Accuracy* in performance of processing work.

-    *Personnel* - ensuring that those with the right skills are employed.

-    *Management* - supervision of all systems by top management using a technique like internal audit.

-    *Organisation* of activities by means of a sub-division of duties.

-    *Segregation* of duties.

-    *Supervision* of one person's work by another.

All of these features will be discussed in this session as the examiner will expect you to be aware of the various aspects of control and security in computer systems.

14.1.2   Organisation of the data processing activity

A fundamental feature of any control system within a business is the requirement of good organisation.

This principle should be upheld when determining the organisation structure of the data processing department.

There is no single form of organisation for information processing. In some large businesses the data processing (DP) function is within the sphere of responsibility of the Management Services Department (MSD). In such a case the MSD will have responsibility for other activities such as internal consultancy, operations research and productivity services (work and method study).

What follows now is a brief description of each key area within the DP department as illustrated in Figure 14.1.

14.1.3   Data processing manager

This title generally assumes that the appointee has overall responsibility for all DP functions. The appointee may delegate responsibilities in two or three areas by dividing up the immediate responsibility for systems development and day-to-day operations.

14.1.4   Systems development staff

The functions of systems development may be carried out in various ways depending upon the management philosophy of the business. The following job titles are not uncommon in the field of development:

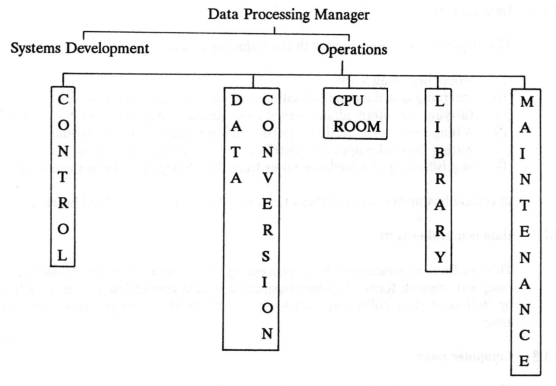

Figure 14.1: A typical organisation chart of a DP department

(a) *Business analyst* - A person so described is generally required to have a good knowledge of the business area and the end users' information requirement.

(b) *Systems analyst* - This person generally requires more technical knowledge than a business analyst and may well be expert in certain programming languages or schemes as well as having a good knowledge of how the computer hardware works.

(c) *Programmer* - A programmer may describe him/herself as either:

    (i)   an application programmer; or
    (ii)   a systems programmer.

An application programmer writes programs for various applications as well as testing and documenting these. A systems programmer is one who works on such matters as operating system design or the preparation of special utility programs.

14.1.5 The operations manager

The person who is responsible for the day-to-day operation of the installation together with all ancillary activities may take responsibility for the various sub-sections of the department such as:

- Data control
- Data conversion
- Computer room
- Librarian
- Maintenance

14.1.6 Data control

This department is concerned with the following tasks:

(a) scheduling of all work;
(b) accepting new data and validating it as authorised and complete;
(c) carrying out intermediate clerical tasks such as hash totals and control totals;
(d) vetting the error/rejection reports and instigating corrective action;
(e) vetting finished output and distributing it to authorised persons;
(f) requisitioning disk packs or tapes from the library as and when required.

In certain businesses some of these tasks may be carried out by the librarian.

14.1.7 Data conversion section

This section is concerned with processing the source data by transcribing it into computer-sensible form. In some businesses a data conversion section may be replaced by individual data collection workstations positioned at the points where source data arises.

14.1.8 Computer room

The computer room, also known as the operations centre, is manned by:

- *a shift leader* - most large businesses may work a two or three shift day;

- *computer operators* - they work under the control of the shift leader and are responsible for loading and unloading peripheral devices, handling finished output, etc.

14.1.9 Librarian

The librarian has custody of the following:

- data files of transactions;
- master files;
- program files.

The librarian also controls the issue of files to the control section for specific processing tasks and the receipt of those files after processing has been completed.

14.1.10 Maintenance

In the large installation maintenance staff are required to carry out the following tasks:

- periodic preventive maintenance of the various devices;

- investigate and repair devices which break down;

- carry out periodic tests on the processing equipment;

- monitor the environment and guard against environmental hazards such as dust, fire, humidity, etc.

14.2 Controls on the integrity of the system

14.2.1 General controls

This is the term given to those **general controls** over the DP department. They include the following:

(a) controls over all computer operations and associated tasks;

(b) controls over program security to guard against unauthorised changes to procedures;

(c) controls over data files to guard against unauthorised changes;

(d) controls over the implementation of new systems to ensure that the system works as originally agreed and specified.

14.2.2 Control of computer operations

Division of responsibility

An important feature of Figure 14.1 is that it illustrates the division of responsibility within the department. It is a fundamental principle of control that no person should have too much responsibility as this could lead to errors remaining undetected, or to acts which could be fraudulent. Students of auditing are familiar with this concept as part of their studies on internal control.

Special features of the chart can be explained as follows:

(a) There is separation of duties between **development** and **operations**. This is necessary in order to ensure that those people with the know-how do not have the opportunity to abuse their skills in order to subvert the operation of the computer system to their own advantage. It is, therefore, of paramount importance to ensure that the organisation structure describes the span of control of the key functionaries and that **their** tasks are clearly set out in job descriptions.

(b) As a general rule the operation of the computer by staff from the development section should be witnessed by a member of operations staff.

(c) The computer room should be an area of restricted access. Computer operators should not be allowed to handle raw data or be involved with any task concerning either validation of data or data capture. (There are certain problems with 'on-line' systems but these will be dealt with later.)

(d) The concept of separation of duties will only be upheld if the management ensure that it is upheld and take steps to ensure that controls are not overridden. Manuals of procedures are one way in which the control philosophy can be communicated.

Control of operator activity

The following are relevant in controlling the operators themselves:

(a) Provision of operating instructions which are sufficiently detailed dealing with all the various routines for each application.

(b)   Recording of times of arrival and departure.

(c)   Maintenance of handwritten operator 'log'.

(d)   Rotation of shifts where multishift working in operation.

(e)   Comparison of machine log and operator by some responsible person.

Controls to check that the correct data files are used

This control consists of ensuring that the files header label is checked in order to ensure that it is consistent with system requirement.

The label generally includes the following:

(1)   an identifier: possibly the word 'HEDR'
(2)   file name
(3)   date written
(4)   number of days for which the file needs to be kept
(5)   purge date = (3) + (4) ie, the date from which the file can be overwritten.

On disk files the header is sometimes called the VTOC (variable table of contents).

14.2.3   Program file controls

These include:

(a)   Segregation of duties so that operators cannot obtain detailed knowledge of program specifications.

(b)   Controls over program files in the library so that they cannot be illicitly copied and used.

(c)   Regular comparison of computer-produced records of processing carried out with actual work done.

(d)   Internal audit procedures to test programs to ensure that the correct version of the program is being operated.

(e)   Regular recompilation from security-held source version programs to remove any 'illicit' object progrms.

14.2.4   Closed shop and open shop programming

In organisations with large development departments there are often controls over the use of computer development time and the activities of programmers. **Closed shop programming** employs a restriction on programmers by requiring computer operations staff to test programs on their behalf and provide the necessary output. The advantages claimed for closed shop programming are as follows:

(a)   It minimises testing time.
(b)   There are no disruptions to processing schedules.

Open shop programming on the other hand allows experienced programmers to use the machine themselves. In many cases programs are tested using remote terminals and routine processing tasks are not disrupted.

14.2.5 Data file controls

(a)   On-line data files should be protected by passwords restricting access to the system.

(b)   Off-line data files should be kept securely in a library which is geographically separate from the computer room.

(c)   The library should be organised so that all files are securely labelled, racked and shelved.

(d)   There should be adequate procedures to control the issue and return of files.

(e)   There should be clearly laid down procedures for file reconstruction.

14.2.6 Hardware security

The following matters are relevant:

(a)   The security of the site is important, all DP staff should carry identification cards and special locks (opened by reading badges) should be used.

(b)   There should be safeguards against environmental hazards such as dust, humidity, strong magnetic fields, extremes of temperature, fire hazards etc.

(c)   Standby facilities should be available in case of breakdown.

(d)   The premises should be suitable for housing the hardware.

(e)   Regular maintenance should be carried out, to minimise the incidence of machine breakdown.

14.3 Controls over processing

The day-to-day controls over processing data must be exercised at two points:

(i)   within the user department
(ii)   within the DP department.

14.3.1 User department controls

By far the largest number of irregularities and errors occur in input data. It is useful to consider the controls exercised by the user in order to highlight and reject invalid data.

The following are typical user department controls:

(a)   Validation of the source data by scanning it to see if it is complete and apparently correct ie, all code numbers correctly transcribed, all fields of data complete and in the right mode.

(b)   Serial numbering of source data for control purposes.

(c)   Control of documents by batching.

(d)   Recording of batches of data in a batch register.

14.3.2   DP department controls

The control section

This section of the DP department is the point of interface between the user and the DP department.

The functions that it carries out are these:

(a)   Examining any batches of data sent to be processed and ensuring that they are complete and properly authorised.

(b)   Keeping records of all incoming work; ensuring that the work arrives punctually; routing the work through the data conversion section and ultimately to the computer room.

(c)   Obtaining output from the computer room and checking it for accuracy and completeness before routing it to the user.

(d)   Obtaining the files from the library and routing them to the computer room.

(e)   Acting upon error reports; dealing with the originating department; progressing the resubmission of rejected work.

Data conversion

This department is responsible for the accurate and timely processing of input data. There should be a separation of duties between originator and verification.

On-line data capture

On-line data capture may be used on a Remote Job Entry (RJE) basis to enter data via terminals to the computer. The input data, therefore, by-passes the data control section. It is appropriate therefore to devise controls to guard against error and fraud. Typical controls are:

(a)   Siting the terminals in areas of restricted access.

(b)   Passwords to guard against improper access to the system.

(c)   Terminal logs to record all operator actions.

(d)   Machine logs to provide a permanent record of all accesses to the system.

(e)   Special keys for operators to guard against illicit use of terminal.

(f)   Batch control records to record all data being entered. Control total proofing would be necessary where sterling data is being entered.

(g) Data encryption software to be used to protect the message while in transit. This operates on a similar principle to the 'scrambler' telephone. The message cannot be decoded in the event of interception unless the correct software codes are used.

14.4   Processing controls

14.4.1   Editing the input

Every commercial data processing system relies on programmed checks which are carried out on input data.

Where data is entered in batches the editing program vets the batch, rejects the invalid records and writes the valid record onto a temporary working file where it is processed further.

If data is entered via a terminal the vetting is done on an interactive basis ie, an invalid record is identified and the keyboard operator then identifies the error.

If the rejection is due to an operations error this is obviously rectified. If the error is an error in the original data then the record is referred back to the originator.

Typical features of a data validation program are as under:

(a) *Sequence* - If input should be in a particular order (eg, ascending customer account number) the data vet can test for this.

(b) *Range/limit checks* - With limits known, it is easy for the program to check that a value lies within a certain range (eg, product code between 1000 and 4999) or below a certain value (eg, invoice value less than £1,000).

(c) *Consistency* - Two or more pieces of data are considered in relation to each other to see if the combination is valid. Incorrect dates, such as 30.02.76, can be picked up in this way, as can orders which exceed a value fixed for a customer by his credit rating code.

(d) *Format* - Each field is examined for invalid characters such as an alphabetic character in an 'amount' field.

(e) *Completeness* - Every field which should hold information is investigated to make sure it does so.

(f) *Check digits* - Calculations are performed to detect transcriptions and transposition errors in numerical codes.

(g) *Control total checks* - If input records contain a standing field this check is essential.

(h) *Record total checks* - Where batches of data are entered a record count guards against lost records.

(i) *Hash total* - A hash or nonsense total is the summation of items of data which have little or no significance in terms of processed output but are useful in controlling the input.

0121z

Example 14.1: Check digits for self-checking code numbers

A common problem encountered with coding systems is the incidence of human error. It is relatively easy to make **errors of transposition** when writing down a series of numbers.

For example 191419794 could be wrongly transcribed as 191491794. Worse may follow; the number might be written down as 191491974.

In the first case there was an error caused by **single** transposition of numbers; in the second case there was **double** transposition of numbers. Random errors may also be made by inattentive clerks. The number could have been written as 191404324.

It is often desirable, therefore, to design numeric codes with a self-checking facility. This generally takes the form of an extra numeric digit added to the right hand side of the number. The purpose of this check digit is to detect either transposition errors or random errors in the transcription of code numbers.

The commonest model user for check digit purposes is the one where each digit in the code number is assigned a rank or position. A prime number constant is used to calculate a check digit which is placed on the right hand side of the number. The calculation is devised so that a valid code number is processed by a computer routine to yield a number which is exactly divisible by the prime number constant, ie, the remainder is 0. If as the result of the calculation the remainder is anything other than 0 then the code number is invalid.

Example 14.2

It is required to create a digit scheme using the code number 1043982.

The check digit scheme is based on the use of modulus 11 (the prime number constant).

Step 1   Determine the position of the check digit
        104 39 82 X

Step 2   Assign ranks to each digit
        104 39 82 X
        876 54 32 1

Step 3   Multiply the numbers by the ranks and sum the products
        8 + 0 + 24 + 15 + 36 + 24 + 4
        = 111

Step 4   Divide by 11

$$\overline{)111}$$
$$\underline{110}$$
$$1$$

Remainder 1 is subtracted from 11 giving 10. This number would be discarded as instead of a single digit we have 10 which is **two** digits.

We shall try   104 3981 X
using weights   876 5432 1

Summing the products

$$8 + 0 + 24 + 15 + 36 + 24 + 2 = 109$$

Apply the modulus

```
                         9
                        ___
              11        109
                         99
                        ___
   Remainder             10
```

Complement of 11 is 1

the check digit is 1 and the code is 104 3981 1

Let us test our scheme by scrambling the numbers as follows:

104 9381 1
876 5432 1

Summing the products

$$8 + 0 + 24 + 45 + 12 + 24 + 2 + 1$$

$$116 \div 11 = 10 \text{ remainder } 6$$

As the remainder is 6 the code number is invalid.

Example 14.3: Hash totalling

A sales order is entered in an RJE system. The keyboard operator is required to key in:

- (i)   the order number
- (ii)   the date
- (iii)   the customer code number
- (iv)   the order reference
- (v)   quantity
- (vi)   stock code
- (vii)   the symbol S (indicating a standard price).

Sales order 11428 has four transaction lines as follows:

Stock code	Quantity
114842	89
171871	26
141819	12
218222	30

207

The stock code column is totalled giving a summation of 646754 which is the hash total. This is keyed in after the transaction lines have been entered. If the operator has omitted a line or duplicated a line this will be detected. Incorrect transcriptions of the stock code will also be detected by this technique.

14.4.2 File processing controls

The controls relevant to file processing are these:

(i) recognition that the correct file has been used in processing
(ii) control totalling procedures and printout of the file control records for audit purposes.

We have already discussed the use of file header labels. The use of control total records however plays an essential part in providing audit trail reassurance for the user.

Example 14.4

A purchase ledger program is operational every fortnight when batches of invoices are entered on the file. The validation program produces a batch acceptance report which prints out the batch number, the number of valid transactions, the details of rejected transactions and a control total. When the invoices are posted to the ledger a control report is printed out as illustrated in Figure 14.2.

Report name:	Bought Ledger Inv Update	Date: 0104X4
	Opening ledger balances	171043.99 +
	Batch 463 INV	21043.42
	Closing ledger balances	192087.41 +
	Total records processed	698

Figure 14.2: Control report for file processing

14.4.3 Matching records

One control that is vital in the processing is the requirement to match master records with transaction records. On most systems the master key and the transaction key must match in order to produce a file update. Any transaction records without a valid key will be rejected from the matching system.

On certain types of updates the matching process is taken further by requiring transactions to be matched within the master record. An obvious example of this is the 'open-item' type. The term 'open-item' has already been mentioned in the section on systems design. In an open-item system an invoice (no 17437 for £71.00) will be matched with a cash receipt for that sum. If this matching is not done, the detail of the master record quickly becomes irreconcilable.

14.5   File control and security

14.5.1   File maintenance

This term refers to:

(i)   the insertion of records on a master file
(ii)   the amendment of records on a master file
(iii)   the deletion of records.

This activity must be carefully controlled by means of:

(a)   registration procedures for taking on new records and allocation of valid record code numbers;

(b)   authorisation procedures for any insertion, amendment or deletion.

14.5.2   File security

Recovering and reconstruction procedures are necessary to guard against the vital loss of data from master files. The techniques vary from system to system but the following techniques are common:

(a)   Back up copies of all program files are made and kept under tight security arrangements.

(b)   Master files that are processed sequentially are generally secured on the grandfather, father, son principle which is explained below. This applies equally to magnetic tape files as well as to disk files.

14.5.3   Magnetic tape file security

The concept of one-way reading/writing on magnetic tape has already been mentioned. This restriction to one direction for reading meant that it was impossible to write updated file records back to the same section of tape from which they had just been read, because that section of tape had already passed the read/write heads. The method of updating a magnetic tape file is therefore to form a new master file on a different reel of tape. If only a few of the records are to be changed this means that the majority of records will simply be copied across from one reel to the other and at the end of the run two master files will exist - the original and the updated version.

The technique may seem rather cumbersome but it can be used to good advantage from a security point of view. While the old version of a file is still in existence it is possible to make a quick recovery, if something goes drastically wrong on an updating run, by merely going back to the old tape. All that is required is to make sure that the old version is not destroyed until the updated file produced from it has itself been updated to produce an even newer version. This can easily be explained diagrammatically (Figure 14.3).

The various versions are known as generations, so that M1 = grandfather, M2 = father, M3 = son. Security dictates that a reel must not be destroyed (ie, re-used) until it has become a grandfather, and the technique is often called the 'grandfather-father-son' method. M1 and M4 can therefore be the same reel of tape. (**Note:** It is no use keeping old master files for review purposes unless the corresponding transaction files are also retained.) The generation number is held in the field header label as part of the writing status to prevent programs over-writing current files.

At least one copy of the file should be kept at a location remote from the main tape library so that if, for example, a fire occurs it should still be possible to recover the data.

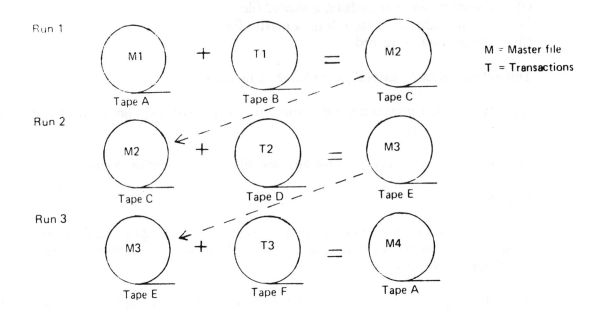

Figure 14.3: Magnetic tape file security

14.5.4   Magnetic disk file security

(a)   *Dumping* - When magnetic disks are organised as DASDs there is obviously a danger that records which are erroneously updated will perpetuate errors in the output. To overcome this problem the system is designed periodically to copy the master file onto magnetic tape. The system also provides for the tape number to be recorded for archive recording purposes.

(b)   *Overflow* - The use of overflow is an essential control.

(c)   *Write protection* - Software that detects written areas on the disk can prevent loss of data caused by accidental overwriting. Some special controls encountered in realtime systems are mentioned below.

14.6   Real time systems

14.6.1   Serial numbering of messages

This is used to ensure that no message is lost. Where a breakdown occurs between terminal and computer there is an exchange of information on the last serial number received so that a correct restart can be made.

14.6.2   Checkpoint tables

These are used in order to validate the status of a computer routine. The real time clock in the system is timed to cause the messages in progress to be recorded on tape.

14.6.3   Test facilities

In a modern system the break or loss of an audit trail is of concern both to management and to the external auditors who rely on the system to produce financial data. Many systems are designed with test facilities built into them.

14.6.4   Embedded code

This term refers to the use of special audit validation routines which can be 'triggered' by the auditors in order to check live data going through the system.

14.6.5   Integrated test facility (ITF)

An integrated test facility implies a set of dummy entities such as employees and debtors, etc. Where live data is entered into the system, records are included which enable the computer process to be tested. The system should provide for the dummy data to be removed from the 'real' records so that confusion does not result.

14.6.6   Databases - a problem for the management

The three elements of a database system are:

(a)   the database administrator (DBA);
(b)   the database;
(c)   the database management system (DBMS).

The control exercised by the DBA makes him or her a potential security risk. A brief list of some of the DBA's functions reveals a number of areas of concern. The DBA's responsibilities include the following:

(a)   designing the physical aspect of databases;
(b)   dealing with demands of users;
(c)   arranging security measures;
(d)   fault finding when things go wrong.

The risks are therefore:

(a)   Lack of audit trail as the only audit trail is a centralised log file which is used primarily for recovery purposes in the event of breakdown.

(b)   As the database approach does not involve the conventional input/validate/sort/update approach of batch processes it is difficult to apply control to all procedures.

(c)   The use of powerful file enquiry languages which allow both enquiry and updating.

(d)   The ability to alter a record in the database (a patch) without visible evider

(e)   The opportunity for the DBA or his/her staff to corrupt the data b their control over it.

These risks present a real danger of serious misstatement in the finan

14.6.7 Controls relevant to databases

(a) Written requisitions to authorise the data extracted from the database.

(b) Control totals to be provided for each terminal operation.

(c) A transaction log to be kept by the computer to record all machine accesses.

(d) At least two persons must be involved in any attempt to alter a record on a data base.

(e) Password security and personal codes for specific users of the data base.

(f) Sensitive data to be protected from general enquiring, eg, payroll data.

(g) 'Before and after' file images. A copy is kept of any record before it is updated and after it is updated.

(h) Other controls such as data encryption and others mentioned in the section on real time systems are also relevant.

14.7 Control aspects of small computer systems

14.7.1 Hazards

Many small computer systems provide accessibility to computer power for the first-time user at modest cost. However the hazards associated with small computer systems should not be overlooked. In the first instance many of the points mentioned earlier with regard to organisational controls do not apply to small computer systems.

Advantages claimed for small machines	Hazard
(i) They are easy to operate.	Inexpert operation could create havoc with data files.
(ii) They are easy to program.	Accessibility of program files often leads to inexpert amendment (with unhappy results).
(iii) They are robust and do not require any special environmental conditions.	Their location in an office environment exposes the machine to risks of unauthorised operation, theft or damage.
(iv) Operation and data entry are interactive.	There is often a loss of audit trail due to short cuts being taken by staff.
(v) Direct access files are used.	The hazard of corruption of data is considerable unless there is the discipline of regularly making the copies.

Advantages claimed for small machines	**Hazard**
(vi) The hardware and software are often purchased in cost-effective package.	Standard software may not suit the needs of the individual user and may require expensive and extensive modification.
(vii) The system only needs one part-time operator.	No opportunity for subdivision of duties. Lack of supervision could allow the system to be abused by the operator.

14.7.2 Other controls on a small computer

(a) Special keys/passwords to restrict access to the system.
(b) Write protection for diskette files to guard against accidents.
(c) Regular back up copies of files held in a fire-proof safe.
(d) Clerical controls over source data so that data entered through the keyboard can be traced back to some handwritten record.
(e) Use of visual checking devices on data entry eg, 'blinking' cursors to prompt a check between screen and source document.
(f) Usage logs in handwritten form.
(g) Some larger minis and micros offer a computer log file facility for preserving audit trail.
(h) Regular print-outs of master files for internal audit purposes.

14.8 Computer bureaux

A computer bureau is an organisation which provides various computer services to users. Examples of these services are:

(a) Complete processing of data from data preparation to production of output.
(b) Programming support.
(c) Time-sharing services via terminals.
(d) Management consultancy.
(e) Application packages.
(f) Do it yourself - customers must provide skilled operators for this service.

Most bureaux in the UK are members of the Computing Services Association (CSA) which lays down a code of conduct and standards with which members must comply. The CSA are particularly concerned with security of information, ethics and the provision of continuity of service. CSA membership therefore implies that the bureau is competent, ethical and financially stable.

14.8.1 Why do people use bureaux?

There are a variety of good reasons that justify the use of bureaux even in these days of powerful, easy-to-use, small machines.

(a) *Familiarisation* - Staff can become accustomed to the type of machine that the company intends to purchase.

(b) *Cost* - It may be cost-effective to use a bureau for processing certain types of transactions as the company may not have the resources to acquire a computer, eg, an executive payroll may be run on a bureau as it saves time for modest cost and preserves confidentiality.

(c) *Stand-by system* - A bureau could provide processing facilities in the event of equipment failure or to deal with peak loads at certain times of the year.

14.8.2   Evaluation of a bureau

If a user decides to enter into a contract with a bureau there are a number of points which should be taken into account when evaluating the service offered.

(a)   Membership of CSA.

(b)   A clearly defined contract setting out *inter alia*:

   (i)   any joining fee;
   (ii)   any fixed standing charges;
   (iii)   the variable processing charges;
   (iv)   the policy for dealing with errors and re-run work.

(c)   A satisfied clientele.

   Many specialist businesses use bureaux (eg, commodity brokers) as a cost- effective way of obtaining computer facilities. Obviously a prospective user would be impressed by a client list of satisfied customers.

(d)   Evaluation by the prospective user to consider whether:

   (i)   management's information needs are met by the bureau package;
   (ii)   the controls built into the system are adequate;
   (iii)   the training and support given to customers are satisfactory.

14.8.3   End user's responsibility

The use of a bureau demands certain disciplines from the end user if the service provided is to be satisfactory. The bureau deals in high volumes of transactions and will therefore lack the insight into a particular business' mode of operation. If source data is incorrect the bureau will speedily and efficiently process it. If certain errors are discovered then those transactions will be reprocessed at extra cost to the end user. It is clear therefore that the end user must maintain controls over the source data, the terminals (where appropriate) and the outputs to ensure that erroneous items are not processed and illegal accesses to files are not made. The controls to be maintained have been mentioned earlier in this session in relation to processing controls on input and output.

14.9   Implementation and systems development controls

14.9.1   What are systems development controls?

The **systems specification** is the blueprint or master plan of how a new system is to be developed. The development of the project from blueprint to reality takes place during the **implementation** program. In order that the implementation can proceed smoothly and efficiently there must be certain controls imposed by the management. These controls can be summarised as follows:

(a) the use of standard methodology;
(b) control over money and time spent on the various activities;
(c) trials and testing of programs;
(d) system listing;
(e) evaluation and acceptance by the users;
(f) training staff;
(g) file conversion and systems validation.

14.9.2 Data processing standards

An important feature of both organisational and development controls is the need for soundly conceived **data processing standards**. This term is taken to mean that there is a standard methodology for *inter alia* the following:

(a) documentation for systems;
(b) terminology;
(c) methods of investigation;
(d) flowcharting conventions;
(e) programming languages;
(f) training methods;
(g) managerial reviews;
(h) specifications of job responsibilities.

Data processing standards are necessary for the following reasons:

- *Communication* - Written down standards of methodology aid the process of communication between those persons concerned with their use.

- *Continuity* - Written down standards aid continuity, eg, when employees leave and are replaced by new staff the disruption can be minimised considerably if there are standard methods that can be applied to tasks.

- *Control* - Laying down written standards of practice provides a benchmark for measuring performances.

14.9.3 Standards manual

A standards manual should be in existence dealing *inter alia* with the following:

Organisation
    Organisation chart
    Job specifications

Documentation
    Systems
    Programming
    Operating
    Clerical

Testing
Errors, malfunctions
Flowcharting conventions
Coding conventions
Logs

Standard procedures
Analysts
Programmers
Operators
Data control personnel
File librarian

Glossary

Management should ensure that these standards are enforced. The appointment of a person with training responsibilities could prove to be worthwhile in the larger organisation.

There should be comprehensive documentation for the user in the form of a finalised version of the systems specification. A manual of standard operating procedures is an important step in establishing integrity controls.

14.9.4   The tasks involved in implementation

Successful implementation of a project requires the wholehearted commitment and involvement of the management if the scheme is to proceed expeditiously. The tasks of implementation should also be carefully planned and sequenced in order to achieve the system's objectives.

The following tasks are associated with the implementation phase:

(a)   making premises available;
(b)   commissioning new hardware;
(c)   program design and testing;
(d)   designing new stationery;
(e)   training staff involved with the system;
(f)   producing manuals of instruction;
(g)   finalising the systems documentation;
(h)   testing for acceptance;
(i)   planning the changeover;
(j)   conversion of files;
(k)   proving the working of the system.

14.9.5   Managerial control

(a)   *Costs* - It is prudent for management to draw up budgetary estimates for the capital and revenue costs associated with the new system and to monitor actual costs against budget.

(b)   *Activities* - The activities involved in implementation should be planned and controlled. The most common techniques used in controlling systems projects are Gantt charts.

14.9.6　Techniques used for monitoring progress

It is not within the scope of this manual to set out the detail of the techniques involved in the construction of a Gantt chart. However, the following illustration will help you to appreciate the use of this technique.

Example 14.5 - Gantt charts

On 1st September 19X4 the directors of ABC Ltd gave their authority to the task of implementing the new computerised sales accounting system. The chairman indicated that the deadline for changeover was 1st March 19X5.

A Gantt chart was constructed to show the various events that the implementation phase involved. No hardware or premises alterations were required.

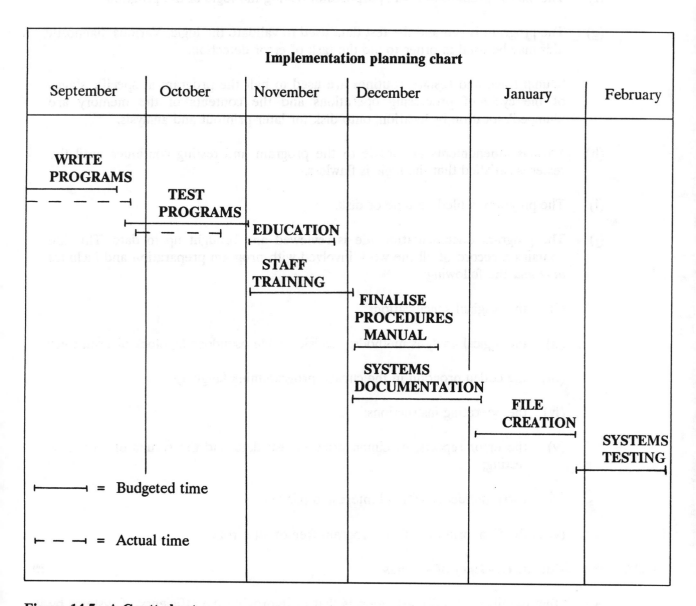

Figure 14.5: A Gantt chart

14.9.7　Program design and testing

The steps associated with the task of program design are set out below:

(a) The system specification is reviewed and the task is divided up between members of the programming team.

(b) Time limits are set and agreed for the completion of the task.

(c) The logic is analysed: common tools of analysis include decision tables, flowcharts and structure charts.

(d) The program is coded in the chosen programming language (the source program).

(e) The program is translated using appropriate software (a compiler or an assembler) and stored on tape or disk (the object program).

(f) The data is prepared for the purposes of testing the logic of the program.

(g) The program is run and the test data used to validate the logic. Various diagnostic aids may be used in order to aid the task of error detection.

'Dump trace and restart' routines are used to halt the program at specific stages of the cycle of processing operations and the contents of the memory are 'dumped', location by location, onto disk for later printout and analysis.

(h) Various amendments are made to the program and testing continues until the tester is satisfied that the logic is flawless.

(i) The program is filed on tape or disk.

(j) The program documentation file is reviewed and brought up to date. This file contains a record of all the work involved with program preparation and includes *inter alia* the following:

    (i) the original specification;

    (ii) the logical analysis methods: decision table pseudocode, block diagrams etc;

    (iii) the coded program in the chosen programming language;

    (iv) the operating instructions;

    (v) the error reports, specimen printout test data and the results of computer testing;

    (vi) correspondence with all interested parties;

    (vii) the final printout of the program free of all errors.

14.9.8 Improving the efficiency of systems

A task that requires specialist attention is that of improving the efficiency of systems by reducing run times. The use of computer time may represent a considerable opportunity cost. Any attempts therefore to minimise costs and increase efficiency should not be overlooked.

Techniques resorted to by analysts to improve the efficiency of systems are these:

(a) *Benchmark tests* - Time standards from similar users are taken and compared with the actual run times.

(b) *Use of spooling software* - The acronym SPOOL stands for Simultaneous Peripheral Operation On-Line and refers to the use of operating systems that attempt to maximise the simultaneity of CPU operations.

A computer will always be constrained by the operating speeds of its slowest working parts. The technique of buffering ie, allocation of areas of memory to peripheral devices aids the speed of data transfer. Simultaneity of operation of peripheral devices maximises the processing capacity of the system and minimises the time that could be lost by being **peripheral bound**.

(c) *Compression of codes used* - It is possible in certain systems to compress EBCDIC characters into BCD characters or to use packed decimal storage to minimise storage space.

(d) *Selecting optimum sizes of data for transfer between backing storage and the CPU* - Research has been carried out on this topic. A detailed knowledge of the mathematics entailed in selecting block sizes for data transfer is outside the scope of the syllabus.

These activities are also known as 'system tuning'.

14.9.9 Education

The involvement of the user is crucial in the successful implementation of the system. Ignorance by the user of system operations can lead to accusations of system inefficiency and ultimately to general dissatisfaction with the system.

It is important therefore to ensure that a programme of education is conceived in order to achieve the following:

(a) inform users of the improvements and benefits provided by the system;

(b) the users' involvement in making the system work;

(c) the interface between the user and the front-line staff (ie, those actively involved in working the system).

Such an education programme could consist of:

(i) lectures/presentations to senior staff;
(ii) seminars/workshops for middle management;
(iii) instructional films, job aids and explanatory manuals for other staff.

14.9.10 Training 'front-line' staff

No system can be expected to work properly if the staff engaged in making it work are ill informed about their tasks. Specialised training will include:

(a) Practical instruction in the classroom for certain types of staff eg, keyboard operators, trainee programmers/analysts.

(b) On-the-job training to simulate real-life experience for all data processing staff.

(c) Adequate training and procedures manuals are to be provided for reference purposes.

(d) Adequate system documentation should be available. System specifications for input, output and files, run charts, operating instructions, etc.

(e) Charts and illustrated job aids for easy assimilation of new procedures.

14.9.11 File conversion

The activity of file conversion must be carefully controlled. If a file contains errors these will propagate further errors every time the file is processed. If a sales ledger file is being created as part of a new computerised accounting system the source records may consist of handwritten records, ledger cards processed from book keeping machines, or a combination of the two.

The work must proceed in an orderly fashion in order that:

(a) Static information is captured correctly.

(b) Any amendments that are necessary to the static information are incorporated.

(c) All data fields are collected and there are no incomplete records.

(d) Source records are carefully checked so that:

   (i) The correct number of records is captured - ie the population of 400 sales ledger 'source' records does not become 402 records because of duplications.

   (ii) The variable data is transferred correctly. Control totals are used here for providing both record numbers and also the totals of variable data fields.

Example 14.6

XYZ Ltd employ a mechanised system of sales ledger accounting. The company have invested in a computer and are about to transfer over 900 live accounts on ledger cards to a new disk file created for this purpose.

What steps should the company take to ensure that the file is created accurately?

Step 1. Determine the cut-off date for closing down the old system and the date for starting up the new system eg, the management decide to close down the system on 20th March and to start the new system on 1st April. This will allow 10 days for the activity of file conversion.

Step 2. Design standard forms which are to be used for transcribing the source data. The form should be compatible with the system specification for the logical file records.

Step 3. At close-down date scan the source data, verify the accuracy of financial data by means of control accounts, scan all static data to ensure that it is correct.

Step 4. Obtain the list of approved code numbers for customers' accounts and allocate a number to each record.

Step 5. Transcribe source data and test check for accuracy.

Step 6. Prove accuracy of items capture by agreeing:

    (a)   control total at start;
    (b)   total number of records.

Step 7. Prepare input file. If using direct data entry methods investigate any rejections of records by validation program. Record reasons for rejection. Amend and re-enter.

Step 8. When file records have been accepted print file and audit in order to agree control totals and test record formatting.

Step 9. Process with live data and validate. Ensure that all registration procedures for inserting/amending/deleting records are carefully controlled and authorised. Scanning of printouts on a regular basis will alert users to errors which should be corrected expeditiously.

Step 10. When the user is satisfied that the new system has been validated the old system is discontinued.

14.9.12 Changeover procedures

The analyst must ensure that there are suitable procedures laid down for the changeover from the old system to the new. There are various choices that can be made:

(a) **Direct changeover**

This type of changeover is either for the very confident system designer or for a system that has been tried out and tested elsewhere. The hazards encountered with direct changeover are threefold:

    (i)   a flaw in the new system may not become apparent until the system is running;
    (ii)   there are no results from the old system to validate the new system;
    (iii) errors are difficult to correct when the system is newly operational.

(b) **Parallel running**

Parallel running is the method adopted when the old and new systems are run together for an initial period. The results of the new system are validated by the results of the old. This method is possibly the safest way of bringing about the changeover from the old system to the new. However there is considerable extra work involved since not only are two systems being run together, but also there are comparisons being made and differences investigated.

(c)   **Pilot running**

The difference between parallel running and pilot running is that the former uses live data as it arises while the latter reruns source data from a previous period. The difference between these methods is illustrated in Figure 14.7.

(d)   **Computer bureau**

The main reason for using the services of a computer bureau rather than installing a computer is normally cost. To establish a computer facility within a company requires a high and continuing cash investment. In addition, many companies reject the idea of their own computer installation because they are not confident of their ability to set up the required management team to organise it. Finally a business may wish to use a bureau rather than purchase a computer of its own because it has an insufficient volume of regular processing to keep an internal machine fully occupied.

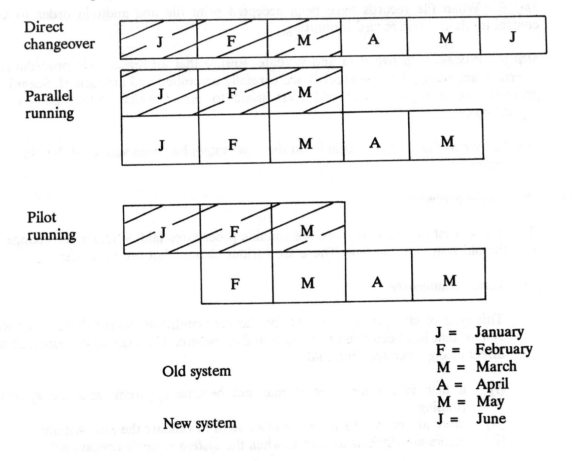

J =	January
F =	February
M =	March
A =	April
M =	May
J =	June

Figure 14.7: Changeover procedures

Even after a company has installed its own computer and established a data processing department there may be occasions when it needs to use a service bureau:

(a)   When the company requires a particular job to be processed on a one-off basis or to a timetable which cannot be met by the internal systems and programming available.

(b)   When a customer arranges to employ a service bureau as a stand-by machine to guard against failure of its own equipment.

(c) If the company's own installation has a fairly heavy work load operationally, but requires a certain amount of machine testing time to develop new applications. The two computers must, as in the previous case, be compatible. In this event, the employment of the bureau to undertake the relevant program trials could significantly reduce the time scale for the new programs becoming operational.

14.9.13 Computer bureaux and turnkey systems

(a) *Bureaux*

A user may well reject the idea of a computer system as the costs may be prohibitive. Instead, he may seek out a computer bureau that specialises in applications particularly relevant to his needs. For example it is not unknown for special types of undertaking, like commodity broking or stockbroking, to be serviced by specialist bureaux.

If a bureau is selected it is by no means an escape from the disciplines of system evaluation. A bureau may offer a standard package which is modified for a user. The user must ensure that those members of staff who deal with the bureau fully understand how the package works as well as its strengths and limitations.

The systems documentation should not be (literally) a closed book to the user. There must be total involvement if the bureau is to give satisfaction. Obviously bureaux can sell sub-standard services. In many cases however the dissatisfaction felt by the user results from an inability to fully understand the type of service that is sold by the bureau. Membership of the Computing Services Association (CSA) is again a desirable attribute of the bureau.

(b) *Turnkey systems*

A turnkey system is one where the hardware and software are sold as a package deal to the user. The vendor often carries out the role of implementation consultant. Here again is an area where many users feel cheated because the system did not match their expectations. There are users who buy turnkey systems without properly evaluating the various alternatives so that the flaws or deficiencies in the chosen system do not become apparent until the user has signed a customer satisfaction note. Thereafter every system change is time-consuming and expensive!

14.9.14 Post-implementation review

It would be prudent for the management to carry out a review after the project has been successfully implemented. A post-implementation review will embrace the following activities:

Computer operations

(a) Comparison of run times with benchmarks.

(b) Examining the reasons for aborted runs and the necessity for re-runs.

(c) Reviewing the scheduling of work loads and the production of output with agreed deadlines.

(d)   Investigation into compliance with operating instructions and laid down procedures for controls and security.

(e)   Reviewing any reports on errors from users in order to establish their cause.

Man/machine interface

(a)   Reviewing documentation for input records in order to assess efficiency of operations. Are the documents designed in order to aid data capture?

(b)   Reviewing the efficiency of man-dominated processes (such as data conversion) in order to evaluate whether manning levels and work loads are reasonable. Noting if standards of output (ie keystrokes per hour) are attainable. Reviewing error rates in keyboarding work.

(c)   Taking account of ergonomic and health and safety considerations. Are machines efficient in terms of the human effort employed in their use? Is there adequate lighting, sound proofing, partitioning, air conditioning so that the environment is conducive to good operations and acceptable health and safety standards?

(d)   Are administrative procedures properly laid down, especially with regard to the division of responsibilities and the maintenance of controls over people?

User attitudes

(a)   Is the user cooperating in the procedures necessary for efficient operation of the system?

(b)   Is the user satisfied with the systems output; its timing and its content?

(c)   Are there procedures which the user would like to see modified?

Costs and benefits

(a)   Are capital costs and revenue costs on target?

(b)   Have the anticipated savings or benefits been achieved?

(c)   Are there any areas of expenditure which were not foreseen? Why did they occur?

This post-implementation review is sometimes referred to as a 'systems audit' and is a necessary step in finally validating the operational system.

14.10   Privacy and data processing

You should be aware of the ethical and social problems posed by the growth in information technology. Concern is often voiced about the need to preserve the privacy of an individual where sensitive data is collected and held by certain types of users. Applicants for credit cards, for example, are usually vetted by a credit intelligence agency who might have access to sensitive items of data dealing with law suits, criminal prosecutions or a past history of defaults to creditors. While it may be perfectly reasonable to collect such data to guard against commercial risk there is a need to ensure that such sensitive records are regulated so that an individual's privacy is not abused. The Younger Report on Privacy in 1972 as well as the Lindop Report of 1978 were influential in the drafting of the Data Protection Act 1984.

14.11 Data Protection Act 1984

14.11.1 Background

The growth of information technology poses both ethical and social problems. Concern is often voiced about the need to preserve the privacy of an individual where sensitive data is collected, held and processed by certain types of user. Applicants for credit cards, for example, are usually vetted by a credit intelligence agency which might have access to sensitive items of data dealing with law suits, criminal prosecutions or a past history of defaults to creditors. While it may be perfectly legal to collect such data to guard against commercial risk, there is a need to ensure that such sensitive records are regulated so that the privacy of individuals is not abused.

Although data held on paper or cards could affect an individual, computers add a further dimension to the problem because they can be used to link and cross-relate data about an individual at high speed.

Following two reports - the *Younger Report* and the *Lindop Report* - the Data Protection Act 1984 was drafted in order to legislate on data protection.

Although the Act was designed to protect the individual, it was also needed because without such an act, companies in other countries could refuse to transfer data to UK companies. This might present a commercial threat to UK companies and computer bureaux.

14.11.2 Definitions and terms used in the Act

(a) *Data.* This is information recorded in a form in which it can be processed by equipment operating automatically in response to instructions given for that purpose.

Note: The Act is not concerned with data processed manually, ie, data on paper or cards, etc.

(b) *Personal data.* The Act seeks to regulate personal data only. This is data consisting of information which relates to a living individual who can be identified from that information (or from that and other information in the possession of a data user).

Thus, if a computer file of data is referenced by a number and, on a manual file, the number could be referenced to a name and address, the computer-held data is regarded as being personal data - provided it relates to a living individual (not deceased persons or corporate bodies).

(c) *Data subject.* The individual who is the subject of personal data.

(d) *Data users.* These are the individuals, corporations or other agencies that control the automatic processing of data.

Note that you do not have to own a computer to be a data user - you could employ a bureau. Also, mere custody of a diskette containing personal data is not enough if you do not have control over its processing.

(e) *Processing.* Amending, augmenting, deleting or rearranging the data, or extracting the information constituting the data and, in the case of personal data, means performing any of those operations by reference to the data subject.

This point is difficult. For example, we could set up a file of students' names showing which firms they worked for and other details. If we could key in a student's name to find out that person's details, then this would constitute processing with reference to the data subject - the subject's name is being used as the basis for the search of the file. However, if we set up a file of firms showing the names of the students with each firm, then provided I could not use students' names to search with, but could only use firms' names, to obtain a list of their students, then this would not constitute processing with reference to the data subject. (Firms cannot be subjects as they are not individuals.)

A specific exemption is given for processing performed only for the purpose of preparing the text of documents. Thus, if I were to set up a list of names and addresses for the purpose sending out standard letters using a word processor, this would not count as processing under the Act. It is likely to be difficult to decide in some cases whether such a list is used only for the purpose of preparing text or whether more complex processing is inevitably carried out.

(f) *Registrar.* The Data Protection Registrar is a new post created by the Act. The Registrar is appointed by the Crown and has a small staff to supervise the legislation. He is given many powers and rights under the Act. In particular, he is charged with creating and maintaining a publically available register of data users and persons carrying on computer bureaux. It is to the Registrar that data subjects may complain if they think that the DPA has been contravened and it is the Registrar who may prosecute data users if they do not comply with the Act.

(g) *Data Protection tribunal.* This provides a right of appeal against the Registrar's decisions.

14.11.3 The major procedures involved in the Act

Registration

The most important procedure for data users is the requirement to register. The DPA also introduces procedures by which data subjects can assert their statutory rights.

The requirement to register becomes necessary if a data user processes personal data automatically. It involves lodging with the Registrar the following details:

(a) The name and address of the data user.

(b)   A description of the personal data held and a statement of the purposes for which the data are held.

(c)   A description of the sources from which the data are obtained and persons to whom it may be disclosed.

(d)   The names of any countries to which the data may be transferred.

(e)   An address for the receipt of requests from data subjects for access.

If data users fail to register, or if the Registrar refuses to accept an application for registration subject to a right of appeal, data users commit a criminal offence if they continue to process personal data.

The exact degree of detail that will require to be lodged will be decided by the Registrar, but it is reasonably safe to assume it will not include disclosing every data field maintained by the users, as this would involve the Registrar in a level of detail and a volume of data too large for the Registrar to process with his limited resources. If after inspection the Registrar is satisfied with the application, it will be entered in a register which will be open to public inspection.

The rights of data subjects

Data subjects, having perhaps consulted the Registrar, have a right to request access to any personal data that a data user holds on them. This may necessitate the payment of a small fee to cover the data user's processing costs. The data user must supply the data within 40 days of the request and must interpret any codes into plain English. If any problems occur in this procedure the data subject has a right to appeal to the courts or a right to complain to the Registrar.

Do remember that the Act does not apply to manually held data even if this is referred to from computer-held data.

If data subjects suffer damage which is directly attributable to the inaccuracy, loss or unauthorised disclosure of data, they may claim compensation. This right is enforced through the courts. A data subject has a further limited right; namely to rectification or erasure of any erroneous data maintained by the data user. Once again this right is enforceable through the courts.

14.11.4   The principles underlying the Act

The DPA is underpinned by eight data-protection principles. The Act gives some guidance on their interpretation for the benefit of the Registrar and the Tribunal, but in general their application will be a matter for the Registrar to decide, having regard to the circumstances of data users or persons carrying on a computer bureau and the interests of data subjects.

The first seven principles apply to personal data held by data users. The eighth principle applies to both data users and persons carrying on computer bureaux.

(1)   The information to be contained in personal data shall be obtained and processed fairly and lawfully.

Data would be said to be obtained unfairly if the data provider were deceived or misled about the purpose for which the data were obtained, held, used or disclosed. 'Lawfully' implies that the data should be obtained and processed in accord with the DPA, the common law and other relevant Acts of Parliament. If data are supplied or obtained under the authority of an Act of Parliament, or are disclosed under an enactment, they will be treated as having been obtained fairly.

(2) Personal data shall be held only for one or more specified and lawful purposes.

This is not, in essence, changing the nature in which data are presently processed: it is merely requiring the purposes to be specified in the registration document.

(3) Personal data held for any purpose or purposes shall not be used or disclosed in any manner incompatible with that purpose or those purposes.

The data must be used or disclosed in accordance with the details registered under the Act.

(4) Personal data held for any purpose or purposes shall be adequate, relevant and not excessive in relation to that purpose or those purposes.

(5) Personal data shall be accurate and, where necessary, kept up to date.

(6) Personal data held for any purpose shall not be kept for longer than is necessary for the specified purpose or purposes.

This principle suggests that data should be destroyed when the specified purpose for which they were collected has been achieved.

(7) An individual shall be entitled:

    (a) at reasonable intervals and without undue delay or expense:

        (i) to be informed by any data user whether he holds personal data of which that individual is the subject; and

        (ii) to access any such data held by a data user; and

    (b) where appropriate, to have such data corrected or erased.

(8) The last principle (which applies to both users and bureaux) relates to the need for appropriate security procedures to be taken to avoid:

    (a) unauthorised access to the data;
    (b) unauthorised alteration of the data;
    (c) unauthorised disclosure to third parties;
    (d) accidental loss of personal data.

The extent of such security measures shall have regard to the degree of harm that would result from contravening the principle and to the ease with which security can be incorporated into the systems.

If the principles are breached, then the Registrar has powers of enforcement which he may exercise supported by criminal sanctions. Data subjects only have rights to compensation in relation to the fifth and eighth principles. However, if a data subject suffers damage arising out of breach of any of the other principles, the existing civil law relating to defamation, negligence, breach of contract and breach of confidence should provide a remedy.

14.11.5 Exemptions

There are four types of exemption (other than that mentioned above) which might apply:

(a) *Data exempt from the whole Act.* Data under this category does not have to be registered under the Act. This type of data includes data of importance to national security, domestic and club data, payroll and accounting data, manually held data of all sorts.

(b) *Data exempt from the subject access provisions.* This means that the data subject has no right or a restricted right to see the relevant data. Examples include data held for the prevention or detection of crime and the collection of tax.

(c) *Data exempt from the non-disclosure provisions.* This means that the data can be disclosed to parties other than those listed on registration under the Act. Examples include crime and taxation, disclosure of data to someone acting on the data subjects behalf, emergency disclosure to prevent injury or damage to someone's health.

(d) *Data exempt from the data protection principles.* This exemption applies to data relating to crime and taxation and to data held for statistical purposes only where, for example, the data can be held indefinitely.

14.12 Conclusion

Controls and security are an essential feature of any computer system. In this session we have considered the three principal areas over which controls are exercised - organisational, systems development and procedures.

The Data Protection Act is outlined and it is important that you are fully aware of the need for, and scope of, the Act.

14.13 Questions

Quick questions

(1) Name *four* checks you would expect to find in a data vet program.

(2) Is the statement 'A data control clerk is responsible for verifying the accuracy of information prepared by a punch operator' true or false?

(3) Name *three* specific jobs that a data control clerk must perform in connection with the main system outputs.

(4) What are the *three* types of file amendment and in which order should they be processed?

(5) If a three-generation magnetic tape file security system is being used, which of the following tapes are used for the brought-forward and carried-forward versions during the **fourth** updating run if the grandfather was the brought-forward tape on the first run?

(1) Grandfather   (2) Father   (3) Son

(6) What are the *two* methods of updating a direct access file called?

(7) Messages in transit in a data communication system are protected by _____ _____ software.

(8) On a header label the purge date is

A   The date on which file was updated
B   The date of the last transaction
C   The date before which no overwriting is possible

(9) The Data Protection Act 1984 applies to

A   Personal data processed manually
B   Manual data processed automatically
C   Personal data processed automatically
D   Corporate data processed automatically

(10) How does the Data Protection Act 1984 classify the following

A   John Smith is a householder with two credit cards
B   Joan Bloggs operates a computer bureau
C   John Smith Ltd has a computerised sales ledger
D   Bill Snooks is buying a TV set on hire purchase

(11) Name *four* ancillary rooms which should be provided when designing a computer area.

(12) Name *two* major hazards for both equipment and data records.

(13) It is rare to find an existing file which can be used in the new system without conversion. This sometimes happens when the existing file is held on a particular medium. What is that medium?

(14) What are the *three* main methods of changeover from a manual system to a computer system?

(15) What information would you include in an operations manual?

(16) What are *three* methods of acquiring computer hardware?

(17) Name *three* factors which could influence a company's decision on the best method of financing the acquisition of a computer.

(18) The computer, its ancillary equipment and all the consumable supplies are major elements of cost. Give *three* other items which must also be added to the bill.

(19) Give *three* reasons why a company may choose to use a computer bureau rather than install an in-house computer.

(20) List *two* reasons why existing computer owners may require the services of a computer bureau.

Objective test questions

(1) Data subjects, as defined by the Data Protection Act, are:

  A   People who control the data
  B   Fields which constitute the data
  C   Hardware devices on which the data is held
  D   Individuals about whom personal data is held

(2) A sequence check will help to ensure:

  A   Accuracy and completeness of input
  B   Accuracy but not completeness of input
  C   Completeness but not accuracy of input
  D   Accuracy and authorisation of input

Written test questions

14.1   Control section

What are the likely functions that a control section would be responsible for in a medium-sized computer installation dealing only with internal work?   **(15 marks)**

14.2   Vetting of input data

What is meant by the vetting of input data? What are the main problems associated with it and how can these be overcome?   **(20 marks)**

14.3   Loss of data

A tape has been damaged and vital data lost. What steps should be taken to retrieve the data?   **(15 marks)**

14.4   Use of a bureau

You have been asked by your managing director to consider the use of a computer service bureau instead of installing an 'in-house' computer. List the advantages and disadvantages of using a service bureau and give two examples of work not suitable for processing by a bureau.   **(20 marks)**

14.5   Security

If you were the last person to leave the computer area at night, what precautions should you take to ensure the security of the installation?   **(15 marks)**

14.6   File conversion

After the formal approval of the system specification, the next stage in a computer project is to implement the newly designed system. An essential part of implementation is file conversion whereby a master file, typically held on a magnetic medium, is created.

Explain, with the aid of a flowchart, the activity of file conversion and indicate the importance of this work.   **(20 marks)**

Answers

Session 1 Introduction to management information systems

Quick question answers

(1)   Any four of: minimising or eliminating losses, cost savings, improved use of resources, increase in sales and/or profits, prevention of fraud.

(2)   False

(3)   The board of directors, senior managers, line managers, (possibly foremen and supervisors also).

Written test answer

1.1   Quality of management information

Management at all levels require information to carry out their own functions, i.e. making decisions, organising, planning and controlling. Although timing is very important, completeness, accuracy, and relevance may be equally important in determining the value of any given set of information to an organisation, or to a particular manager.

Obviously the quality of management information is partially dependent upon its timing, but this in itself may be linked to the particular situation giving rise to the need for the information in the first place. The following examples will help to illustrate this point:

(a)   Information for control purposes, for example, as in stock and credit control. Speed and accuracy are important, so as to avoid costly stockouts, or eventual bad debts.

(b)   Historical information, such as annual accounts, where there is no conflict between speed and accuracy, since there is plenty of time in which to produce the required information, and to check it thoroughly. Most organisations have a clearly laid down timetable for doing this at their period- and year-end.

(c)   Information for planning purposes is rarely required in a desperate hurry, and there is probably little need for precise figures, although the need for accuracy (ie between 100 and 100,000) is still present in the general magnitude of each value provided.

By accuracy, one is referring to 'an acceptable level for the prevailing circumstances' - cost/benefit should be borne in mind, so that more cost is not incurred than the figuring deserves.

A well designed management information system will provide the various levels of management with appropriate information to enable them to manage effectively. Thus the starting point will be the uses to which the information is likely to be put.

Amongst the factors influencing the design of such a system will be:

(a)   The organisation structure, and the number of levels of management between the source of the information and its destination.

(b)   The data processing cycle - what operations are involved? Where do they take place? How long do they take? Who is involved in them?

(c)   The form (or format) of reports required - too much transcription can delay a report. Delays can often be avoided by the use of a visual display unit, providing 'instant' information as and when it is required, from an on-line system, rather than the traditional once weekly reports, which may be too late for effective management action to prevent further losses or waste occuring.

The overall criterion will always be the cost of producing management information, compared to its usefulness.

Session 3 Electronic data processing

Quick questions answers

(1)   (b) and (c)

(2)   ASCII

(3)   Four (assuming packed decimal storage was used)

(4)   A bus

(5)

	7	6	5	4	3	2	1	0	
	2	2	2	2	2	2	2	2	
	(128	64	32	16	8	4	2	1)	
(a)		1	1	0	0	0	1	0	= 98
(b)			1	0	0	1	0	1	= 37
(c)		1	1	1	1	0	1	1	= 123

Objective test answers

(1)   C
(2)   C
(3)   D
(4)   B

Written test answers

3.1   Microcomputers

Five characteristics that distinguish the microcomputer are:

(a)   *Size* - It is a compact device that occupies little more space than an office desk.

(b)   *Environment* - The microcomputer is robust and does not require a controlled environment. It can be used in an office environment.

(c)   *Modularity* - The microcomputer's hardware centre enhanced by further additions of memory modules.

(d)   *Skills required by staff* - A microcomputer can be operated by staff without specialist skills who are trained in its use.

(e)   *Price* - The continuing development of mass production in micro-electronics has lowered the price of the hardware.

3.2   Micros in the office

Microcomputers have had a considerable impact on office procedure in recent years. The applications which are worthy of note are the following:

(a)   *Word processing.* The use of microcomputers has revolutionised the task of processing the printed word. The task of typewriting large volumes of work was traditionally slow and prone to errors which required correction or even retyping of manuscripts. The finished product was dependent upon the skills and application of the typist and therefore infinitely variable. The use of dedicated word processors has made this task more efficient and less labour intensive. The term 'dedicated word processor' refers to a microcomputer with an operating system especially designed for the processing of the printed word as opposed to carrying out computational tasks. The typical word processor offers the following facilities:

     (i)   visual display of text for editing purposes;
     (ii)   automatic page length and page numbering;
     (iii)   margin definition;
     (iv)   automatic centring of text;
     (v)   choice of different typefaces;
     (vi)   'search and replace' facilities ie, a word or phrase that recurs in text could be removed and an alternative substituted;
     (vii)   'glossaries' of standard words or phrases that can be brought into use;
     (viii)   spell-checking, using English and foreign-language dictionaries;
     (ix)   a thesaurus function.

(b)   *Electronic mail.* This application combines word processing skills with data communication techniques. Standard letters that are prepared on a word processor can be distributed through telecommunication links without the need for the physical transmission of documents. Thus a Head Office can distribute the latest price lists to branches without laborious reproduction and expensive postage costs.

(c)   *Facsimile reproduction.* This is used if documents are to be transmitted between locations in an identical format. The use of Facsimile reproduction enables the document to be scanned by an optical reader and transmitted through a data communication system where the process is reversed in order to produce the finished product.

Session 4 Data capture techniques

Quick questions answers

(1)   (1)   OCR - Optical Character Recognition
       (2)   OMR - Optical Mark Reading
       (3)   MICR - Magnetic Ink Character Recognition

(2)   The code is known as the European Article Number, or bar code. It can be scanned by an optical reader or sensed with a light pen in order to eliminate the keying of individual amounts and codes.

(3)   Punched cards are now prepared with an interpretation across the top edge. Paper tape is not interpreted.

(4)   (a) True
       (b) True

(5)   (a) 7
       (b) 3
       (c) 6
       (d) 4
       (e) 1 or 2

(6)   (b)

(7)   OCR

(8)   False

(9)   Entering stock items during a stock count; recording weights of carcasses in a slaughterhouse.

(10)   Point of Sale System

Objective test answers

(1)   B
(2)   A
(3)   D

Written test answers

4.1   Data capture methods

Data capture refers to the original entry of source data into the computer system - not to retrieval of information from files which have been stored within the system for any length of time.

(i) *Magnetic Ink Character Recognition (MICR)* - In this system a line of characters in a special font is printed on the source document. The printing ink used contains a metallic substance in suspension which enables the printed characters to be magnetised. The magnetic image can be sensed by suitable reading equipment and the detected character converted automatically into code for direct storage within the computer. The method is widely used by banks for the encoding of cheques. It has the merit of being a convenient, fast method of entering data into the computer system and is very suitable for high-volume applications where many thousands of documents need to be processed in a short time. Once the stylised fonts have been learnt, the encoding can be read by the human eye without difficulty.

(ii) *Optical Character Recognition (OCR)* - Like MICR, this system allows data printed in special characters to be interpreted visually. With OCR, however, ordinary printing ink is used and the shapes of the characters enable them to be converted for input to the computer. The absence of the need for special inks enables the characters to be printed by standard typewriters having suitable type-bars, or even by modified on-line printers. In the latter case, the computer is able to encode its printed output for subsequent use as input - a method called turn-around documentation. A typical application for such a system is reading electricity meters. Cash registers can also be fitted with the necessary typeface to allow the tally rolls to be printed in OCR characters. When installed in a busy shop, such machines provide computer input as a by-product of normal trading activities. The encoded tally rolls can be processed through a suitable reader directly into the computer to enable analyses of sales and stock to be printed for management control. Recent developments of this OCR technique will allow normal typewriter fonts to be read and converted.

(iii) *Kimball tags* - These are small tickets having numerical information pre-printed and also punched in pin-size holes. The tickets are used as identification tags on goods, such as clothing and are removed at the point of sale. The tags can be processed through a special convertor and the coded information transferred to punched cards, paper tape or magnetic tape for subsequent computer input. The system has the merit of providing clear details of the goods showing size, price etc, while being capable of swift conversion for computer processing. The elimination of transcription from manually-raised sales dockets reduces the chance of error in subsequent computer-produced sales analyses.

4.2 Data capture in two different systems

(a) *TV rental company*

Each customer is equipped with a rent book with vouchers. Each voucher has the customer's account number, the branch number, and monthly rental encoded in an OCR typeface. When the customer visits the shop the voucher is torn out of the book and processed by a document reader which encodes the data onto magnetic tape. The tape can be read off and the data transmitted to the Head Office computer by means of a terminal link at weekly intervals. The customer's record consists of a voucher stub which can be stamped by the branch staff.

Advantages of above

(i) The human effort of keying and verifying data is eliminated as the source document is machine-sensible.

      (ii)   Errors at source are eliminated as the amount and key code numbers are preprinted.

Disadvantages

      (i)   Customers may lose their rent books or forget to present vouchers when making payments, thus creating additional work in preparing source documents.

      (ii)   The costs of specialist form design may be prohibitive if rentals are subject to reviews at regular intervals.

(b)   *Factory costing system*

The method of data capture will be as follows. Terminals are sited at strategic points in the factory. A terminal with a full QWERTY keyboard and VDU is sited in the works office.

Materials

A parts list and progress card are prepared by the works office. One part of the parts list is used to draw out materials/components, and is returned to the works office who match it with its counterpart. (No entries are made through the terminal until this matching is done.)

The data keyed in by the terminal operator is as follows:

-     job number;
-     product number;
-     number of units;
-     stages in production.

As the components are assembled they are accompanied by the progress card.

Labour

The terminals used for recording labour are badge readers equipped with a numeric keyboard and certain control keys. Each operator has a plastic badge on which is encoded the following:

-     operator number;
-     department number.

As each batch of components reaches each operator the following tasks are carried out:

-     the operator inserts his plastic badge and encodes the job number using the terminal keyboard;

-     the task is then carried out;

-     on completion the operator depresses a key to retrieve his card.

The system is linked to a real-time clock which records the start and finish times of each operator.

The job number keyed in must match with the job number on the work-in- progress file.

The system has the following advantages:

(i)   the recording of material usage is integrated with stock recording so that one operation in the works office 'sets up' the job on the work-in- progress file and records the issue of materials thereto;

(ii)   the system for recording labour times is a considerable improvement on clerical methods, which are never error-free.

The possible disadvantages that might occur are as follows:

(i)   the cost of specialised equipment may not be matched by the benefits;

(ii)   errors by operators may result in poor quality input;

(iii)   breakdowns (such as computer failures) may cause considerable disruption to operators.

4.3   Alternative data capture methods

Further to your instructions I have carried out a review of the existing methods of data capture employed in the company and have considered various alternatives which may serve as a basis for further discussions. I have not, as yet, calculated the costs and benefits of the alternatives.

Faults of existing method

While the existing systems for preparing punched cards as input for the various accounting routines are tried and tested, there are various drawbacks which can be identified as follows:

(a)   *Error rates* - Punch card preparation is prone to transcription errors. These are time consuming to correct.

(b)   *Labour intensive* - The preparation of cards involves considerable human effort to:

    (i)   punch cards;
    (ii)   verify cards;
    (iii)   handle the cards as input; and
    (iv)   store the cards.

(c)   *Bulky and slow* - Card reading is now one of the slowest input methods. The punched card is not an efficient medium for input as its storage capacity is limited to a maximum of 80 characters.

(d)   *Card fixed format* - The fixed format of an 80 column card is a bar to further streamlining of systems.

(e)   *Portability* - Cards are durable but they can be lost or mislaid or fall out of sequence due to careless handling.

Alternatives

Key-to-cassette encoder

This device consists of a keyboard, a screen/panel and a spool of magnetic tape. Data is keyed in from source documents and can be visually checked by the operator. The record is then encoded on magnetic tapes. Verification can take place by keying the machine into its 'search/verify' mode. Each record can be read in and validated by re-keying the original document.

The advantages are:

(a)   Magnetic tape is a dense, cheap medium which records continuously instead of in discrete physical units like punched cards. There is less need to worry about record lengths.

(b)   Tape is also more portable and easier and quicker to process as an input medium.

(c)   The device has a limited degree of intelligence and can be wired up to validate code number transcription. This method, however, although superior to punched card preparation, is inferior to the concept of a separate computer system dedicated to data entry, which is described below.

Key-to-disk system

A key-to-disk system is the name given to a configuration where a number of key stations with visual display screens are linked to a central computer. The computer may be a minicomputer or a microcomputer with a resident program which controls each keyboard. On such a system the resident program is designed to recognise a number of data entry 'formats'; for example sales order entry would require a typical format of:

(a)   date;
(b)   order number;
(c)   customer code;
(d)   customer reference;
(e)   stock order; and   )
) X repeated n times
(f)   quantity.   )

The resident program would validate each format and reject those which contained errors, were incomplete or were otherwise incompatible with system requirements. The disk is then read out onto tape and the tape input file is used as the medium of input.

The advantages are:

(a)   The central computer's intelligence controls the whole process and a greater rate of productivity is claimed for such systems.

(b)   Keying errors can be reduced by the validation procedures.

(c)   As a logical outcome of (b) verification procedures can be reduced.

(d)   The computer can also be used as a terminal which can interface with our main machine.

Conclusions

There is no doubt that the key-to-disk system is superior to both key-to-cassette or the use of remote terminals due to the facility of controlling the data capture function by a separate system.   However the costs must be evaluated in terms of the hardware, software and training required.   Benefits that come to mind include the possible reduction in salary costs and overtime payments coupled with greater efficiency in day-to-day operations.

Session 5 Output methods and media

Quick question answers

(1)   (a)   N
        (b)   I
        (c)   I
        (d)   N
        (e)   I

(2)   (b)

(3)   'Paging'   'Scrolling'

(4)   (c)

(5)   (c)

(6)   (b)

(7)   (a) or (b)

(8)   (a)   1
        (b)   4
        (c)   3
        (d)   4 or 3
        (e)   5

(9)   Some printed output is often produced in a special typeface so that it can be read by an OCR device as input.

(10)   True

Objective test answers

(1)   C
(2)   A

Written test answers

5.1   **Line printer, incremental graph plotter, cathode ray display tube**

(a)   Line printers have similar characteristics to a normal office typewriter in that the printed impression on the paper is created by a type slug and an inked ribbon. Unlike the situation with typewriters, however, the paper is normally struck against the type by a small hammer, rather than the other way round.

The various types of line printer are distinguished by the arrangement used for the type itself. Methods available are:

(i)   Chain printers. Type characters are embossed on the outer edge of a closed metal chain which revolves continuously. As the required letter or symbol passes the printing position a hammer strikes the paper and pushes it against the ribbon, which in turn is pressed against the type itself so that the character is printed.

(ii)   Barrel printers are similar to the above in printing method, but the type characters are embossed around a solid barrel.

(iii)   Bar printers contain a complete character set on a vertical bar. The bars move up and down to form the complete line of print and the paper is struck in one stroke against the type.

(iv)   Wheel printers are similar in action to bar printers, but the vertical bars are replaced by wheels which turn on a common axis to form the required line of type. Each wheel contains all the characters in the set.

(v)   Dot matrix impact printers. At each printing position is a matrix of small pins arranged as a rectangle of, say, seven by five. Characters are formed by moving the pins slightly forward to outline the letter or figure required. The resulting print is made up of small dots.

(b)   An incremental graph plotter is an output device in which one or more pens are moved over a sheet of paper in such a way that graphs and other diagrams can be drawn. The vertical and horizontal movement of the pens is controlled by the computer and the plotter can be accurate to within one hundredth of an inch. Models differ in their design and sophistication and the paper can be flat or rolled around a drum depending upon the particular make of the device. The advantage of such a unit is that the results of calculations made by the computer can be output directly as a graph, thus avoiding any intermediate manual effort.

(c)   Cathode-ray display terminals enable computer output in alpha-numeric or graphical form to be seen on what resembles a television screen. The units have keyboards enabling the user to communicate with the computer and amend or update the display currently being shown. Another means of man-machine communication is via a light pen. This device, which is like a small torch, can be used to draw graphs and diagrams on the face of the cathode-ray tube in such a way that they are stored in the computer's memory. Diagrams input in this way can be reproduced again under program control and if required, rotated on the screen through all planes to enable the user to view the pattern from different angles - a requirement often met in building design.

5.2 **Graphics**

To   Training Officer

From   E A Moonshine

Re: 'Graphics' on small computers.

It is now possible to obtain not just printed output, but also graphical displays (graphics) from small computers. These provide an additional dimension to the reporting systems provided. Many managers have an inbuilt distrust of tabulations of figures. Graphical display as a visual image often provides an insight into a report which is not provided by columns of figures.

Graphics possess the following advantages:

(a)   they emphasise relationships;
(b)   they uncover previously hidden facts;
(c)   they focus interest;
(d)   they save time in analysing data;
(e)   they help recall; and
(f)   they break down the barriers of language.

Accountants are often criticised for providing too much detail. Graphics can be used effectively to explain matters to non-accountants simply and effectively. Graphics can be used in three ways:

-    information graphics
-    report graphics
-    presentation graphics.

Information graphics is, essentially, presentation of information to the computer user on the VDU.

Report graphics is presentation of information in the form of a printed page.

Presentation graphics is used when it is desired to present information by projection onto a screen or a TV monitor. It is possible to print output directly onto a transparency and use these in a slide projection presentation.

Conclusion

In order that the use of graphics is successful there are certain guidelines which must be followed:

(a)   Simplicity - over complicated displays are self-defeating.

(b)   Use of familiar terms and concepts - the display is directed at the likely level of audience understanding.

(c)   Consistency in layout - this applies to style, colour, and typeface.

I hope you will find the above useful.

5.3   **Page printers, dialogues and COM**

(a)   *Page printers*

The term 'page printer' is used to describe the device that is capable of producing complete pages of output at a time by means of a process which:

(i)   produces the output page by a laser 'writing' on a sensitive surface;

(ii)   transfers the image onto a page by a heat transfer process (xerography) similar to that used in photocopiers.

Page printers produce high quality single part documents in a fast silent process.

(b)   *Dialogues*

Many small computers operate in an interactive mode ie, the user and the machine engage in a conversational exchange by means of visual displays which require some sort of reaction by the user. A typical dialogue may be initiated by the display of a menu which offers various options to the user. On choosing a particular option the user is guided through various stages of operation by means of a series of 'prompts' on the VDU screen. A typical dialogue is set out below:

'ENTER TRANSACTION TYPE INV = 1 CRN = 2 JNL = 3'

'1'

'ENTER AMOUNT'

'129.77'

'CORRECT? TYPE Y/N'

'Y'

'ENTER TRANSACTION TYPE INV = 1 CRN = 2 JNL = 3'

Dialogues can be highlighted by blinking display lines, reverse video or **BOLD** displays.

(c)   *COM*

These letters stand for computer output on microfilm. This is a specialised output production system which can be explained in the following way.

Output from a process is collected in computer-understandable form on say magnetic tape. The output file is then read by a COM logic unit which converts the binary digits to a character display on a cathode ray tube. The display on the cathode ray tube is directed towards a camera lens which enables the image to be captured on a spool of microfilm. The microfilm can be manipulated by another process to provide several units or frames of microfilm to a larger unit called the microfiche. Retrieval of the stored information is possible by a microfilm reader.

Session 6 Backing storage

Quick question answers

(1)   Drum, Tape, Disk
(2)   Interblock gap
(3)   (b)
(4)   By key fields
(5)   False
(6)   False
(7)   LAM (Laser Accessed Memory)
(8)   Non volatile
(9)   Header label
(10)   (a)

Objective test answers

(1)   B
(2)   C

Written test answers

6.1   Interblock gaps, cylinder concept, tape cycling

(a)   *Interblock gaps on tape*

The interblock gap is an area of blank non-magnetised tape which separates two record blocks of data. The purpose of the interblock gap is to provide a 'braking mechanism' for the magnetic tape reel, ie, on receiving a command to read a tape file a block is read past the read/write head and the tape stops when the blank area is sensed by the head.

(b)   *Cylinder concept*

The cylinder concept refers to the method commonly used for organising a disk file when a disk cartridge consists of several platters. Data is loaded onto the disk from the outermost track to the inner track but on **successive common** heads. Assuming five platters with ten recording surfaces, data will be recorded as follows:

Surface 0	Track 0
Surface 1	Track 0
Surface 2	Track 0
Surface 3	Track 0
Surface 4	Track 0
Surface 5	Track 0
Surface 6	Track 0
Surface 7	Track 0
Surface 8	Track 0
Surface 9	Track 0

The assembly of common tracks (track 0 on ten surfaces) is said to comprise a cylinder. The cylinder concept is fundamental to the concept of the addressability of disk storage. If there are 200 concentric tracks in a disk with ten recording surfaces, each surface being divided into ten sectors, then the disk comprises 200 x 10 x 10 addresses each one capable of being addressed by a code number consisting of a hierachy of

cylinder number 0-199
track number 0-9
sector number 0-9

(c) *Three generations system of tape cycling*

A magnetic tape is a serial access medium which is read from end to end. If a magnetic tape file is to be updated it is not practicable to overwrite the last records with the new data. Instead, it will be necessary to create a totally new tape as illustrated in the diagram below. Tape A contains the transaction data, Tape B the data to be updated and Tape C is the updated version of B.

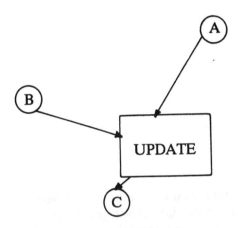

By analogy, B is the father (earlier generation) and C is the son. If any errors are discovered in C, the routine can be rejected and the new 'blemish-free' version of C is created. This process can be projected so that 'C' becomes the input file (father) and a new file created 'D' B, C and D then represent the three generations of file in existence. The theory behind the practice is that three generations of file should be retained in case of corruption. Should errors be discovered, the relevant files can be reconstructed from earlier generations.

6.2   **Magnetic tape versus magnetic disk**

Magnetic tape

(a) Serial access medium.

(b) Non-addressable storage. Each record can only be located by an identifier such as an account number.

(c) Tape files can only be used in schemes of batch or sequential processing.

(d) Tape can only be updated by copy.

Magnetic disk

(a) Can be used to provide serial access and direct access.

(b) Can be organised as bulk addressable storage as the disk can be subdivided into individual sectors each with its own identifying address.

(c) Disk files can be used for both batch and demand (transaction) processing.

Magnetic tape	Magnetic disk
(e) Magnetic tape update by copy provides an inbuilt security feature.	(d) Disks can be updated by copying or updated by overlay (overwriting).
(f) Because of its reliability, slow reading and handling speeds tape is relegated to the role of a secondary storage medium.	(e) Disks updated by overlay are copied for security purposes onto magnetic tape.
	(f) Magnetic disk is now in widespread use as a primary recording medium.

6.3 Sectored diskettes, header and trailer labels

(a) A diskette is a device widely used in microcomputer systems for backing storage. A typical diskette consists of a flexible device made of magnetisable material 8", 5¼" or 3½" in diameter. Data is recorded on concentric tracks; each track is capable of being divided up into smaller units called sectors. The sector is therefore the smallest addressable unit on a diskette for storing data. Hard-sectored diskettes are those with a fixed sector size determined by the manufacturer. On most hard-sectored diskettes, a circle of punched holes around the centre indicates the sector boundaries.

Diskettes can also be soft-sectored; this means that the user can determine sector size and the boundary of each sector is marked by special computer-understandable data.

(b) The header label is the name given to the first record on a magnetic tape or disc file. The header label enables the computer's control or operating system to recognise the correct file in any processing run. The header label usually consists of the following:

   (i)   a code identifying the record as the label;

   (ii)   the file name;

   (iii)   date last written;

   (iv)   date before which no destructive overwriting can take place. (This does not apply to a 'direct access file'.) Should a file be loaded incorrectly, the header label will be read and an error message will be signalled to the operator.

(c) The trailer label is a record placed at the end of a file which contains the following features:

   (i)   some code which signifies that it is a label;

   (ii)   a count of the total number of records;

   (iii)   a reference to another file if the file is continued on another reel of tape or another disk cartridge.

The trailer label, like the header label is written to the tape by the operating system and serves as a signalling device that there have been no reading errors and that all the records have been processed. It is part of the system of software controls exercised over backing storage.

Session 7 Data communication systems

Quick question answers

(1)   Local Area Network
        Packet Switching System
        Automatic Repeat Request

(2)   A modem

(3)   (a)

(4)   (c)

(5)   (a)   transmission one way only
        (b)   transmission in two directions simultaneously
        (c)   transmission in two directions but not simultaneously

(6)   Polling

(7)   (c)

(8)   Hierarchical

(9)   Data encryption

Objective test answers

(1)   D
(2)   C
(3)   B

Written test answers

7.1   Data transmission

(a)   The term data transmission refers to the transfer of data between either:

       (i)   a terminal and a computer;
       (ii)   one computer and another;
       (iii)   one terminal and another.

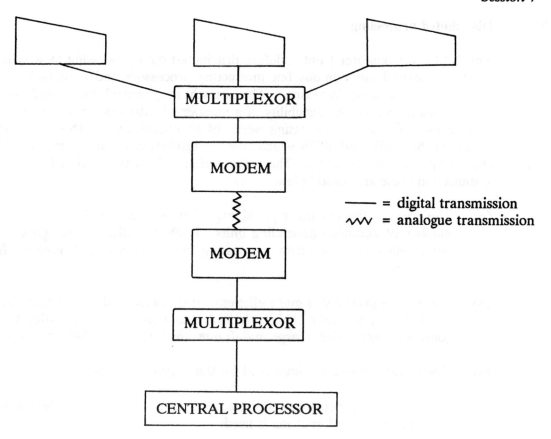

Data transmission is generally achieved by means of a switching system such as British Telecom's Packet Switching System (PSS). The medium of transmission is, most commonly, the telephone line but other devices may be used; satellite links are used for inter-continental transmission and cable for totally distributed devices. The diagram illustrates a conventional data transmission system which has the following features. Three terminals are linked to a host computer by means of telephone lines. The binary coded data transmitted through the terminal is converted to analogue signals by means of a device called a modem (modulator demodulator). Another modem converts the analogue signals into digital data so that the computer can receive and handle it. When a number of terminal devices use the same telephone line they require a hardware device called a multiplexor which receives and compresses the signals for several data channels into one. The multiplexor nearest the central processor is called a **multidrop** multiplexor as it is monitoring and controlling three terminals but using the same telephone line.

(b) (i) Synchronous transmission is the method used where data is transmitted with a constant time interval between each binary digit as opposed to a continuous stream of bits which require 'start' and 'stop' bits to indicate the extent of each character.

(ii) Half duplex transmission occurs when data can be transmitted in two directions but not simultaneously.

(iii) Polling is the name given to the means of controlling the multiple use of transmission lines. The computer signals each terminal device in turn to ascertain whether they wish to transmit data. Polling is resorted to when multiplexors are not available and each terminal device has its own independent line to the host computer.

7.2   Distributed processing

The National Computer Centre define distributed data processing as a system in which there are several autonomous but interacting processors and/or data stores at several different geographical locations. The growth in powerful mini- and microcomputer systems has permitted the feasibility of a number of autonomous data processing systems serving the information processing needs of an organisation. This is a reversal of the trends of the 1960s and 1970s which saw the institution of large centralised DP systems shared by a number of users. There are various advantages claimed for distributed DP systems and these are listed below.

(a)   The concept favours the type of organisation which is itself decentralised into a number of autonomous trading units. Each unit/division has greater freedom in determining its own data processing requirements and greater flexibility of operation.

(b)   The service provided is more efficient. It is reasoned that it is more sensible to use small cheap powerful machines dedicated to a particular application than to rely on continually upgrading a large mainframe which is less flexible and responsive.

(c)   The service provided is improved for the following reasons:

   (i)   the data processing system is faster as it takes place at the point where data arises and information is used;

   (ii)   the data on file is more accessible to the user;

   (iii)   there is a reduction in the amount of effort expended on data transmission; and

   (iv)   the incidence of machine breakdown is claimed to be reduced.

(d)   Greater security is claimed for the system as (i) machine breakdown does not paralyse the entire system and is restricted to the particular unit, and (ii) data files are not centralised at one location and the risks of physical hazard are therefore reduced.

The disadvantages are:

(a)   Small computers have restricted memory sizes (8 bit/16 bit memories) with limited addressability and file handling ability for batch type processes and their interaction mode of operation may not suit high volumes of transactions. The disadvantage is less serious with the development of the 32 bit micro and improved software for advanced file structures.

(b)   There may be cost disadvantages in that certain costs are duplicated.

(c)   There may be difficulty in controlling and monitoring data processing standards and hardware material with a variety of geographical locations.

7.3   LANs, password controls, protocols

(a) *Local area networks*

A local area network (LAN) is the name given to a number of interconnecting computer devices within a local geographical area. The devices in a LAN are generally 'hard-wired' by some transmission medium such as coaxial cable, fibre optic cable or twisted pairs. The design of the network can also vary; common physical design shapes are illustrated diagrammatically below:

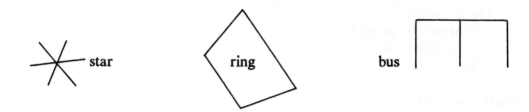

LANs can have a number of devices for handling text, data or graphics and may feature machines such as other computers, facsimile reproduction devices, proprietary disk stores etc.

There is now a greater awareness of LANs and various property control systems are now marketed by manufacturers such as IBM (Systems Network Architecture) or Xerox (Ethernet).

(b) *Password controls*

Data transmission systems bring both the benefits of improved communications and the hazards of illicit access to files of data by unauthorised users. Passwords are therefore used as devices to permit access to files only to those persons who are authorised. The password is a unique code which may incorporate some form of mnemonic as well as the identification of the user's terminal device. The password is keyed in as part of the 'logging on' process and once the system acknowledges the password, data transmission can commence. The password should be restricted to key staff; passwords may also be hierarchical in that they may provide access to files on a selective basis to certain users.

(c) *Protocols*

The term protocol (also known as 'data link control') refers to the set of rules used to govern the information flow between devices in a communication system. Protocols are needed in order to guard against loss or corruption of data. The simplest protocol is the concept of parity bit checking; an ASCII character is represented in 7 bits with one extra bit to ensure that each character is transmitted as a valid collection of bits. More complex protocols can also exist, eg, automatic repeat request (ARQ) systems. The protocol breaks up the message into blocks of characters each with a check character computed by some algorithm. The blocks are then reassembled and by recomputing the check character it is possible to determine (to a certain level of probability) if an error has occurred. The receiving terminal can then send a message to indicate that the block was error-free or, if an error was detected, to request re-transmission of the block.

0122z

Session 8 The electronic office

Quick question answers

(1)   Word processing
(2)   False
(3)   Facsimile reproduction
(4)   Spreadsheet models
(5)   Electronic funds transfer using SWIFT
(6)   A programmable telephone exchange
(7)   Electronic mail
(8)   Global search and replace
(9)   Shared logic systems
(10)   False

Written test answers

8.1   Modernisation of typing pool

To: E A Mond - Managing Director
Re: Modernisation of typing pool

There is no doubt that an organisation of our size should not rely for typing services on a pool staffed by typists using outmoded electric typewriters, for the following reasons:

(a)   The rate of finished throughput is erratic.

(b)   There is an unacceptable incidence of error; even if the machines are equipped with self-correcting ribbons the appearance of the finished product could be improved.

(c)   There is little scope for economy of effort. Brochures and catalogues need extensive retyping when they are updated.

(d)   Staff costs are a significant expense; it may be possible to redeploy some typists by assigning them to other parts of the organisation if alternative methods of providing typing services are installed. Alternatively, it may be possible to reduce staff levels or fail to replace those typists who leave for more lucrative and demanding employment elsewhere.

Many organisations such as ours have installed word processing systems in order to provide both typewriting services and document retrieval systems. Considerable advantages are claimed for word processing systems. Some of the obvious points are stated as under:

(a)   The word processing devices enable text to be entered and stored on magnetic diskette and displayed on a VDU screen so that the operator can edit his/her own work. It is possible therefore to proof-read documents and amend the stored version so that the printed copy is free of error.

(b)   The appearance of the document is improved by such devices as left and right justification, automatic line counting and alignment of decimal figures.

(c) Rate of throughput is increased as the keyboards are touch-sensitive and almost silent in operation. Certain keying operations are eliminated through the use of automatic carriage returns at the end of the line, automatic centring of text and the use of pre-prepared words or phrases termed 'glossaries' which can be inserted into text.

(d) Updating of documents is facilitated by the use of techniques such as 'search and replace' by which certain key words in text can be replaced by others **throughout** the text without additional keying.

(e) Replicated documents can be prepared swiftly by keying a name and address file with the standard letter so that each letter can be individually addressed.

These are **some** of the various features of the word processing systems.

The machinery can be obtained in various combinations:

(a) Stand alone WPs, which are individual machines consisting of keyboard, VDU, processor, diskette drive and printer sold as one unit. The machines are **dedicated** WPs, ie, their control system is specially designed for text handling as opposed to computational work.

(b) Shared logic WPs, which consist of one processor linked to tape/disk storage and capable of controlling a number of individual work stations (each work station comprising a keyboard and VDU).

This type of installation may well be suitable as a replacement for the centralised typing pool as additional keyboards can be linked to it from certain offices or departments.

If there is any further information that you require, please let me know as soon as possible.

8.2   Processing of credit card vouchers

To: Managing Director
From: Gloria Zizzbaum - Accountant
Re: Processing of 'PASSPORT CARD' vouchers

The growth in volume of transactions involving the use of PASSPORT CARD is causing considerable administrative problems. Customers complain that the processing of cash transactions results in unacceptable delays. Additionally, the depot staff dislike the task of processing the card because of the ancillary tasks that result such as:

(a)   summarising the vouchers;
(b)   preparing the banking;
(c)   filing the copies.

While it is clear that a delay of possibly three days occurs between processing the transaction and crediting the company bank account with the proceeds there are still various hazards such as:

(a)   loss of vouchers;
(b)   errors in summarisation;
(c)   fraudulent use of cards.

We could streamline our systems quite considerably by the use of electronic funds transfer at point of sale (EFTPOS). This technique has already been tried by certain garages who accept the VISA card and offer self service. The system operates as follows:

(a)   A petrol dispenser linked to the pumps displays the petrol purchased.

(b)   The petrol purchase displayed is transferred to a computer terminal together with any other purchases (oil, spares, confectionery) which are entered using a keyboard.

(c)   The terminal has a badge reader and the customer's credit card is inserted into the badge reader so that the card number is obtained.

(d)   A tally roll printer produces two receipts; one receipt is for the customer. The other receipt is retained by the cashier.

(e)   The day's transactions are recorded on disk and transmitted overnight to the PASSPORT CARD computer centre.

Such a system will speed up customer card processing considerably and reduce the incidence of errors. Future developments could allow for real time checking of card status as well as encoding the customer's details by fitting the petrol pumps with badge readers.

I should be grateful if I could have the opportunity of discussing these points with you more fully.

8.3   Viewdata, teletext, electronic mail

(a)   *Viewdata*

Viewdata is the name given to a communication system which falls within the classification of videotex systems, whereby certain computer databases are made accessible to users through the medium of a telephone line. A feature of the viewdata system is that it is a two-way communication medium; the user is able to enter data via a keypad or keyboard as well as retrieve data which is displayed on a screen. In the UK the viewdata service is known as Prestel which, at its simplest, requires a user to have a TV set equipped to receive Prestel and a telephone connection. Prestel allows information providers (IPs) to display their services and they are remunerated out of the fee charged for Prestel services. Well known IPs are American Express, the Stock Exchange and the Central Statistical Office. Travel agents can use Prestel to make bookings for their clients by accessing travel company IPs.

(b)   *Teletext*

Teletext is another type of system which is covered by the generic term videotex. Examples of teletext systems in the UK are Ceefax and Oracle. Teletext is a one-way read only communication system, in that the user can access a data base which is displayed in pages using a domestic television set. The main purpose of teletext is to provide information of a general nature such as weather forecasts, sports results etc. In order to make use of this information, a keypad and an adaptor are needed. A menu on the screen offers a list of options which can be selected by keying in the appropriate numeric code.

(c) *Electronic mail*

This development is concerned with the use of communicating word processors which are operated through the use of packet switching systems such as British Telecom's PSS. Letters and documents typed in one office can be transmitted and scanned in another office within the network. Security of the message in transit can be achieved by an address code so that the letter is directed along the correct route. A pass code enables the message to remain confidential while in transit until the authorised recipient is able to match the code and 'open' the message.

Session 9 Computer processing systems

Quick question answers

(1)   R, M, R, M, T

(2)   Tapes, disks

(3)   Random, sequential, indexed sequential, random/algorithmic

(4)   Random, sequential

(5)   Key

(6)   Head movement time, latency, read time

(7)   False - a bucket may hold several records

(8)   (a)   Volatile or soft copy
      (b)   Hard copy

(9)   Data output in a form suitable for direct re-input

(10) Decollating (multi-part sets)
      Bursting (continuous stationery)
      Enveloping/franking/mailing (outgoing documents)
      Copying (microfiches, for internal distribution)

Written test answers

9.1   Master file

In an operational computer system the data employed is either of a temporary or a permanent nature. The customer's orders received today are essentially temporary data, because they will be processed through the system and follow an identical path to orders received on any other day. Once the information about the orders has been analysed and translated into action instructions (delivery notes, production schedules, etc.) they cease to be significant in their own right. Permanent data, on the other hand, retains its significance within the system on every processing cycle. An example of such permanent data is the details of all piece-parts, sub-assemblies and assemblies that go to make up a given product. Every order received from a customer for this product would have to be compared with the constituent parts' stock balances to determine whether it could be completed.

Files containing permanent data of this kind are termed master files. Those containing temporary data are normally referred to as transaction files. Because of the permanent character of any master file, the system must provide for it to be amended as required. The file amendment system will allow for:

(a) Insertion of new records as extra items need to be added.

(b) Deletion of unwanted records to remove items that have become obsolete **within** the system.

(c) Amendment of existing records to allow changes to be made to items for which revised information has been received.

An example of a master file would be a stock file, whose purpose within the system is to maintain the current stock balances for all finished goods items in a warehouse.

The following diagram illustrates the updating procedure.

Product	Stock balance	Product	Quantity sold	Product	Stock balance
3A	40			3A	40
3B	90	3B	50	3B	40
3C	30			3C	30
3D	120	3D	10	3D	110
3E	80	3E	100	3E	20
3F	70			3F	70
ORIGINAL FILE (MASTER BROUGHT FORWARD)		TRANSACTIONS		UPDATED FILE (MASTER CARRIED FORWARD)	

The updating process is as follows:

(a) Sort the transaction data to the same sequence as on the master file, if serial type processing is involved. If the master file is accessed randomly, sorting is unnecessary.

(b) Compare the transaction records one by one against the original master file.

(c) If the product on the master file has a reference number which is less than the transaction record, copy the original record to the updated file. Read the next master record.

(d)   If the products on the master and transaction files have identical references, subtract the transaction quantity from the original balance and write the new balance to the updated file. Read the next master and transaction record.

(e)   If the product on the master file has a reference number greater than that on the transaction file, all transactions have been processed and the remainder of the original file can be copied unchanged to the updated file.

In this process the use of two master files, an original and an updated version, is not only a security measure, but is necessary also because it is not possible to read from and write data to, the same physical magnetic tape simultaneously. If the original file is held on a random access device the balances can be amended 'in situ', thereby avoiding the need for a second file but increasing the security risk.

9.2   File organisation

File organisation refers to the relationship between the key fields of consecutive records within a file; the record key being a piece of information which identifies a particular record and distinguishes it from all other records. For example the key field in a payroll file would probably be **clock number**. There are four basic methods of file organisation and an exchangeable disk pack is capable of using any one of them.

(a)   Random organisation may be thought of more simply as lack of organisation. Information (records) is stored on the file as it arises with no particular thought for the sequence.

(b)   Sequential organisation implies that the keys on consecutive records are in a defined sequence - usually ascending numerical order.

(c)   Indexed sequential is essentially the same as sequential but with the added advantage of an index to say exactly where each record is held. This saves the computer reading through the whole file to look for a record: it merely looks up the record key in the index and goes straight to the correct **address** or location. This facility is only available on direct access devices.

(d)   Random/algorithmic organisation establishes a connection between the record key and the record address. The connection, generally a simple mathematical calculation known as a **randomiser** or **addressing algorithm,** is used to generate the address from the record key and allow the data to be accessed directly. The advantages over indexed sequential are savings in both time spent searching the index and space in core storage to hold the index, but it is not always feasible to hold randomly organised files if regular listings are required from the file in key order.

    (i)   For **direct access** either indexed sequential or random organisation could be used. More details would be needed to be able to decide which would be the better of the two in a particular case.

    (ii)   For **sequential file processing** either sequential or indexed sequential organisation would be permissible although it would be a waste of time using indexed sequential if the whole file is to be processed every time (ie, the hit rate is very high). On the other hand, if a direct accessing facility such as indexed sequential is available it might be a good idea to take advantage of the facility as there are always some instances of file maintenance (eg, additions or deletions) where only one or two records need to be accessed. With ordinary sequential organisation a disk pack is acting like a magnetic tape from the processing point of view.

9.3 Input techniques

Note: Arrange your selection in order to demonstrate your knowledge of input techniques, rather than your knowledge of business!

The three types of selling business chosen for this question are:

(a) A 'corner shop' tobacconist, selling sweets, ice cream, newspapers and magazines, etc.

(b) A mail-order firm, selling household goods from a large catalogue.

(c) A book club, selling 'monthly selections' to its subscribers.

In the case of the corner shop-keeper, he has just installed a modern cash register, which is used for keeping a record of sales via 'commodity-group' keys which are depressed at the time each sale is made, to identify the nature of each transaction rung up by the shop assistant. The cash register uses the by-product technique to capture sales data (time of day, commodity code, amount of sale, cash/cheque/credit account) onto a magnetic tape cassette. Because the shop is not big enough to justify its own computer, this cassette is sent each week to a service bureau, who extract the daily data from it, and produce a weekly sales analysis for the shop-keeper.

The mail-order house uses an order form supplied inside each catalogue as the document on which orders are received. Because these are completed by the general public, no 'clever' techniques are possible, but by efficient form design, the scope for errors has been eliminated over the years, and a keyboard operator (key-to-disk - punched cards or paper tape (unlikely these days), more probably tape or disk, or even direct entry) transcribes all details from the forms. The item codes are check digited to detect erroneous entries by the customer or miskeying by the operator, and quantities are usually singles, or item-specific.

The book club, since it knows who all its subscribers are, sends them a monthly 'selection' card, indicating that the 'selection of the month' will be despatched unless they either refuse it by returning the card, and/or choose an alternative selection by simply marking a box on the card with an 'X'. The returned cards are put directly into an optical reader, which reads the customer's wishes from the pattern of marks he has entered, and identifies the customer from the optically-readable number or mark pattern printed on the card by the computer before it was sent out. This is a classic turnaround application. After a given 'closing date', all subscribers for whom a card has not been processed have the 'selection of the month' despatched (and invoiced) by default.

Session 10 Problem definition and analysis

10.1   **Halls of residence**

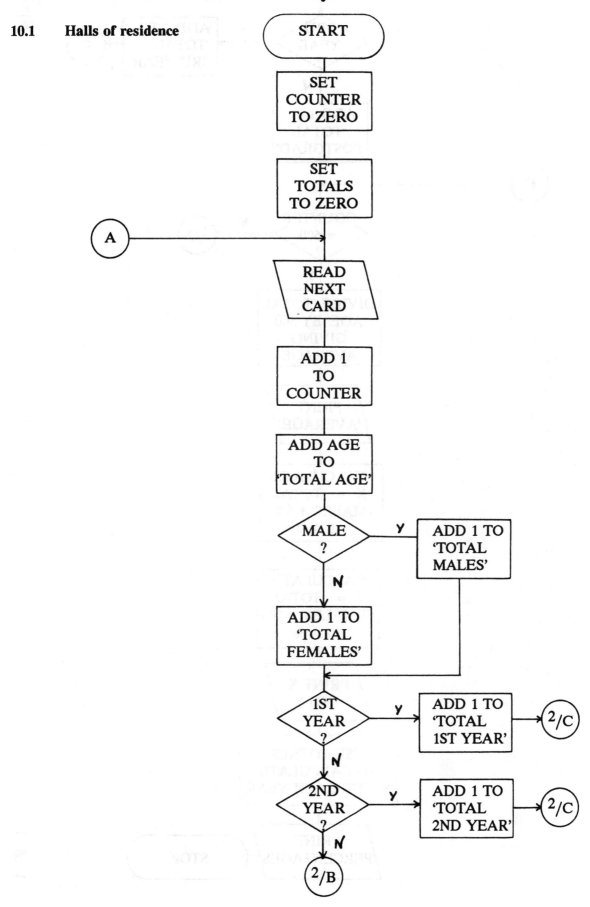

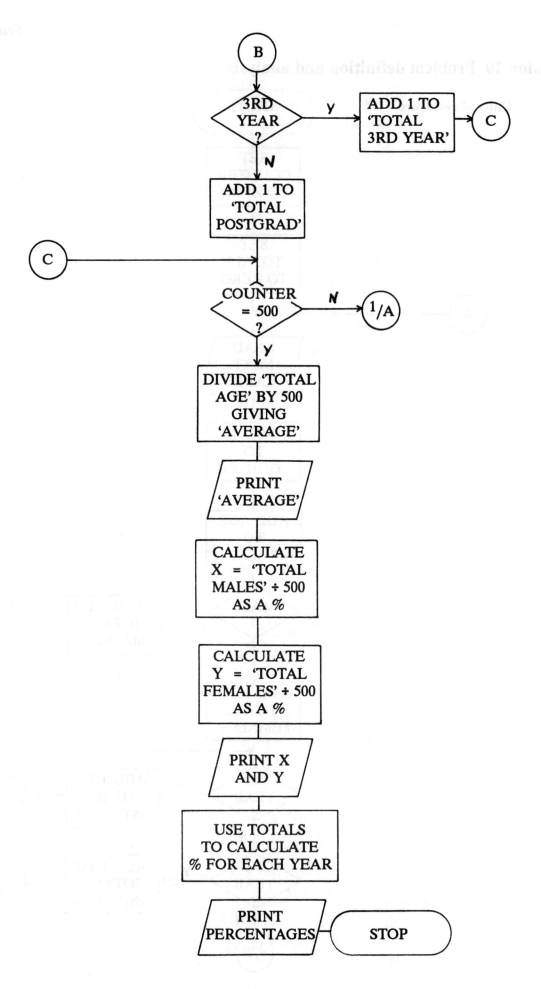

10.2   West Ltd

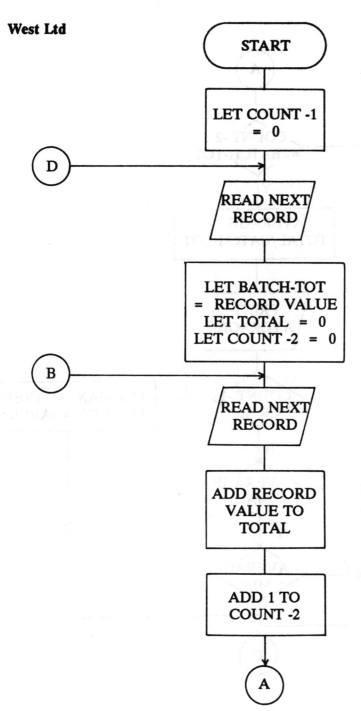

Key

COUNT -1   counts the batches.

COUNT -2   counts the records in each batch.

BATCH-TOT   holds the number of records in each batch.

TOTAL   totals each batch.

MAX   holds maximum average batch value found so far.

MIN   holds minimum average batch value found so far.

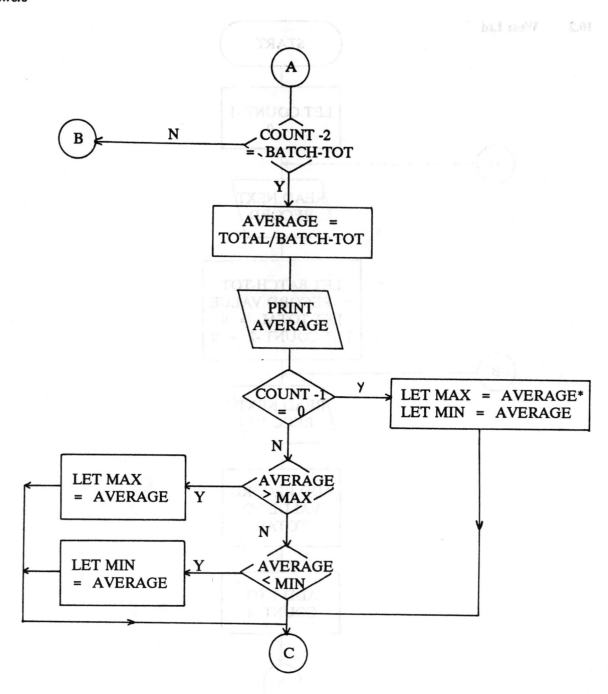

*   This is to allow for the possibility that the average of the first batch is potentially the maximum average ever to be found or the minimum average ever to be found. Future batch averages are then compared to this amount, replacing it when required.

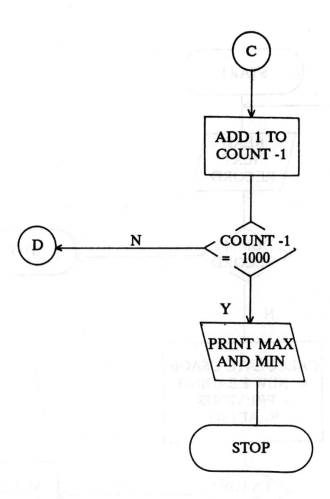

0122z

10.3   Gas invoices

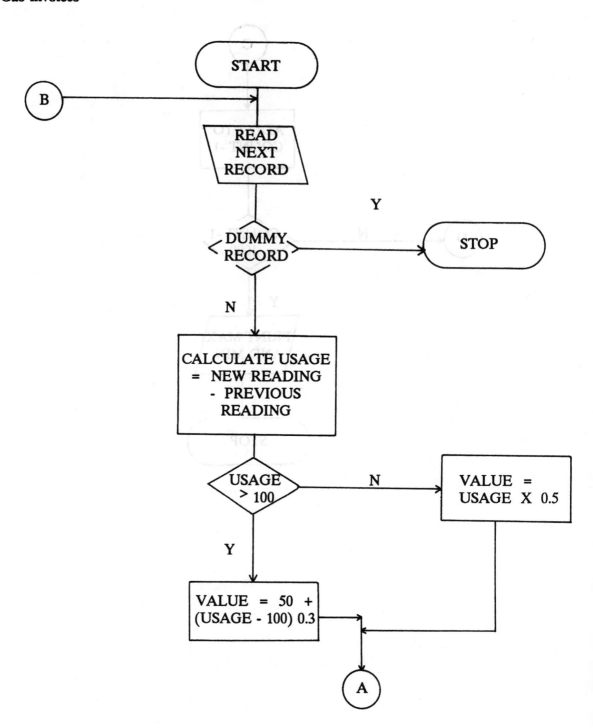

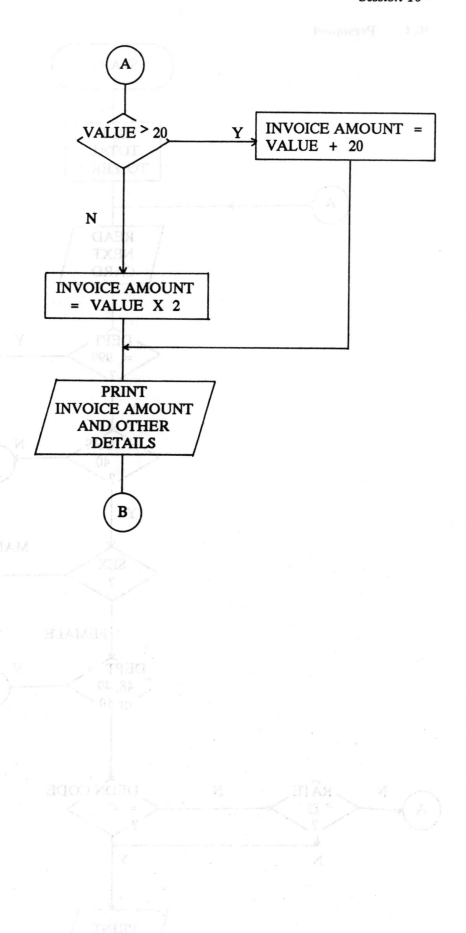

10.4   Personnel

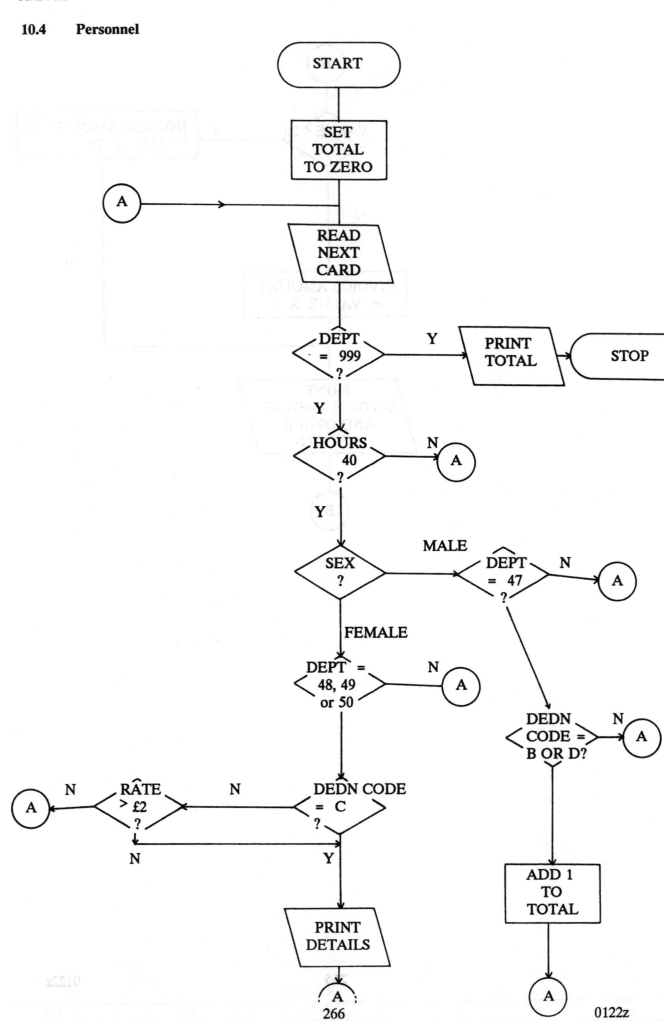

10.5   Inequitable Life Assurance Company

Conditions \ Actions	1	2	3	4	5	6	7
Age < 45	Y	Y	Y	Y	N	N	E
Dangerous Occupation/Sport	Y	Y	N	N	Y	N	L
Good health	Y	N	Y	N	Y	Y	S
Age > 45 < 65	-	-	-	-	Y	Y	E
Normal terms			X				
10% Loading						X	
15% Loading				X			
20% Loading	X						
30% Loading					X		
35% Loading		X					
REJECT							
EXIT							X

See workings and note for rule reduction.

Workings

Conditions / Actions	1	2	3	4	5	6	7	8	9	10	11	12	13	14	15	16
Age < 45	Y	Y	Y	Y	Y	Y	Y	Y	N	N	N	N	N	N	N	N
Dangerous Occp/Sport	Y	Y	Y	Y	N	N	N	N	Y	Y	Y	Y	N	N	N	N
Good health	Y	Y	N	N	Y	Y	N	N	Y	Y	N	N	Y	Y	N	N
Age < 65									Y	N	Y	N	Y	N	Y	N
Normal terms					X	X										
10% Loading													X			
15% Loading							X	X								
20% Loading	X	X														
30% Loading									X							
35% Loading			X	X												
REJECT										X	X	X		X	X	X
EXIT																

Note: Rules 1-8 can be reduced by half. Rules 10, 11, 12, 14, 15 and 16 can be eliminated by use of the ELSE rule.

10.6   Passport card: credit vetting procedure

Conditions / Actions	1	2	3	4	5
Age > 21	Y	Y	Y	Y	E
Full-time employment	Y	N	N	Y	L
Earnings £8,000	Y	Y	N	N	S
Good bank reference	Y	Y	Y	Y	E
Married to card holder	-	Y	Y	Y	
ACCEPT	X	X	X	X	
REJECT					X

Session 11 Programming principles

Quick question answers

(1)   False
(2)   (b)
(3)   (b)
(4)   (d) and (f); the others are programming languages
(5)   False
(6)   (c)
(7)   (c)
(8)   (b)

Objective test answers

(1)   B
(2)   D
(3)   A
(4)   B

Written test answers

11.1   Assembler program, compiler program, syntax errors

(a)   When a programmer writes his program he may write it in a machine language or he may choose a high-level or low-level language to write the program, using symbols and certain English verbs and nouns to express each instruction.

The use of machine language is complicated and laborious, as data is referred to both by name and by address and this method of program preparation is only used for the very small computers.

A programmer may select a program language which uses symbols and mnemonics and is unique to the machine in use, ie, it is machine-orientated. Such computer language is termed a low-level language and requires a translation program to convert the source program into a program that the computer can use. Such a translation program is termed an assembler program.

(b)   When the programmer selects a high-level language, such as COBOL, a translation program is again required to convert the source program into a program that the computer can use. Such a translation program is termed a compiler program.

(c)   A syntax error is a grammatical error made by a programmer when writing a source program; this means that he has broken the grammatical rules of the particular low-level or high-level language which he is using.

When attempting to convert a source program into an object program, a translation program checks each instruction to ensure that it is syntactically correct. Any syntax errors found are reported on an error listing, and they prevent the source program from being converted into an object program. When this happens, the programmer must correct the erroneous statement(s) and attempt the assembly or compilation process again.

11.2   Instruction format, branching

(a)   *Instruction format*

In a typical computer, an object program in machine code occupies successive locations of store. In each location or word of store, there is one program instruction which the control unit first interprets and then acts on. These program instructions are regular in structure, ie, they are of a similar pattern and this regular pattern is termed the 'instruction format'.

Typically a program instruction consists of four main parts. The first part indicates to the computer what action is to be taken, eg, read, add, print and so on. It is known as the operation code and the full range of these codes is known as the instruction set.

The second part of the instruction indicates the address of the data which is to undergo the operation specified. It is known as the operand.

The third part of the instruction gives the address of one of 7 or 8 different registers in the computer which are used to hold or accumulate temporary or intermediate results.

The last part of the instruction holds a single digit whereby the address of the operand may, if required, be modified.

The instruction will, of course, exist in the computer in binary code. But the programmer is able to write his instructions in a language in which the precise instruction format may not be apparent.

Other types of computers have different formats in which, inter alia, reference may be made to 2 or 3 operands.

(b)   *Branching*

A program is stored in computer core storage as a series of sequential instructions.   When the program is operating, the control unit in the central processor starts by executing the first instruction in the list and then executes each instruction in turn sequentially unless it encounters a branch instruction. This type of program instruction is used to point the control unit to the next instruction to be executed when it is not the next instruction in sequence and such an action is known as 'branching' or 'jumping'. It is a very important feature of computer programming particularly when a program is required to take different courses of action depending on certain conditions.

Branch instructions can be conditional or unconditional. An unconditional branch automatically directs the control unit to the next instruction to be executed but a conditional branch instruction will direct the control unit to one of two instructions depending on the outcome of some condition which is being tested. This facility gives the computer its 'decision-making' ability. Often a set of program instructions need to be repeatedly executed until a certain condition is met. A conditional branch instruction enables the programmer to do this without repeatedly coding the same instructions and the result is known as a program 'loop'.

11.3   High-level language

The source program, as coded by the programmer, is keyed to diskette or disk, depending upon the configuration.   An additional set of instructions, known as job control parameters, is also keyed in and added to the diskette or disk.   The job control parameters tell the computer that a compilation is required.

Parameters and program are then fed into the computer and a first compiler listing is printed out. This listing is in two parts. The first part contains an exact copy of the input, with each program instruction appearing on a new line. Format errors are detected at this stage. Invalid instructions cannot be handled by the compiler and thus are ignored in subsequent processes. If the source program is going to be stored on some magnetic media, the compiler will allocate a serial number to each program instruction. These serial numbers will be printed against the instruction on the initial listing. To allow for subsequent amendment of the program and more particularly, the insertion of new program instructions, serial numbering often commences at ten and increases by ten for each subsequent instruction.

The second part of the compiler listing repeats the source program, but this time indicates any syntactical errors that have been made in the coding. These are normally indicated by an error message printed alongside the instruction, on the next line, or at the end of the listing. Error messages may be in coded form, eg, ERROR 031/10, or they may be explicit, eg, FULL STOP OMITTED or INVALID BRANCH ADDRESS.

In the former case, reference will have to be made to the relevant language manual for an explanation of the error.

If errors have been detected by the compiler then, depending on the job control parameters submitted, the compiler may or may not go on to produce a machine language version of the program.

When the programmer gets his compiler print-outs, he has:

(a)   to check each source statement against his original coding sheets to ensure that nothing has been miskeyed;

(b)   to examine every error message, determine its cause, decide how it should be corrected and prepare the necessary coded amendment.

In making amendments to correct errors, it is not necessary to have the whole program keyed in again. Corrections can be made by quoting the serial number of the erroneous line together with the corrected instruction. If new instructions are to be introduced, they are given any of the ten serial numbers available between successive lines on the original listing. For example, to add three new source instructions between lines 0130 and 0140, it is only necessary to number them 0131, 0132 and 0133. The computer will then insert them in their correct sequence. At the option of the programmer the source instructions can be renumbered each time a program is compiled so that the original gaps of ten are maintained.

Session 12 Software - an appreciation

Quick question answers

(1)   Supervisor (monitor or control module)

(2)   None: a sort routine is a utility

(3)   Square root calculation; calculation of statistical measures; calculating length of time between two dates; trigonometric functions.

(4)   Source, object

(5)   (c)

(6)   (c)

(7)   (c)

(8)   (b)

(9)   Dump trace and restart routines

(10) Manufacturers of hardware, software houses, other users

Objective test answers

(1)   A
(2)   A
(3)   C
(4)   D

Written test answers

12.1 Operating systems

Operating systems aid computer operations by allowing better use to be made of the computer's potential. This is achieved by giving the computer control over certain of its own activities thus eliminating much manual intervention and delay.

The areas which are affected include:

(a) job scheduling;
(b) file handling;
(c) disk access;
(d) timing;
(e) multiprogramming and virtual storage;
(f) communication;
(g) store allocation;
(h) library procedures;
(i) peripheral allocation and spooling;
(j) error diagnostics.

Operator intervention in these tasks is minimal and thus they are executed at machine speeds. Not all of the above processes will need to be carried out at the same time or even for the same program. For example, if a program does not use disk files then there is no need for the operating system to include the instructions which would allow disk access to be carried out. Thus, operating systems are modular, ie divided into sections. The relevant modules are called into main store as required so that the minimum amount of main store is occupied by the operating system. One module, the supervisor, executive or control module is always present in main store whenever the computer is running. This handles communication and looking after the retrieval of the other modules when they are needed.

12.2 Compiler and interpreter programs, spreadsheet model

(a) A compiler program is one that translates a program written in a high-level language into machine code. It thus

   (i) allocates areas of main memory to data fields;
   (ii) checks each statement for syntax errors;
   (iii) prints an error list; and
   (iv) prints out a source program listing.

   Compilers process the entire source program from beginning to end without a break. Syntax errors then have to be detected and the process continued until there is total compliance with language selection.

   An interpreter, on the other hand, is a program that is resident in the computer for the purpose of translating program statements entered on a line-by-line basis through a keyboard directly to the computer. Any syntax errors in a line will be identified immediately and rejected.

(b) A spread sheet model is a commonly used application package for financial modelling with microcomputers. It consists of a matrix of rows and columns each accommodating a cell for storage of a variable. For example if it was desired to produce a twelve month cash budget with 60 possible lines of data there would be 12 X 60 = 720 analysis cells.

The user enters data via the keyboard and by moving a cursor any individual cell can be found and amended.

The model is useful when carrying out 'what if' type calculations, eg, 'what if interest rates rise and certain debtors do not pay'. The model incorporates this change in the variables and alters all other variables connected with the change.

12.3   Programming languages

(a)   BASIC is a high-level or problem-orientated language and possesses the following features:

(i)   It is written in English or near English and is therefore easy to understand.

(ii)   It uses a number of reserved terms and conventions to which the programmer must adhere if he is to avoid syntax errors.

(iii)   It uses macro instructions - ie, instructions which can be interpreted into several operations in machine code.

(iv)   It is an interactive language and especially useful for small machines operating in an interactive or conversational mode.

(b)   Languages like BASIC were developed (and are increasingly used today) for the following reasons:

(i)   To make computing skills more readily available to the non-specialist.

(ii)   To aid the non-specialist in being able to specify his programming requirements.

(iii)   To speed up the production of program and aid the process of data retrieval by facilitating the interactive mode of operation.

(c)   Programming languages are also available in what is known as low-level or assembler code. These languages generally use symbols or mnemonics for describing computer operations and operands. They are used by expert programmers for designing either systems software or application programs.

The lowest level of programming language is machine language where the operations and operands are described in binary notation. Their use demands expert knowledge by programmers and may only be used for very specialised diagnostic routines.

Session 13 Databases

Quick question answers

(1)   (A), (C) and (E)
(2)   False

(3)	(A)
(4)	(C) and (D)
(5)	Expert system
(6)	Attributes, lists
(7)	Data Description Language
(8)	Chain
(9)	Ring structure
(10)	$\sqrt{625} = 25$
(11)	C
(12)	D

Written test answers

13.1   Inverted files, tree data structures

(a)   *Inverted file*

A record on a traditional computer file consists of a key identifier followed by a number of fields or attributes. Each record is retrieved by reference to its key field. An inverted file however consists of a collection of records; each record consists of a number of attributes and these attributes are listed one list per attribute. A group of lists make up an inverted file. The difference between conventional and inverted fields is shown in the diagram below:

Conventional record

KEY	FIELD$_A$	FIELD$_B$	FIELD$_C$	FIELD$_D$	FIELD$_E$

LIST$_A$	LIST$_B$	LIST$_C$	LIST$_D$	LIST$_E$
KEY 1	KEY 1	KEY 1	KEY 1	KEY 1
KEY 2	KEY 2	KEY 2	KEY 2	KEY 3
KEY 3	KEY 3	KEY 3	KEY 4	KEY 4
KEY 4	KEY 4	KEY 4		
KEY 5	KEY 5	KEY 5		

Assume that 'Key' in the example above corresponds to the name of an employee. If KEY 3 = JONES then it would appear that JONES possesses attributes A, B and C but not D and E.

(b)   *Tree data structure*

A tree data structure is a logical arrangement of data in a hierarchical form. The highest point in the hierarchy is the root and from the root stems a number of nodes (each representing an attribute). It is a convention of the structure to allow only one node at a higher level linked to several nodes at a lower level (by analogy the lower level are 'child' nodes and the higher level are 'parent' nodes; no child can have more than one parent).

0122z

A simple example of tree data structure is given below:

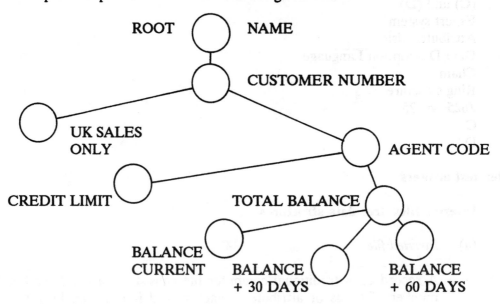

13.2 Schema

The term *schema* refers to each software option that permits data extracted from a data base to be sorted, calculated or reformatted in the style required by the user of the information. As there are no specific application programs (the data base being program-independent) each schema is drawn up to enable the data in the data base to be manipulated for various purposes. These various schemata are controlled by the data base administrator who is responsible *inter alia* for:

(a) defining the data elements;

(b) liaising with users to determine their information needs; and

(c) defining the processing requirements necessary (the schemata) to provide the various reports and outputs.

13.3 Databases

(a) A database can be defined as one common collection of data which is substantially non-redundant and program-independent.

(b) The advantages associated with the use of a database are:

(i) The quality of information is improved as the database can be constructed to reflect the total information needs of a business.

(ii) Resources are used more efficiently as there is less duplication of effort.

(iii) The system is more flexible to the needs of the business.

(iv) Management can react more quickly to situations as information is readily available.

(v) Inconsistencies in the collection and storage of data are eliminated.

(c) Three major problems associated with a database are:

    (i) The database administrator exercises considerable influence over the database and security of data may be difficult to achieve.

    (ii) The complexity of such systems means they are expensive.

    (iii) The integrated nature of such systems complicates the correction of processing errors.

(d) The logical structure of data refers to the identification of each relevant facet of the data record which ultimately affects the completeness and comprehensiveness of the information extracted from the system.

The physical structure of data refers to the physical storage of each data record, eg, a disk file containing 20 megabytes of storage is used for the customer data base. This is the *physical* structure of data. Each customer record contains facets as follows - area code, customer number, agent code, units sold per annum, total sales to date, balance to date, etc. This is the logical structure of the data.

Session 14 Controls and security in a computer-based system

Quick question answers

(1) Any four from relevance, duplication, sequence, range, limit, consistency, format, completeness, check digit verification, batch control.

(2) False

(3)   (1) Spot checking of printed output
    (2) Checking file totals and file control reports
    (3) Investigating error report

(4) (1) Deletions   (2) Insertions and (3) Amendments (in that order)

(5) Brought-forward (1) and carried-forward (2)

(6) (a) Copying and (b) overlay

(7) Data encryption

(8) (c)

(9) (c)

(10)   (a) Data subject
    (b) Data user
    (c) Data user
    (d) Data subject

(11) File library, stationery store, engineer's store and office, data control room, data preparation room, programmers'/analysts' offices.

(12)   Fire; water.

(13)   Punched cards

(14)   Direct, parallel running, pilot operation.

(15)   Timetable; list of programs; input; files; output; operating instructions; error routines; restart procedures.

(16)   Purchase; leasing; rental.

(17)   Capital available; expansion; stability of system.

(18)   Preparation of site (air conditioning, power supplies, double glazing etc)
Purchase of software
Salaries (programmers, analysts, operators)
Insurance
File conversion costs
Changeover costs

(19)   Cost; lack of organisation ability; low volumes.

(20)   One-off jobs; as a stand-by program testing; as a stand-by machine in case of breakdown; for program testing.

Objective test answers

(1)   D
(2)   C

Written test answers

14.1   Control section

The control section within the installation is part of the operations department. It is staffed by data-control clerks, who may be headed by a supervisor if their number is sufficiently large. The section's prime responsibilities are to control the flow of data through the operational activities and to act as liaison centre between the computer staff and all user departments.

Data-control clerks will check input documents received and record their arrival in a suitable register. They may also be responsible, when the system design requires, for the preparation of certain job control parameters that must be added to the input before processing. The types of information needed could be batch-header details of run numbers, frequency of run (daily, weekly, monthly, etc.) and so on, which the originator of the source documents would not know. Only after the input was collected together would it be practical to assign this additional data and the function is, therefore, performed by the control clerks. A related duty is to confirm the accuracy of the main systems outputs after production. This involves checking that file end totals reported as carried forward on master files and shown on the control reports printed, agree with the brought-forward total plus insertions less deletions after allowing for rejected input. When rejections have occurred the data control clerk must examine the error reports in detail and determine the corrective action needed. He, or she, will be responsible for checking the progress of action taken on the queried items to ensure that all input is successfully processed. Apart from action on error reports, the clerk must also be certain that all accepted data has been processed correctly. Comparison of batch control totals input against those shown as accepted by the system enables this to be done. All file-amendment printouts must also be checked back character by character against the original amending documents as a precaution against punching errors or misprocessing.

Finally, the control section will be the point to which all user departments will refer if they require to know when specified outputs are scheduled for production, or to clarify the action needed on particular inputs. To answer enquiries, the data-control staff must maintain up-to-date and accurate records of every job from receipt until final despatch back to the user. These records may also be employed in audit investigations, as they form a linked trail which is unlikely to be available from the computer files themselves, since these are continually updated.

14.2   Vetting of input data

In commercial computer systems it is normal for all input to be processed by a data vet program before it enters the main system. Such a program checks the validity of the input in an attempt to ensure that only accurate information is processed. Before this stage is reached, however, two other vetting operations are possible. The first is to ensure that the source documentation being used for creation of input is accurate in all respects. The second is to include checking facilities within any data-preparation system that is employed.

The main problems that can occur with computer input, and ways of overcoming them, are as follows.

(a)   *Non-receipt of documents* - Prevented by collecting batches of like documents together in manageable quantities, say 50 per batch and supplying a slip with each one showing the number of documents submitted and a pre-listed control total for subsequent reconciliation with a computer-derived figure after acceptance.

(b)   *Loss of documents after receipt* - Prevented by logging receipt of batches and recording subsequent handling through each operational stage. Serial numbering in sequence upon receipt is an alternative control system.

(c)   *Transcription errors in punching* - Prevented by verification, the use of check-digit systems, or derivation of control figures after punching to agree with pre-lists.

(d)   *Misinterpretation of fields on punched cards or tape* - Prevented by adequate range and content checks performed by the computer during the data vet stage. For example, a field used to carry data into the system can be checked to see that the day number is in the range 1 to 31 and the month number in the range 1 to 12. The extent of these types of check is the responsibility of the analyst who designs the system.

(e)   *Incorrect data presented to the system* - This can be one of two main types. Either data is presented that belongs to another system (for example, cash receipts entered into an invoicing program instead of into the sales ledger run) or data is presented twice to the same operation. Both types of error can be detected by

0122z

suitable checks on the header information. The use of distinctive data types will prevent the first occurrence. The application of sequential run numbers will stop the second.

(f) *Illegibility or unsuitability of input documents* - Normally prevented by a manual screening process prior to batching, before documents are passed for data preparation. Rejected source documents are returned to the originator for clarification and re-submission to the system.

14.3   Loss of data

With a magnetic tape system it is normal practice to provide security against loss of data by using the **generation** method. The word is used in the sense of a family and the method used in a three-generation system is commonly referred to as the grandfather-father-son technique.

With such a system, three versions of any file are always available and are updated on a cyclical basis with the frequency demanded by the overall processing system. For the first three updating runs of a new program, the carry-forward tape used is a blank one. These tapes become:

First update run	Grandfather tape (file 1)
Second update run	Father tape (file 2)
Third update run	Son tape (file 3)

With the fourth updating run the generation cycle proper begins. Tape 3 (son) is used as the brought-forward version and the updated carry-forward of the file is overwritten to tape 1 (grandfather). The fifth update uses tape 1 and outputs to tape 2. The sixth update run uses tape 2 and outputs to tape 3. The cycle is now complete and repeats itself continuously. The advantage this offers is that recovery is always possible, by re-running the program with the relevant input plus the tape that was not employed in the erroneous run. For example, if the new data on file 3 were found to contain some errors, the job could be repeated using file 2 again with the input. If files 2 and 3 were both damaged during processing, file 1 is still available to create a new file 2 and this can be used in turn to create file 3 again.

14.4   Use of a bureau

Advantages

(a) No capital investment is required on equipment, buildings and staff specialists.

(b) Rapid introduction of computer systems is possible, if a standard bureau package can be employed. Examples are payroll preparation and sales analysis.

(c) Cost savings are probable, if the computer application can replace manual effort by a large number of clerks.

(d) Using a bureau service is a good introduction to the internal disciplines required when processing by computer and can form a sound basis for conversion to an 'in-house' machine at a later date.

(e)   The benefits of better control information for management can be obtained from the relevant application without pressure to expand the areas of usage simply to fill unused machine capacity and recover a high initial investment.

(f)   It is probable that the experienced bureau staff have met similar problems before and this prevents each company from 're-inventing the wheel'.

Disadvantages

(a)   There is a possible loss of control over the program design, if it is left to people who are not familiar with the overall philosophy of the company. This is minimised by close liaison during the design and implementation stages and by the client's insistence upon accurate and comprehensive documentation.

(b)   It may be necessary to transport source documents or data over long distances if the bureau is a remote one.

(c)   There is a need for very tight scheduling if results are to be processed on time and the last-minute changes in run dates that can be accommodated on an internal machine will be unacceptable to a bureau.

(d)   A minimum weekly or monthly charge may be imposed, even when the volume of data to be processed is small.

(e)   A contract will be required, so that it may not be possible to stop using the system without a financial penalty even if the benefits expected do not materialise. This only applies, of course, if the client's original job specification has been implemented as requested.

(f)   If a change to an internal computer is visualized for some time in the future, the choice of the machine may be limited by the number of programs already implemented on the bureau computer. When this is large, there is a tendency to want to keep the machine compatible to save the extra cost of re-programming.

As the number of computer bureaux increases there are fewer and fewer applications that they cannot tackle. In theory, all jobs that can be done on an internal machine could be processed by a bureau. With the rapid advance in the use of data transmission facilities and on-line terminals this becomes even more valid. However, real time applications have only limited suitability for bureaux because of the need to have a large data bank available for one customer at all times. Similarly process control is not really a bureau job because of the requirement for instantaneous corrective action to be taken.

In the normal commercial field however, the only serious adverse factors would be a high volume of input and a great distance. Neither of these completely precludes the use of a computer bureau, but they would certainly make it less likely that such usage would be more economical than having an internal data-processing department.

14.5   Security

The following precautions should be taken.

(a)   Ensure that computer peripherals are unloaded and equipment shut down.

(b)   Lock all relevant magnetic and other media in a fireproof safe or cabinet, as specified by the operating instructions, to allow master copies of programs and files to be preserved in the event of a fire.

(c)   Check that all air-conditioning equipment is running satisfactorily and that the recorded temperature and humidity are steady within the prescribed tolerance limits.

(d)   Switch on and check operation of any automatic fire and burglar alarm systems in use within the installation.

(e)   Make a tour of the site to detect possible fire hazards, eg, electric fires left on or lit cigarette ends.

(f)   See that all windows are closed and securely fastened.

(g)   Lock the computer room door, if this is normal practice within the installation.

(h)   Close all interior doors.

(i)   Switch off all lights.

(j)   Lock and secure the main door and deposit the key with the security guards if relevant to the site.

14.6   File conversion

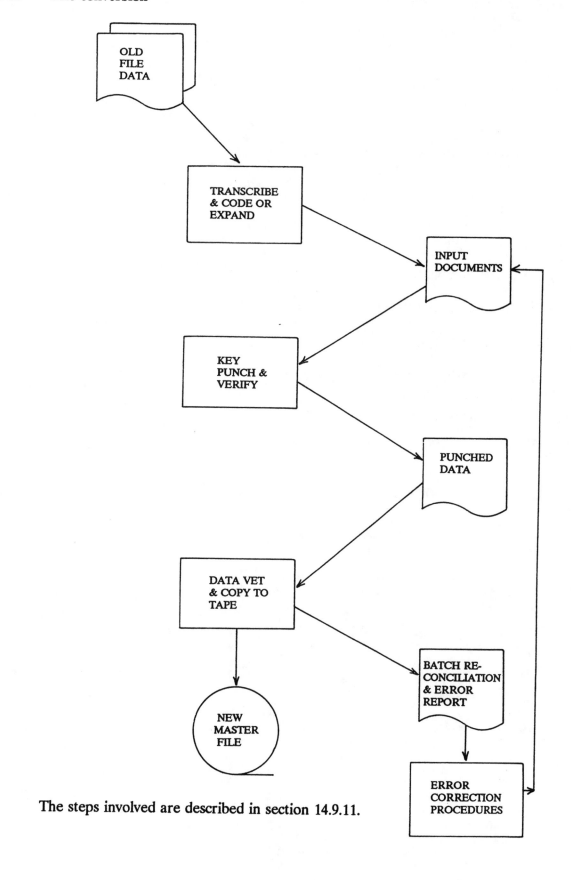

The steps involved are described in section 14.9.11.

0122z

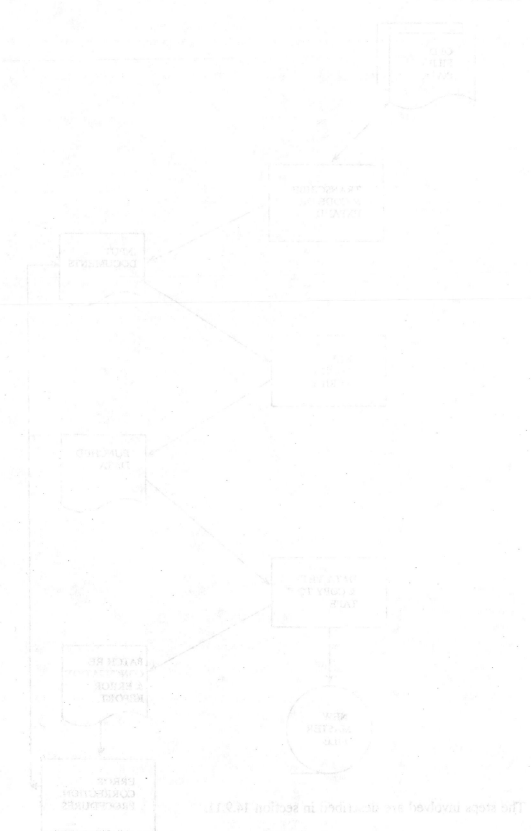

The steps involved are described in section 14.9.11.

Glossary

The following are terms and phrases commonly used in data processing. This glossary is provided to help you when you read the Study Pack or even if you hear a term that is not immediately familiar. Fashionable 'buzzwords' have been avoided; certain trade names (eg. Visicalc) have been included due to their familiarity in business life.

Expression	Meaning
Access mode	The method adopted for reading/writing to a file (ie direct access mode or sequential access mode).
Access time	The interval between an item of data being requested from file and that item being available for processing
Acoustic coupler	A device which is used to enable a telephone handset to be used in data transmission as an alternative to a modem in order to encode/decode digital data and analog signals.
Action entry	The bottom right-hand quandrant of a decision table, in which is entered the specific action(s) to be taken under each permutation of conditions (or **Rule** qv).
Action stub	The bottom left-hand quadrant of a decision table listing all possible actions to be taken.
Actuator	A device, or stage in a process, which receives feedback information from the comparator and initiates appropriate control action within the system or process.
Address	An area of computer main storage for holding data which is individually identifiable.
Address generation	A method for computing the disk address of a record from the record's key field.
ALGOL	ALGorithmic Orientated Language - a powerful scientific programming language.
ALU	Arithmetic Logic Unit - part of the central processing unit reserved for mathematical/logical functions.
Analog computer	A computing device that measures data in terms of continuous physical magnitudes.

Expression	Meaning
ASCII	American Standard Code for Information Interchange. A 7-bit code offering 128 states of representation; commonly used by micro-computers.
Assembler	Program translation aid for converting machine-orientated languages to machine code.
Asynchronous transmission	Transmission in a continuous stream of bits without any timing regulation by the computer.
Audit trail	The ability to follow the stages in a business transaction from input to final output.
Badge reader	Input device for reading embossed plastic badges for data encoding (eg, time recording systems).
Bar code	Code used in packaging in retail trades which can be sensed by wands (qv) in order to record sales data. In UK convention is commonly that of the European Article Number (EAN).
BASIC	Beginner's All purpose Symbolic Instruction Code. A powerful high level language using common English words and mathematical symbols.
Batch processing	A way of processing data in batches, rather than processing individual transactions as they arise. (Implies relative non-urgency of process.)
Batch register	A handwritten record of the details of each batch of transaction data entering the system.
Baud	Limit of measuring analog signals in a data transmission system. 1 Baud = 1 binary digit. (Derived from Baudot who invented the five digit telex code.)
Bench mark	A time standard used for evaluating efficiency of program performance.
Binary coded decimal	A six digit code offering 10 numbers, 26 upper case alphabetic characters and symbols.
Block	An area of storage either on a magnetic tape or a disk.

Expression	Meaning
Block code	Coding system in which blocks of numbers (or letters) are allocated to logical groups within the items being coded.
Boot	Term used to describe the transfer of operating system (qv) from backing storage to main memory (also 'booting' or 'bootstrapping').
Bucket	A section of a disk holding items of data. May be used synonymously with 'block' (qv).
Bus	A central channel to which component parts of a micro computer can be wired.
By-product (input)	A technique by which data is input to (or captured for) a computer, as a by-product of an existing operation being performed (eg, ringing up items on a cash register).
Byte	An eight-bit binary character, normally used as the unit of measure for expressing the capacities of computer storage devices.
Byte machine	A machine whose memory architecture is based on 8 bit units of storage. Utilising $2^8(256)$ states of representation.
Ceefax	An example of a system utilising videotext (qv) techniques, operated by the British Broadcasting Corporation.
Check digit	The key figure within a check-digited value which confirms whether or not the whole value has been recorded or transcribed correctly.
Check digit system	A system for 'proving' the correctness of a code number by subjecting it to a predetermined series of arithmetical processes. If the number has been wrongly recorded or transcribed, it fails to generate the required key value (check digit) imbedded in or appended to the value itself.
Checkpoint table	A control used in real time systems to determine the status of messages in progress.
Clerical procedure flowchart	Diagrammatic representation of the detailed operation performed on documents within clerical procedure, or within a department.

0123z

Expression	Meaning
Closed system	A system completely insulated from its environment.
COBOL	Common Business Orientated Language. A high-level language designed for general business purposes using a standard or reserved English vocabulary.
COM	Computer Output on Microfilm. A technique for converting machine-sensible output (tape or disk) into spools of microfilm.
Communication theory	A set of 'laws' concerning the transmission, reception and distortion of information-carrying messages in any form of communication system.
Comparator	A device, or stage in a process, which receives information from the sensor (qv) compares it to the required standard and passes an appropriate control message (feedback) to the actuator.
Compiler	A translation program for converting high-level languages to machine code.
Computer log	A running record of the events occurring during a computer run. Usually kept on the computer/by the computer, as most events are reported by the operating system rather than the computer operator.
Computer run (flow) chart	Diagrammatic representation of the sequence of programs to be run for defined areas of work (eg, payroll), showing all relevant inputs, outputs and files.
Computer system	Note the two different meanings: (a) a particular hardware configuration; (b) the overall system, both hardware (as above) and software, for carrying out a specific data-processing problem.
Condition stub	A top right-hand quadrant of a decision table, listing all possible conditions which are covered by that table.
Control unit	That part of the control processing unit which decodes, executes and sequences program operations.

0123z

Expression	Meaning
Conversational mode	A method of computer operation where computer operation is achieved by means of dialogues between man and machine.
Conversion (within a system)	The process of converting the various inputs (money, materials, energy, information, etc) to a system into the required output(s) of that system.
CP/M	Control Program for Micros - an operating system (qv) for microcomputers.
CSA	Computing Services Association. A body which acts as a professional association for computer bureaux and similar.
Cursor	A marker (either a symbol or spot of brightness) on a VDU (qv) screen which is used for data editing purposes.
Cylinder concept	The concept of storing data on a disk in common tracks. The assembly of the relevant tracks is known as a cylinder.
DASD	Direct Access Storage Device.
Data	Raw facts, which are fed into a data-processing system. (**Note:** The 'data' input to one system may be the 'information' output from a preceding process.)
Database system	A system in which all data relating to an organisation are held in a single, integrated storage system, rather than on several (application-oriented) files.
Data collection	(a) The process of gathering computer input data from its point of origin, and conveying it by appropriate methods to the computer for processing.

(b) The process of gathering data about an existing or proposed system, as part of the analysis process. |
| **Data control section** | That part of the computer operations concerned with controlling and validating input data and output. |

Expression	Meaning
Data vet/validation	The process, performed as early as possible for checking the overall accuracy and consistency of data input to a computer program.
DBMS	Data Base Management System.
DDE	Direct Data Entry (via keyboard or similar device).
DDL	Data Description Language. A means of communicating with DBMS in order to define data structures, ie, records, field keys, lengths and values.
Decimal (or hierarchical) code	A form of group classification code in which each successive digit indicates the next lower level of classification into which that item falls.
Decision table	A detailed tabulation of what actions are to be performed (by a clerk, or by a computer program) under each specific permutation of all possible conditions likely to arise in a given situation.
Decollator	An electro-mechanical device used for handling multi-part computer stationery in order to produce single strands.
De-coupling	A deliberate disconnection of specific links within a closely integrated system to eliminate unnecessary sensitivity and oscillation.
Denary	A numbering system based on ten states of representation.
Deterministic system	A system in which a known input produces a predictable output.
Direct changeover	A policy under which a new system is introduced fully, immediately the previous one is discontinued, with no overlap. (see also Parallel running and Pilot running.)
Direct entry (input)	Data is keyed (or otherwise input) directly into a computer (see DDE).
Distributed data processing	A system made up of individual processors providing a decentralised DP service but linked together in a network.

0123z

Expression	Meaning
Document analysis form	Specialised form designed to cross-reference data items, their characteristics, and the documents on which they appear.
Documentation	The complete set of written descriptive material about a (computer-based) system, required for day-to-day operations and general reference.
Document flowchart	Diagrammatic representation of non-computer processes and document flows outside the computer system.
Duplex	Term used to describe two-way simultaneous transmission in a data communication system.
Electronic funds transfer	The transmission of financial transactions by electronic means (eg, interbank transfers).
Electronic mail	The transfer of information between users by means of a computer network.
Emulation	The use of a separate hardware device equipped with simulation software (qv) in order to make machine code for one machine understandable to another.
Encryption software	System for scrambling messages in transit between computer and terminal in order to render them unintelligible if illicitly intercepted.
Entity	General term for a logical record (also term used to describe any unit, individual, etc).
Executive	A control program part of operating systems occasionally permanently resident in memory.
Extended binary coded	An 8-bit code providing 2^8 (256) states of representation.
Extended-entry decision table	A form of decision table, in which both conditions and actions are specified in words or numerical value (rather than the simple Y, N and X of the limited-entry table).

Expression	Meaning
E13B	A typeface for Magnetic Ink Character Recognition. Commonly used by UK clearing banks.
Faceted code	A form of group classification code in which each specific digit (or group of digits) represents a specific characteristic of the item being coded.
Fax	Generic term to describe the technique of micro processor-based systems for facsimile transmission of documents.
Feasibility study	A preliminary study undertaken to determine the general parameters of business problems, and the feasibility of using a computer to solve it.
Feedback	A control signal transmitted back from the comparator to the activator, to modify the input or process, in the light of deviations from a required norm.
FEP	Front End Processor. A processing device often used to handle input/output functions for a 'host' computer.
Field	A section of a record.
File	A set of related records (see also Master file, Reference file, Transaction file and Report file).
File amendment	The process of revising the (relatively permanent) data items held on a master file, in the light of new circumstances (eg change of address, tax code, etc).
File analysis form	Specialised form designed to show the characteristics of the data items in each file in a computer system.
File conversion	The process of creating new files for a new computer application, by a process of converting existing files, but normally requiring considerable additional data, reformulating, and careful checking.
File label	Can be either: (a) an external, human-readable 'stock label' on the outside of a tape reel or disk pack; (b) an internal, computer-readable record at either the start or end of a file (and possibly at intermediate points within it).

0123z

Expression	Meaning
File maintenance	The process of keeping a master file up to date by amending any revised data, deleting obsolete records, and inserting new records into their correct position in the file.
File updating	Processing a master file so as to update the balances and other running totals held within it.
First generation computer	Early computers (up to 1959 approx) characterised by large physical size, utilising thermionic valves, and various experimental memory systems.
Firmware	Term used to describe 'hard wired' modules of programming (see **ROM**).
Fixed word length	A unit of storage with a fixed number of bits for character representation.
FORTRAN	FORmula TRANslation language. A powerful high-level language suitable for both business and scientific application.
Fourth generation computer	Computer produced post-1974, essentially 'modular' in concept rather than specific 'model' and with plentiful, cheap backing storage capable of holding complete data bases.
Generation technique	A security measure for safeguarding a file by retaining the two previous versions (or 'generations') for which it was produced. In case of loss or damage, the file is reconstituted by re-running the previous generation file against the transaction data which originally produced the damaged file. Also referred to as the 'grandfather/father/son' technique.
Grandfather, father, son	A system for securing sequentially processed master files by preserving three generations of the file at any time in the processing cycle. (See Generation technique.)
Graph plotter	Output device for producing hard copy graphical displays.
Group classification code	A coding system in which one or more digits (or letters) indicate particular classifications of items.
Half duplex	Transmission in two directions but not simultaneously.

0123z

Expression	Meaning
Hard sector	Sector on disk determined by manufacturer.
Hardware	The physical parts of a computer (the 'machinery') as distinct from programs (see also Software).
Hash total	A control total produced by adding together apparently meaningless values (eg, weights in dissimilar units or serial numbers). The hash total has no intrinsic value in itself, but each time it is calculated, it should yield the same value. If it does not, this is an early warning of a missing document, or other error.
Header label	First part of file used for system identification.
High-level language	Problem-orientated programming language.
Hit rate	The proportion (or percentage) of records in a file for which there are transactions to be applied.
Home track	Usual location of a disk record.
Indexed sequential file	A file in which the records are in sequential (but not consecutive) order, and whose precise storage location is determined by reference to an index.
Information	The processed, meaningful output from a system. (Distinguish from the 'raw' data which is input to that system.)
Information groups	The different groups of people who may require information at different levels from an information system.
Information system	Any system for recording, collating, summarising and reporting the essential data about an organisation's operations and performance. (Usually appears as 'management information system' MIS (qv).)
In-house (computer, etc)	Any facility on an organisation's own premises.
Integrated system	A system where all aspects of a business transaction are capable of being reflected in any processing application.
Intelligent terminal	A terminal equipped with its own processor capable of being programmed with certain routines to aid operation, eg, a key-to-cassette system is based upon a small processor system.

0123z

Expression	Meaning
Inter block gap	The blank non-magnetised area of magnetic tape (also known as the inter record gap).
Interpreter	A special translation system that acts upon program language statements entered on an interactive basis (eg, with BASIC language).
Inverted file	A file which is made up of a variety of lists each showing an attribute of the entity.
IT	Information Technology - general term for the study of information processing methods.
Job control language	A language used to control the sequence of tasks in processing which is understood and interpreted by the operating system (qv).
K	One thousand (as in kilometre = km = 1000 metres). Used to abbreviate large numbers: when measuring computer storage used to indicate 1,024 (2^{10}) rather than 1,000 exactly.
Key-to-cassette	Data encoding system using intelligent terminal to encode a tape via keyboard/VDU entry.
Key-to-disk	Data entry system based on a small data control computer with linked workstations.
Kimball tag	A pre-punched tag used in the retail trade containing a computer-sensible code generally describing the product group and price.
Library	A collection of files - physical library - off-line filing.
Light pen	Electronic device used for changing visual displays by contact with screen.
Limited-entry (decision) table	A form of decision table, in which condition entries are limited to 'Y(es), N(o)' or '-', and action entries indicated only by 'X' in appropriate positions.
Liveware	Expression used (by analogy with 'hardware' and 'software') to describe the people involved in a computer system.

Expression	Meaning
Log	A record produced either by the computer (machine log) or by the operators (duty log).
Logical file	An assembly of related records.
Looping	A repetitious cycle of operations in a computer program.
Low-level language	A machine-orientated language using symbols or mnemonics to express program instructions.
Machine code	The machine-understandable program instructions and data expressed in binary code.
Magnetic strip card	A card used in Visible Record Computer applications for collecting printed output. The strip is encoded with the data on the card.
Mainframe (computer)	Large, centralised computer, offering a general purpose data-processing service to an organisation.
Management information system (MIS)	A system in which defined data are collected, processed and communicated to assist those responsible for the use of resources.
Mass storage	High-volume backing storage system using lengths of magnetic tape or individual disk cartridges stored in cells.
Master file	A file containing relatively permanent information about an item or person which is kept up to date by processing against it all transactions relating to that item or person.
Megabyte	One million bytes (see Byte), used to express the capacity of large storage devices.
Menu	A visual display of program options together with 'prompts' for user guidance. Used in interactive systems esp. small computers.
MICR	Magnetic Ink Character Recognition. Special typefaces (E13b or CMC7) are used to encode characters on forms using ink containing magnetic fluxes. Commonly used in cheque sorting systems.
Microcomputer	Small computer, capable of sitting on a desk-top generally costing £5,000 or under, but with proportionately limited facilities.

0123z

Expression	Meaning
Microfilm	Miniaturised man understandable data for storage purposes. Can be combined to form a microfiche. (See Microform).
Microform	See **Microfilm**.
Mini-computer	Small to medium computer often dedicated to one specific application, rather than offering a general-purpose service.
Mnemonic code	A coding system using alphanumeric characters from the name of the entity, eg, NY = New York.
Modem	Diminutive of MOdulator/DEModulator. A device for encoding/decoding binary data and analog signals in data communication systems.
Modulus 11	A prime number constant used in check digit verification schemes to validate code number transcription.
Multi-access computer	A system offering many users access to the processor via remote terminals and 'time slices' of processor use.
Multiplexor	A hardware device converting many channels of data (usually from remote terminals) into a single channel.
Multi-Programming	The capability of running several programs apparently simultaneously.
Nanosecond	One (US) billionth (ie, one thousand-millionth) of a second.
National Computing Centre (NCC)	National body set up to develop standards, etc, for computer-based systems.
Negative feedback	A control signal which causes a system to act in the opposite direction whenever an abnormal output is detected, and hence return the system to within its predetermined operating limits.
Noise	An extraneous distortion within a system which causes errors or misleading output to be produced.
O&M (organisation & methods)	The specialist function concerned with analysing and improving an enterprise's organisation and (paperwork) methods.

0123z

Expression	Meaning
OCR	Optical Character Recognition. Man understandable characters which can be scanned by a document reader to render them computer-sensible.
OMR	Optical Mark Reading. Assigning values to marks which are sensed on documents by a document reader.
On-line processing	A way of processing data (wholly or partially) as soon as it is input to the computer.
Open-item ledger	A ledger system (eg, sales ledger) where each transaction is specifically identified and matched with input transactions in order to identify and list all unpaid or open transactions.
Open system	A system that interacts with its environment.
Operand	The address of the data described in a program word.
Operating system	A large control program, which 'manages' the efficient processing of the computer's workload by scheduling jobs, allocating computer facilities in the light of previously established priorities and available facilities, and automatically handling error conditions.
Operation code	The instruction to be carried out on data expressed in a numeric code.
Operations Manager	Controller of the day-to-day operations of the computer and related departments.
Oscillation	A situation in which a system or process fluctuates repeatedly (and often unnecessarily) between two extremes.
Overflow	An area on a disk file used for storing variable length records which are too large for their home track (qv).
Package (program)	A ready-written program, to perform some common processing function (eg, payroll, sales ledger). So called because it is a 'package deal': you take it as it stands, with little scope for modifying it (unless modification facilities have been incorporated from the outset).

Expression	Meaning
Paging	Programming context otherwise VDU display of complete pages of text (as opposed to line or character displays).
Parallel running	The process of testing out a new system by running it in parallel with the existing system, and carefully cross-checking the results produced by each, and only discontinuing the old system when full confidence in the new one has been established (see also Direct changeover, Pilot running).
Parity check	A security technique for checking the accuracy of data transferred from one part of a computer system to another, by counting the number of bits sent and received. There should always be an even number (ie, parity) at every stage in the process.
PASCAL	A high-level 'all purpose' language often used on small machines.
Password	A coded name or phrase keyed into a terminal in order to access a system.
Pilot operation (or running)	The process of implementing a new system piecemeal, by gradually introducing it (on a 'pilot' basis) to selected areas one at a time, so that the previous system can easily be reverted to in case of catastrophic failure of the new one (see also Direct changeover, Parallel running).
PL/1	Programming Language One - An IBM language designed for 'all purposes' (real time, business and scientific language).
Point of sale system	Generic term for cash registers linked to a small processor to provide an integrated stock/cash recording system.
Polling	A system for sending signals according to some protocol from a computer to a network of terminals.
Positive feedback	A control signal which tends to increase or exaggerate an output which is already excessive, and hence causes the system or process to get further and further out of control.

0123z

Expression	Meaning
Probabilistic (system)	A system in which, whilst the general nature of the output is predictable, there is considerable variation each time the process is performed.
Program	A set of coded computer instructions for carrying out a defined set of tasks.
Program flowchart	Diagrammatic representation of the logical steps to be performed within a computer program.
PROM	Programmable Read Only Memory - see also **Firmware, ROM**.
Protocol	A recognition system for signalling between a computer and a terminal.
PSS	Packet Switching System. A form of data communication system where data is formed into packets of a fixed size (say 256 bytes) and transmitted with an address protocol from computer to terminal or from terminal to terminal.
Pseudocode	A term used to describe the use of program language type statements used for logical analysis. Also called structured English.
Query	A file interrogation package marketed and developed by Hewlett Packard Limited.
Questionnaires	A fact-finding technique in systems investigation.
QWERTY keyboard	Term given to describe full typewriter keyboard (from the arrangement of the first line of keys).
RAM	Random Access Memory. Synonymous with internal storage (commonly used in context of small machines).
Random/algorithmic file	A file in which the records are apparently stored in random sequence, but whose storage location is determined by applying a predetermined algorithm to the code number or key field.
Random file	A file of records which are in a random sequence.
Real time processing	A way of processing data in which all relevant files are updated immediately each transaction is processed.

Expression	Meaning
Record	A set of data elements which have some logical relationship in common.
Reference file	A file of relatively permanent data about the items or persons concerned (eg, names and addresses, prices and descriptions, etc).
Remote job entry (RJE)	The entry of batch processing data via remote terminals on-line to a computer.
Response time	A measure of the speed of a computer system, ie, how soon after the input of data are the results of processing available?
ROM	Read Only Memory. Memory units containing non-erasable program (see also **Firmware**).
Rule	Each vertical column within a decision table specifying a particular permutation of conditions, and what actions are to be carried out for that permutation.
Run chart	See **Computer run (flow) chart**.
SASD	Serial Access Storage Device.
Scrolling	Term used to describe VDU output in which data is displayed on a line by line basis.
Second generation (computer)	A computer built in the early 1960s: often as one of a 'family' of related models, featuring transistors (in place of valves), core storage and magnetic-tape backing store.
Sensor	A device, or stage in a process which inspects the output from the processes and feeds it to the 'comparator' (qv).
Sequence code	Coding system in which items are identified by a simple alpha or numerical sequence.
Sequential (or serial) file	A file in which the records are sorted and stored in sequential (usually ascending) order for processing and reference.
Service bureau	An organisation selling computer services.
Significant digit code	A coding system in which successive digits (or letters) indicate various characteristics of the item being coded.

Expression	Meaning
Silicon chip	Miniaturised assembly of metal oxide silicon holding a module of memory; a logic unit or a complete microprocessor.
Simulation	*Generally* - Running different experimental values through the mathematical model of a business or similar organisation to see how it behaves under various conditions.
	Also - Software device for making programs written in one machine code understandable on another machine (see also **Emulation**).
Soft sector	A sector which can be determined by the user, eg, soft-sectored disk - one where sector sizes can be allocated by users system.
Software	Computer programs. Sometimes extended to include operating instructions, whether written down or known from experience.
Spooling	Acronym for Simultaneous Peripheral Operation On Line.
Spreadsheet	Financial modelling system for small computers based on a display matrix of rows and columns providing cells for each variable in the model. Commonly used in cash budgeting systems on small computers.
Stand alone	Term used to describe a data processing device as a single entity (ie, not part of a larger system).
Sub-optimisation	An improvement in one or more sub-systems which results in a deterioration in the performance of the larger overall system.
Subroutine	A module of a program to carry out a set routine that occurs several times in a processing run eg, calculation of VAT on a sales invoice.
Sub-system	A system (qv) which is part of a larger system.
System	A set of things connected, associated or inter-dependent so as to form a complex unity.

Expression	Meaning
Systems analysis	The process of investigating the requirements of an information system, and analysing these requirements critically and quantitively (before proceeding to systems design (qv)).
Systems analyst	A person who undertakes the detailed study of a business problem area, with a view to its solution by computer.
Systems design	The process of devising a (computer-based) system to meet the requirements revealed by the systems analysis process.
Systems flowchart	Diagrammatic representation of all inputs, outputs, processing and files within a system.
Systems investigation	The detailed study of a business problem or application area, usually prior to applying a computer to it.
Systems life cycle	The concept that a system has various stages from initial feasibility through to cessation when obsolete.
Systems proposal	The 'end-product' of a systems investigation (qv), containing all details of how a new computer-based system is to be implemented.
Systems specification	An updated version of the systems proposals (qv) indicating the exact details of how each aspect of the system has been (or is to be) implemented, as the basic reference point for all concerned.
Systems theory	A general theory about systems - their nature, classification and general characteristics, derived from the study of systems in widely different areas (eg, biology, economics, astronomy, etc).
Third generation (computer)	A computer produced in the late 1960s and early 1970s, featuring integrated circuits, operating at nanosecond speeds.
Time sharing	A system under which several different users are apparently utilising the computer's facilities simultaneously.
Timing	(a) Calculating (or measuring) the running-time of each element of a computer system to determine the overall 'production-time'.

0123z

Expression	Meaning
Timing (continued)	(b) Determining the optimum frequency for producing management information, consistent with accuracy, economy and effectiveness.
Trace routine	Diagnostic software routine whereby the contents of memory are dumped at set stages so that the cycle of operations can be traced.
Transaction file	A collection of the items of data to be passed against one or more master files.
Transcription	The process of inputting data into a computer by copying it character by character, through some form of keyboard device.
Transient monitor/ executive	An operating system module not resident in memory and requiring to be booted (qv **Boot**) into memory.
Turnaround (technique, document)	The technique of originating an output document by computer, processing it clerically, then turning it around, back to the computer as a directly readable input document.
Turnkey installation	A computer installation run on a contract basis by a service company.
Update by overlay	The process of updating by overwriting original data in a logical record (disk storage) also known as update 'in situ'.
Utility	Standard housekeeping program eg file sorting.
VDU	Visual Display Unit. Cathode ray tube display for input/output systems.
Visicalc	Spread sheet model popular with small computer users.
Videotext	Generic term for computer transmission systems which employ such techniques as teletext systems (Ceefax, Oracle) and viewdata system (Prestel) etc.
Voice data entry	Data entry device capable of sending human speech (certain reserved words) as computer sensible input.
Volatile storage	Storage that is lost when power is off.

0123z

Expression	Meaning
VRC	Visible Records Computer. Small office computer combining features of a book-keeping machine with records in visible and machine sensible form (see Magnetic strip).
Wand	Electronic reading device used as alternative to keyboard for sensing coded data - typically bar codes (qv).
Winchester	IBM disk in sealed container. Heads are positioned close to surface. Airtight construction makes disk head crash almost impossible. Smallest mode 5.25" in diameter.
Word processing	Technique using computers to process the printed word, ie, typewriting applications in offices.
Work measurement	Technique for measuring content of manipulative tasks (eg, clerical work measurement).
Workstation	Term for keyboard and VDU unit.
Zero proof	Test used in book-keeping machines to validate pickup of opening balance.
Zero remainder	Convention used in check digit calculations (modulus 11) in order to test for valid code description.

Index

0124z

0124z

0124z

0124z